Perspectives on Change

"This book demonstrates that organizational change is not as difficult as some academics make it sound, not as easy as some consultants suggest, and more painful than most practitioners expect."
—*Stewart Clegg, University of Technology Sydney*

"This is the most insightful book on organizational change I have read. The concept is brilliant—getting leading academics, consultants, and practitioners to 'tell it like it is.' Informative, thoughtful, and challenging, it is simply a great read."
—*John Hassard, Manchester Business School*

Despite the plethora of books on change, there appears to be a notable gap in the field; rarely are the authentic and candid voices of change practitioners heard. Seldom are those most closely involved in the management of change given (or seek) the opportunity to write about their personal experiences and reflexiveness. Nor is this just a case of practising managers not being given a voice or feeling that they cannot be frank and open about what they do. How often do academics candidly state what they actually do when they are faced with managing change in their own institutions or when they are called on in a consultancy capacity? Similarly, it is rare for full-time consultants to be candid about what it is they actually do: instead they tend to have a well-honed sales pitch which lays out a logical change process directed at helping the client to achieve success. Yet when academics, consultants, and practising managers are prepared to speak candidly about what they really do, a richer, messier, but more illuminating picture of change emerges.

The aim of *Perspectives on Change* is to move beyond the 'do as I say' approach of most change books and to encourage academics, consultants, and managers to say candidly what it is they really do and what they really think about change and how it should be managed. The editors of this book, Burnes and Randall, have over 60 years of experience between them of studying and teaching change management, acting as consultants, and actually managing change projects. They are, therefore, well aware of the differences and contradictions between what academics, consultants, and managers say about change in public and what they say in private and do in practice.

Perspectives on Change will offer students and practitioners of change a unique opportunity to understand change in practice. In addition, it will also contribute to the rigour-relevance debate by giving a different and perhaps more realistic perspective on the nature of the gap between theory and practice.

Bernard Burnes is Professor of Organisational Change at the Stirling Management School.

Julian Randall is Senior Lecturer at the University of Aberdeen Business School.

Routledge Studies in Organizational Change & Development

Perspectives on Change

What Academics, Consultants and
Managers Really Think about Change

**Edited by Bernard Burnes
and Julian Randall**

NEW YORK AND LONDON

First published 2016
by Routledge
711 Third Avenue, New York, NY 10017

and by Routledge
2 Park Square, Milton Park, Abingdon, Oxon OX14 4RN

First issued in paperback 2018

Routledge is an imprint of the Taylor & Francis Group, an informa business

© 2016 Taylor & Francis

Library of Congress Cataloging-in-Publication Data
  Perspectives on change : what academics, consultants and managers really think about change / edited by Bernard Burnes and Julian Randall.
     pages cm. — (Routledge studies in organizational change & development ; 13)
   Includes bibliographical references and index.
  1. Organizational change. I. Burnes, Bernard, 1953– editor. II. Randall, Julian, 1945 editor.
   HD58.8.P4724 2015
   658.4'06—dc23
   2015025791

ISBN 13: 978-1-138-33996-5 (pbk)
ISBN 13: 978-1-138-93012-4 (hbk)

Typeset in Sabon
by Apex CoVantage, LLC

Contents

PART II
Consultancy Cares
JULIAN RANDALL AND BERNARD BURNES

PART III
Managers as Consultants
JULIAN RANDALL AND BERNARD BURNES

Tables and Figures

Tables

Figures

Introduction

Change we need[1].

(Barack Obama)

Change? Change? Why do we need change? Things are quite bad enough as they are.

(Lord Salisbury to Queen Victoria[2])

This is a unique book in two key respects. First, it brings together academics, consultants, and managers to write about their experiences of managing change and the advice they can offer to others who have to bring about change. Most books and articles on change are written by academics for other academics and their students. By giving a voice to consultants and managers as well, this book helps to focus on what change agents actually do and why they do it. Second, it is unique in that the contributors do not tell the reader what they should do or promote their favoured approach to change. Instead, the contributors tell us how they manage change and what they really think works and does not work when they consider it from their own viewpoint as change agents.

In compiling this book, we recognise that many of us have an ambiguous relationship with change. We accept its inevitability and may be inspired by those politicians like Barack Obama who promise it, but—as the quote from the former British Prime Minister Lord Salisbury shows—change is not exactly welcome. Even up to some 30 years ago, Salisbury's words would have found support from most people, including those who led organisations. Indeed, it was only in the 1990s that Hammer and Champy (1993: 23) declared that, 'change has become both pervasive and persistent. It *is* normality'.

This implies that before then 'unchange', stability, was the norm, which of course it was not. After all, Heraclitus's famous comment that 'Change is the only constant in life' was uttered over 2500 years ago. However, the point is that only in recent times have organisations, or those who lead them, come to see change as something to be desired rather than something to be feared and resisted. Similarly, it is only in recent times that the ability to manage change has become seen as a key and difficult skill for managers. Previously, change tended to be viewed as a break from the norm, which managers needed to muddle through until stability reasserted itself.

For most of human history, those who led societies and institutions tended to manage change by trying to avoid it or suppress it. There was a distinct preference for stability. We can see this across the ancient world. In Egypt, Greece, and Rome the structure, laws, and practice of the state and social norms, such as ancestor worship and respect for age, promoted tradition and stability over newness and change (Antonaccio, 1994; Beyer, 1959; Jones, 1984). This was because stability, control, and power tended to be synonymous. In England, for example, Prince John opposed Magna Carta because it threatened the stability and power of the established order, which at that time was enshrined in the concept of the 'divine right of kings' to rule under God. Similarly, the various guilds that controlled manufacturing and commercial activities in Medieval Europe opposed change, not because they were innately opposed to progress but because new technologies, practices, and competitors had the potential to destabilise the established order and undermine their economic and social standing.

It was only with the British Industrial Revolution in the eighteenth century, buttressed by the new thinking of the Enlightenment, that this preference for stability began to break down (Hampson, 1990; Hobsbawm, 1979). The emergence of the factory system led to the creation of a new entrepreneurial-industrial class who saw stability and tradition as obstacles to their pursuit of wealth and power. Even so, this preference for change often resulted in one set of immutable rules being exchanged for another. This can be seen in Scientific Management, which its originator, Frederick Taylor, argued was the first attempt to establish a systematic and fair approach to change. It was designed to identify the 'one best' way to organise work and then to ensure that was not challenged or changed in any way (Burnes, 2014). Indeed, even the work of Kurt Lewin, the great 'Practical Theorist' of change, is characterised by his critics as a pursuit of an unachievable stability (Kanter et al., 1992).

Nevertheless, we undoubtedly live in an era where, rightly or wrongly, change is seen as both the normal order of things and desirable, at least by politicians and those who lead organisations. However, and perhaps paradoxically, successful change is seen as elusive. Though there are many approaches to change and certainly there is no shortage of advice or advisers, it is commonly agreed that the vast majority of change initiatives fail, although some organisations seem better able than others to bring about successful change, and some types of change seem easier to achieve than others (Burnes, 2014). A wide range of explanations have been offered for this high failure rate, ranging from impractical theories to ill-informed practice (Burnes and Jackson, 2011). Certainly, academics in their ivory towers are often accused of holding up the mirror of perfection to the real world and finding it wanting, whilst managers are seen as simplistic in their approach and keen to get from start to finish as quickly as possible so that they can move on to the next change project. As far as consultants are concerned, the common view seems to be that they are only in it for the money and—once paid—will rush off as quickly as they can. These are unfair caricatures, but they are not unrepresentative of how each of these groups views the other two.

In essence, as academics, managers, and consultants, we are seen as ignoring or falling short of Lewin's (1943/4: 169) famous dictum that 'There is nothing so practical as a good theory'. For Lewin, the interdependence of theory and practice was essential to understanding and changing organisations and communities. To this end, theorists, i.e. academics, should also be practitioners, and practitioners, i.e. managers and consultants, should also be well versed in the theory which underpins their practice. The difficulty of achieving this has been the focus of the 'rigour-relevance' debate of the last 20 years or so, where academics have argued about how or if it is possible to provide managers and consultants with theories and practices which combine both academic rigour and practical relevance (Bartunek, 2007; Polzer et al., 2009).

Unfortunately, since Lewin's time, there does not seem to have been any narrowing of the gap between theoreticians and practitioners. In some respects, as organisation theorists—in seeking to understand change better—have adopted ideas from other disciplines, the gap has grown. The exotic ideas and vocabulary of postmodernism, social constructionism, and complexity science, to name but a few, seem to act as a barrier to academics, consultants, and managers developing a common perspective on change and a common language in which they can talk about it. Similarly, managers and consultants seem wedded to encouraging more and more change, regardless of the failure of past initiatives. Yet this is a very misleading picture based on a misunderstanding of what these three groups actually do when they manage change themselves, as we will show in this book.

The common assumption that academics merely sit back and study change, but have no practical experience of it, was not true of Kurt Lewin, hence his reputation as the 'Practical Theorist'. Not only was he involved in working with governments, businesses, and community groups to bring about change but he also established and ran organisations himself and had to lead and develop these. Many of the leading change scholars since Lewin have also operated along these lines. For example, Rosabeth Moss Kanter and John Kotter, two of the most prominent figures in the change field today, run their own very successful consultancies whilst still being professors at Harvard Business School. The academics writing in this book not only act as consultants to businesses, but they have also held and hold senior managerial positions in their own organisations—hardly the profile of the unworldly academic.

The same goes for the consultants writing in this book. Whether consultants run their own businesses, are employed in larger consultancies, or are employed as internal consultants, they are also involved in managing and changing their own businesses as well as working with clients. In general, consultants are not divorced from research; most are accredited by professional bodies such as the UK Institute of Consulting or the British Psychological Society, which require them to undertake continuing professional development so that they understand the theory as well as the practice of change. The big consultancies also undertake their own research and develop their own theory-based approaches to change (Jones et al., 2006). Furthermore, most consultants have at one time or another worked as managers in organisations, and it is not unusual for senior consultants to move to senior roles in either the private or public sectors, including academia.

In terms of the managers who have contributed to this book, they have business qualifications and/or undertake periodic training and development in which managing change now tends to feature quite prominently. Like many managers, they are often in close contact with academia, for example, acting as guest lecturers or visiting professors. They may also be involved as sponsors of research by undergraduates, postgraduates, or academic staff. Therefore, the notion that most managers are 'uninformed' as to how change should be managed is as much a misrepresentation as seeing academics as unworldly or consultants as only interested in money.

This book allows these three groups the opportunity to write about how they see and manage change. It also offers them the opportunity to challenge the caricatures that have built up around academics, consultants, and managers, which can and do act as barriers to working together to bridge the theory-practice gap. This book will also show that in terms of the practice of managing change, there is far more that the three groups share in common than the myriad theories and approaches to change might suggest.

On a final note, in case you are wondering how the contributors to this book were selected, the answer is simple: we just asked people we know. This once again emphasises the closeness of academics, consultants, and managers. We may inhabit separate worlds, but these are worlds which heavily overlap and where we meet and share our experiences. Also, we all work in organisations, we all find ourselves involved in changing and developing our organisations, and we all have to do this in circumstances which are not always as we would wish them to be. However, in actually writing about our experience of change, there is a distinct difference. For academics, writing is a core part of our job—it is what we are paid to do. For consultants, it can be considered as part of their professional development and as contributing to promoting themselves and their abilities, although it does have to be fitted in around paid work. However, for managers, it is something that is very distinct from the day job and does have to be done in their own time, which is often a scarce commodity. This is why we have fewer contributions from managers than the other two groups.

We started out with an equal number of contributors in each the three sections of this book, but a number of managers dropped out owing to the pressure of their daily workloads. Therefore, although we are very grateful to the academics and consultants who have contributed to this book, we are even more grateful to the managers who have sacrificed their own time to undertake activity that is somewhat alien to them but from which a great number of people—academics, consultants, students, and other managers—will benefit.

Bernard Burnes and Julian Randall

NOTES

1. Barack Obama 2008 presidential election campaign slogan.
2. Quoted by Wilson (1999).

REFERENCES

Antonaccio, CM (1994) Contesting the Past: Hero Cult, Tomb Cult and Epic in Early Greece. *American Journal of Archaeology*, 98 (3), 398–410.
Bartunek, J (2007) Academic-Practitioner Collaboration Need Not Require Joint or Relevant Research. *Academy of Management Journal*, 50 (6), 1323–1333.
Beyer, WC (1959) The Civil Service in the Ancient World. *Public Administration Review*, 19 (4), 243–249.
Burnes, B (2014) *Managing Change* (6th edition). Pearson: Harlow.
Burnes, B and Jackson, P (2011) Success and Failure in Organisational Change: An Exploration of the Role of Values. *Journal of Change Management*, 11 (2), 133–162.
Hammer, M and Champy, J (1993) *Re-Engineering the Corporation*. Nicolas Brealey: London.
Hampson, N (1990) *The Enlightenment*. Penguin: Harmondsworth.
Hobsbawm, EJ (1979) *The Age of Revolution*. Abacus: London.
Jones, A H M (1984) *The Greek City from Alexander to Justinian*. OUP: Oxford.
Jones, Q, Dunphy, D, Fishman, R, Larne, M, and Canter, C (2006) *In Great Company: Unlocking the Secrets of Cultural Transformation*. Human Synergistics: Sydney, Australia.
Kanter, RM, Stein, BA and Jick, TD (1992) *The Challenge of Organizational Change*. Free Press: New York, NY.
Lewin, K (1952) [1943/4] Problems of research in social psychology. In D Cartwright (ed) *Field Theory in Social Science*. Social Science Paperbacks: London, pp. 155–169.
Polzer, JT, Gulati, R, and Khurana, R (2009) Crossing boundaries to increase relevance in organizational research. *Journal of Management Inquiry*, 18, 280–286.
Wilson, R (1999) Permanent revolution? Yes, minister—From the inaugural Vice Chancellor's lecture at City University given by the head of the Home Civil Service. *The Independent*, 11 May. Available at www.independent.co.uk.

Part I

An Academic Debate and Practice

Julian Randall and Bernard Burnes

Academics devoted to the subjects of business and management are keen to establish the credentials of their discipline in terms of its scientific foundations of valid and reliable knowledge which can, on occasion, be applied by others reading the results of their research. But there is an ongoing debate which indicates that they are not always convinced about the impact they have on the wider world of management practice. A recent fiftieth anniversary for the *Journal of Management* featured several articles which raised the questions of relevance and applicability of academic theories or whether that should even be a goal for those who are engaged with pure rather than applied science.

For example, there is a classic divide between science and 'stories'. For some academics, the positivistic approach of measuring factors affecting work is preferable to the qualitative approach, which focuses on what people at work say about themselves to management researchers. The editorial suggests that:

> We have become to some extent at least rather 'insular' and 'narrow' in our approach to theory, focusing on a particular theoretical tradition . . . We rhetorically position our work separate from other related approaches and do not sufficiently look across the fence even to what close colleagues are doing within management studies.
>
> (Corbett et al, 2014: 13)

Certainly there have been times when the closely argued beliefs of academics can be lost on managers. Why can academics not speak in plain language about the things that matter to ordinary people at work? Why are the theoretical and philosophical underpinnings of a topic so densely expressed that ordinary management practitioners can make little or nothing of what seems to them an arcane debate?

The authors suggest that the resolution of this dilemma may be found in process and agency. They suggest that:

> *Process refers to how we balance exploitation and exploration issues in our development and assessment of research. Meanwhile agency refers*

to what we do as authors, reviewers, editors, educators, and leaders and managers within educational institutions to promote plurality, while supporting the ever difficult and ever present trials of striking a balance between careerism and purity in the pursuit of research, and a balance between rigour and imagination in research.

(Corbett et al., 2014: 16)

We like to think that the academics who have contributed to this book have demonstrated an ability to bridge the divide between theory and practice in their work. Perhaps those of us involved in the management of change are fortunate that there is no other way of approaching the evidence about change events than the voices of the people who undergo it. As one PhD supervisor was once overheard telling his student, 'Let these people have a voice.' And without that voice, empirical data can be somewhat sterile and under-illustrated. But capturing the voices presents another challenge: How can we generalize from the data that we receive as researchers? This may make an interesting case study for those interested in the sector researched, but it may mean much less to those who attempt to manage themselves and others elsewhere in the diverse fields that management and organization studies encompass.

We begin this section with an author of change who is prepared to challenge many of the assumptions of traditional management of change narratives. The title of David Buchanan's chapter leaves no doubt about his own experience of the popular beliefs about change: 'I Couldn't Disagree More: Eight Things about Organizational Change that We Know for Sure but Which Are Probably Wrong'. He challenges the claims that change is on the increase, that the distinction between leaders and managers is a useful one, that we need transformational leaders, that a change manager is needed to make change happen, that bureaucracy is dead, or that best practice is the best guide for implementing change successfully. He does believe that change agents should be aware of and work with the politics of change. The work of change, he suggests, is always contentious and getting involved in the dynamics of the organizations is something that is frequently underestimated or disregarded.

Our second contributors are David Boje and Tonya Henderson, whose writing on antenarrative are well-known in the field of the management of change and management generally. The assumptions that people have about themselves, their jobs, their work, and their organizations are all part of the context in which the researchers become immersed. But those stories and accounts reveal the narratives which underlie the perceptions of individuals about themselves and the roles that they have had to play. Significantly, David has chosen to devote his time to those suffering from the after effects of military action in which those narratives become crucial for finding resolution and healing. And he explains how his work has developed from theory into practice.

Thus far, then, the researcher engages in the accounts of others in a process which our next chapter writers, Nic Beech and Rob McIntosh, describe as dialogic. By this they mean that key events are processually linked in organizational narratives in what they describe as anchor points and that these anchor points are created, interpreted, manipulated, and retold over time, because these are the processes by which change (and not changing) are justified. For the change agent, there is a similar interaction that occurs which they refer to as 'dialogic encounters'. They conclude with an Enquiry Action Framework which focuses on 'questioning and understanding the context, content and process of change . . . as well as developing a repertoire of alternative ways of enacting change'.

Our remaining chapters include accounts of actual change encounters which their authors had with individuals and groups researched during change events. For Patrick Dawson, 30 years of research into change events has reinforced his view of processual change and recognising that stories are 'powerful vehicles during times of change (in terms of sensemaking and sensegiving for individuals and groups), and they can be used to support change, to resist change, and to engage multiple stakeholders in opportunities for new pathways to change innovations or to curtailing change initiatives'. He illustrates this with accounts of individuals encountered over his research career and explores their responses to change events.

Stephen Procter and Julian Randall reflect on a 20-year journey in HM Customs and Excise, including their final merger with Inland Revenue in 2005, which illustrates how change agents are not always as adept at managing change as they would like to believe and the lessons that follow from that. But they also offer an example of a mixed group of doctors and counsellors working with the survivors of childhood sexual abuse whose meetings became a vehicle for sharing insights into effective caring of their patients and appreciation of the benefits that different approaches can bring to their patients.

Finally, Richard Badham unfolds the account of his work in Cokemaking Oz where his work provided him with contact with several memorable individuals with whom he shared a close, personal, and frank exchange which probably less experienced change agents might avoid. As he says 'involvements and relationships in the field involve a whole range of bargains, favours, trade-offs and ethical dilemmas, as the researcher strives to obtain access, data, time and resources, and those observed seek insight, relief, advice, and even material, reputational, or career enhancement'. Change affects the researcher and should be welcomed for that.

None of these contributors sound as if they have lived in an ivory tower. Indeed the benefit of exploring the issues surfaced during change events offers a direct route into the basic assumptions that individuals have and which may be shared within a working group. Failure to engage with your research subjects as a researcher means engagement in failure—the same applies to all change agents.

Returning to the debate 'Has management studies lost its way?' there is a view that the requirement to research and write in a predictive way has blunted the topic's ability to attract groundbreaking work. Alvesson and Sandberg suggest that:

> *A researcher identity engineered to only produce similar-looking journal articles for a limited group of sub-specialists is counterproductive to the ideal of interesting and influential studies, in which assumption-challenging is a key characteristic.*
>
> (Alvesson and Sandberg, 2013: 148)

We hope you will agree that these chapters satisfy the authors' aspirations for challenging accounts of change written by academics who have been immersed in their work to monitor what organizations generate among their people during imposed change at work.

REFERENCES

Alvesson, Matts and Jorgen Sandberg (2013) 'Has management studies lost its way? Ideas for more imaginative and innovative research', *Journal of Management Studies*, 50 (1), 128–52.

Corbett, Andrew, Joep Cornellisen, Andrew Delios and Bill Harley (2014) 'Variety, novelty and perceptions of scholarship in research on management and organization: An appeal for ambidextrous scholarship', *Journal of Management Studies*, 51 (1), 3–18.

1   I Couldn't Disagree More

Eight Things about Organizational Change that We Know for Sure but Which are Probably Wrong

David A. Buchanan

I am Emeritus Professor of Organizational Behaviour at Cranfield University School of Management and Visiting Professor at Nottingham Business School, Nottingham Trent University. I work freelance as a consultant, presenter, and author, specializing in change management and organization politics. I have a doctorate in organizational behaviour from Edinburgh University, I was director of Loughborough University Business School from 1992 to 1995, I have held visiting posts in Australian and Canadian management schools, and I work regularly in Australia. I am author/co-author of over two dozen books, including the bestselling *Organizational Behaviour* (with Andrzej Huczynski; eighth edition 2013). I have also co-authored several books on change management, including *Take The Lead* and *The Expertise of the Change Agent* (with David Boddy), *The Sustainability and Spread of Organizational Change* (with Louise Fitzgerald and Diane Ketley), and *Power, Politics and Organizational Change: Winning the Turf Game* (with Richard Badham). I have also written numerous book chapters and articles on organizational behaviour and change and research methods.

Most of my experience of organizational change is based on my work and observations as a field researcher. However, I also have some direct experience of change management from various senior roles in higher education. It has often been observed that change is a paradoxical process. From my experience, two paradoxes stand out. The first concerns the tension between rationality and creativity. Practical advice, from both management consultants and academics, often seeks to codify and simplify the change process; 'Follow these steps to success.' That generic advice has to be translated into action that 'fits' the context—presenting problems, past history, local cultural norms, available resources, stakeholder views, and so on. That translation process is a creative one, based on locally informed managerial judgement. The creative dimension of the change design and implementation process is often overlooked or considered unimportant. The second concerns the tension between rationality and politics. Organizations are political systems, and change is a politicized process. The change agent, manager, or leader who is not able and willing to play the organization politics game will fail, sooner or later, and probably sooner—because most if not all other stakeholders are playing that game, too, to protect or advance their own interests. The politics of the change process seems also to be a 'missing ingredient' in much of the practical commentary in this area, and training and development in change leadership often avoids the development of political skill.

Recent research has concerned managing change in extreme (post-crisis) contexts, the changing roles of middle management in acute health care (funded by the UK National Institute for Health Research, Health Services & Delivery Research Programme), the prospects for transformational change in acute hospitals, and medical change leadership capabilities.

EVERYONE KNOWS THAT 'CHANGE IS THE NEW NORMAL'

Everyone knows that progress is inevitable, that resistance to change is a natural human response, that the pace of change is increasing, that bureaucracy is rigid and bad, and so on. Welcome to contemporary conventional wisdom concerning organizational change. However, from experience as a researcher who has observed many organizational change programmes (and who has some successful, but not necessarily painless, personal experience in the area), conventional wisdom is mostly wrong. The aim of this chapter, therefore, is to take eight 'obvious' claims about the nature of change and to suggest that these are misguided. This is not an academic sniping exercise. Management beliefs and assumptions about the nature of the world in general, and about people and organizational change in particular, have implications for management decisions and actions. Driving change is one area where, if you get it wrong, you can cause a lot of individual and corporate damage.

The following conventional wisdoms have been culled from conversations with managers and management consultants, comments from national politicians, articles by journalists, and from academic publications. (Government ministers in the UK appear to inhabit a unique fantasy world with regard to their understanding of the nature, pace, and implications of change in the departments for which they are responsible.) The choice of targets is inevitably based on personal bias and judgement; however, with regard to each of these eight issues, sustaining an unshaken belief in conventional wisdom means consistently ignoring the research evidence.

THE PACE IS PICKING UP

> That this is an age of change is an expression heard frequently today. Never before in the history of mankind have so many and so frequent changes occurred. These changes that we see taking place all about us are in that great cultural accumulation which is man's social heritage. It has already been shown that these cultural changes were

> in earlier times rather infrequent, but that in modern times they have
> been occurring faster and faster until today mankind is almost bewil-
> dered in his effort to keep adjusted to these ever increasing social
> changes. This rapidity of social change may be due to the increase in
> inventions which in turn is made possible by the accumulative nature
> of material culture (i.e., technology).

Conventional wisdom says that change today is affecting more aspects of our lives, at a faster pace than ever before. This is nonsense. People have been complaining about the pace of technological and social change since the nineteenth century, and probably earlier. We just think that we are dif-ferent. We are not. Do the armchair experiment for yourself. Look around, at home, at work, and across society as a whole. What has *not* changed over the past ten years, the past fifty years, the past century?

Does the previous quote sound like a description of the early twenty-first century? William Fielding Ogburn wrote that in 1922 (p.199). Half a century later, Alvin Toffler (1970) rediscovered Ogburn's concerns, claim-ing that we were being overwhelmed by too much technological and social change too quickly. This led, Toffler argued, to 'future shock', and to stress and information overload—complaints that are commonplace now, more than 40 years later.

Perceptions of pace and of the need to respond by accelerating the rate of change accordingly are being heightened by advice from management con-sultants and academics. Sarah Fraser (2002) provides suggestions on how to accelerate the spread of new ideas in health care. Christopher Worley and Edward Lawler (2009) argue that organizations must be 'built to change', which means reorganizing constantly and naturally. From the results of a survey concerning best practice in organizational redesign, Giancarlo Ghis-lanzoni and colleagues (2010) from McKinsey found that one of the top-five strategies for success was accelerating the pace of implementation to deliver results as quickly as possible. John Kotter (2012b) describes eight 'accelerators' that are necessary to ensure rapid change. The management consultancy firm Deloitte (2013) advises clients with a methodology called 'organization acceleration', based on the argument that many change pro-grammes move too slowly. Bringing this argument down to a personal level, Todd Buchholz (2011), who has no time for 'work life balance', argues that we are 'built to rush'. Speed, stress, and competition at work are good for us and make us healthier and happier.

Changes may have to be implemented rapidly in some circumstances, such as responding to crises. Constant rapid change, however, can be dam-aging and is unnecessary. Eric Abrahamson (2000; 2004) argues that this is destabilizing and causes burnout. He advocates 'painless change', inter-spersing major initiatives among carefully paced spells of smaller changes, which he calls 'tinkering and kludging'. Heike Bruch and Jochen Menges (2010) also argue that fast-paced change leads to corporate burnout.

In many organizations, market pressures encourage management to increase the number and speed of activities, raise performance goals, shorten innovation cycles, and introduce new systems and technologies. When the chief executive makes this furious pace 'the new normal', the result is chronic overloading. Working constantly under time pressure, with priorities frequently changing, focus is scattered, staff become tired and demotivated, and customers get confused. Bruch and Menges call this 'the acceleration trap', claiming that in companies that were 'fully trapped', 60 per cent of employees felt that they lacked the resources to get their work done, compared with only 2 per cent in companies that were not 'trapped'.

Henry Mintzberg (2000) argues that each succeeding generation tends to perceive its own situation as more turbulent than that of its predecessors'. Perhaps we should not overreact. Change is accompanied by continuity and is defined by and with reference to what has not changed. In addition to considering with more care the timing and speed of change, organizations launching new initiatives may be advised to indicate what is going to stay the same, to reassure those who are implicated, and alleviate unnecessary anxiety.

LEADERS, NOT MANAGERS

Conventional wisdom says that change management and change leadership are different roles, and that this is an important distinction. This is nonsense. Whereas it may be possible to define clear categories in theory, in practice these roles are overlapping and indistinguishable.

One of the main advocates of this distinction is John Kotter (2012a). For him, change management refers to the basic tools and structures with which smaller-scale changes are controlled. Change leadership marshals the driving forces and visions that produce large-scale transformations. His main point, of course, is that we need more change leadership.

This argument has two flaws. The first concerns the assumption that large-scale transformations are more meaningful and potent and are therefore more valuable than small-scale change. They aren't. The second concerns the belief that the contrasting definitions of these management and leadership concepts will survive contact with practice. They won't.

Moore and Buchanan (2013) report a change initiative that was deliberately called 'sweat the small stuff'. Staff in one clinical service in an acute hospital were asked to identify small annoying problems which had not been fixed for some time. These included broken equipment and faulty administrative processes. The five problems were addressed by a three-person team, including an 'animateur' who set up and coordinated the project, a clinical champion who engaged medical colleagues, and a 'who knows who knows what' person whose administrative background and networks helped the team to identify shortcuts, 'workarounds', and 'the right people' to solve these problems quickly. All five problems were solved within five days. The total costs came to £89 for a piece of equipment and the 40 minutes which the animateur spent in conversations. The benefits were financial (income generation), processual (safer patient allocation), temporal (tasks performed more quickly with less waiting time), emotional (less annoyance, boredom, frustration), and relational (improved inter-professional relations).

If management had decided instead to launch a major transformational change in this service, it may not have succeeded. One of the overarching benefits of 'sweating the small stuff' was improved management-medical relationships, laying the foundation for further improvements (this idea was spread to other services in the hospital). Fixing the small stuff was beneficial in its own right and was the precursor for future major changes. The animateur's job title was 'operations manager'; was she a change manager or a change leader?

The general distinction between management and leadership has been challenged by Henry Mintzberg (2009, p.8) who argues; 'Frankly, I don't understand what this distinction means in the everyday life of organizations. Sure, we can separate leading and managing conceptually. But can we separate them in practice? Or, more to the point, should we even try'? He also asks, how would you like to be managed by someone who doesn't lead, or led by someone who doesn't manage? 'We should be seeing managers *as* leaders, and leadership as management practiced well' (Mintzberg, 2009, p.9).

In short, this is not a distinction worth arguing over and may be more simply resolved by a combination of personal and contextual preference. In any case, the effective change manager or change leader rarely changes anything; their role is to orchestrate the conditions that allow others to design and implement the necessary changes for themselves.

WE NEED TRANSFORMATIONAL LEADERS

Conventional wisdom says that we need transformational leaders to deliver the scope and pace of the changes required by the current uncertain, competitive, and rapidly changing environment. This is nonsense. Transformational leaders can destabilize an organization and create burnout with too much rapid and major change.

Transformational leaders are defined as charismatic, visionary individuals who motivate and inspire their followers to excel, to lift their game, to 'go the extra mile'. To check the popularity of this concept, google 'transformational leader/leadership' and see how many millions of 'hits' are returned. This concept was first popularized by James McGregor Burns (1978), and the idea remains fashionable today. With the pace of change accelerating (allegedly) and with the accompanying (presumed) need for radical, transformational change, there appears to be a logic behind the attractiveness of such heroic figures.

The arguments in favour of transformational leaders, however, do not survive contact with the evidence. Exploring the success of organizations that had consistently outperformed the stock market, James Collins and Jerry Porras (1995) found that their success was partly attributable to internally appointed leaders with skills in institution-building and the consistent pursuit of performance improvement. Consistency of leadership with a strong sense of purpose thus outperformed charismatic heroics. Rakesh Khurana (2002) argues that charismatic, transformational leaders are not indispensable organizational assets but 'a dangerous curse', particularly as they can destablize an organization in dangerous ways (Jeff Skilling's role at Enron is a popular example of this phenomenon). Khurana also warns against attributing an organization's success to a single individual, pointing to the combination of social, economic, and other forces that shape and constrain individual efforts.

Joseph Badaracco (2001; 2002) argues that 'we don't need another hero', and that a more subtle approach is effective, emphasizing small changes, careful moves, controlled and measured efforts—as Abrahamson (2000; 2004) also suggests. Debra Meyerson (2001a and b) offers a similar argument stressing the importance of the behind the scenes, 'below the radar' efforts of middle managers in particular. These 'tempered radicals' are not senior managers, but they are instrumental in initiating and driving change.

David Buchanan and Steve Macaulay (2014, p.48) argue that the successful change leader is not the champion who drives change on his or her own and takes all the credit, but one of several champions, among whom responsibility is distributed and who 'share the prizes'.

WHO IS IN CHARGE OF THIS PROJECT?

Conventional wisdom says that responsibility for change implementation must be clearly focused on one individual or a small project team for the duration of the programme. This is nonsense. This is only one model of change implementation, which today is more often accomplished by large numbers of people working in collaboration. Distributed change agency works through responsibility and accountability being shared across an organization, migrating from one individual or team to another as the programme develops.

Related to the generic concept of 'distributed leadership' (Gronn, 2002; 2011; Denis et al., 2012), several commentators note the dispersed, decentred, pluralistic, or distributed nature of change agency or change leadership. Pettigrew et al. (1992) describe team-based approaches to change in health care. In a hospital study, Brooks (1996) found that implementation involved the chief executive, a cadre of managers, and a diagonal slice of a dozen staff designated as 'networkers'. Denis et al. (1996; 2001) focus on 'leadership constellations', whose members play fluid and complementary roles.

Gronn (2002) argues that the defining characteristic of distributed leadership is 'concertive action'; steps initiated by one individual are developed by others through the 'circulation of initiative'. Buchanan et al. (2007) describe the implementation of a complex change agenda which dramatically improved the treatment given to men with prostate cancer in an acute hospital. Whereas the contributions of four individuals (one of whom was employed by an external agency) were key, there was no project leader and implementation involved a further 23 individuals and 26 managerial, administrative, and clinical groups, patients, representatives, and other organizations. As Gronn (2002) suggested, responsibility for the changes in this case shifted between individuals and groups as the work progressed, apparently without the need for any supervisory or coordinating roles or structures. Many of those implicated in this process had little or no change leadership background or training.

Does this mean that everyone is now a change leader? No, but the current probability of becoming involved in a change initiative is high, and having some basic skills in this area is helpful. It may therefore be appropriate to offer change leadership development opportunities to staff other than those in formal change management roles.

BUREAUCRACY IS DEAD

Conventional wisdom says that, to cope with constant change, slow and rigid bureaucratic hierarchies must be replaced by organization structures that are flat and flexible. This is nonsense. Most of us need order, stability, and predictability. Bureaucratic structures help to achieve this. Customers and suppliers also want to deal with businesses that are predictable.

Weber Max (1947) defined bureaucracy as a rational and efficient mode of organization based on division of labour, written guidelines, a hierarchy staffed by career professionals, and with authority residing in the position rather than the person. Although bureaucracy has become a contemporary hate term, this is a model with significant strengths, with regard to order, stability, predictability, standardization, and control. Harold Leavitt (2003; 2005) argues that many large bureaucratic organizations are innovative and successful. Clear hierarchical structures, he notes, contribute to our sense of place and status, self-esteem, and also to our identity. He also argues that, 'multilevel hierarchies remain the best available mechanism for doing complex work' (Leavitt, 2003, p.102).

Bureaucracy is especially associated with the public sector. But here unity, coordination, precision, predictability, impartiality, and continuity across changes in government are significant considerations (Olsen, 2006). The British National Health Service (NHS), for example, is criticized for being fragmented, uncoordinated, confused, unpredictable, partial, and forgetful (Donaldson, 2000). In other words, the NHS is not bureaucratic enough.

Bureaucracy is also popularly associated with inflexibility. Forrest Briscoe (2007) inverts this view, showing how the temporal flexibility of professional service workers can be enhanced by intensifying bureaucratic processes. Temporal flexibility means the ability to adjust work schedules to accommodate personal circumstances. Professional service work is seen as temporally inflexible, because it demands responses to the unpredictable needs of clients with whom professionals have personal relationships. This makes it difficult to hand clients over to colleagues. However, processes that can increase flexibility in this context include managing client expectations by routinizing the 'service encounter'; the use of rules, procedures, and decision protocols to standardize the handling of common problems; and codifying client knowledge by developing knowledge management systems. This formalization of working practices, relying on rules and procedures, means increased bureaucracy and hierarchical control. For most of the professionals in Briscoe's study, these constraints were offset by increased flexibility, and the protocols were themselves flexible in response to circumstances and not treated as binding. In sum, those organizational processes generate a more bureaucratic, and more flexible, workplace.

Johan Olsen (2006) concludes that bureaucracy is not *the* way to organize public services but is part of a repertoire of overlapping and coexisting organizational forms. He rejects the fashionable 'dinosaur scenario' in which the undesirable presence of obsolete bureaucratic forms and their accompanying bureaucrats wither and disappear because they are incompatible with a complex, individualistic, rapidly changing society.

SIMPLY BEST PRACTICE

Conventional wisdom says that, to manage change effectively, we must learn from organizations that have done it well and then use 'best practice'. This is nonsense. Effective management practice is highly contingent. What worked well in one setting is unlikely to work well in another. Management actions must be sensitive to context.

There is no shortage of 'best practice' change implementation recipes. One of the most well-known is the eight-step transformational programme developed by John Kotter (1995; 2008). His ingredients include sense of urgency, powerful guiding coalition, vision, communication, empowerment, short-term wins, consolidation, and institutionalization. The management consulting company McKinsey has a recipe for transformational change with only four ingredients: aspirational targets, clear structure, maintaining energy and involvement, and strong leadership (Keller et al., 2010). Some recipes are accompanied by snappy acronyms. One is the DICE framework developed by the Boston Consulting Group: Duration, performance Integrity, Commitment, Effort (Sirkin et al., 2005). ADKAR is another, from the consulting company Prosci: Awareness, Desire, Knowledge, Ability, Reinforcement (Hiatt, 2006).

Unlike the recipes in your kitchen cookbook, however, these guidelines list the ingredients without explaining how to cook the dish. You have to work that out for yourself—and this is a source of frustration for many practising managers looking for concrete advice on 'what works and what doesn't'. These guides simply identify the factors that need to be addressed; the challenge is to construct a change process that fits the particular organizational context (Rod et al., 2009). That is the hard part. Change is thus to some extent a technical exercise, understanding the issues that have to be taken into consideration, and also a creative exercise, designing a process that recognizes local history, context, resources, and objectives.

Contingency models of change recognize the limitations of simple recipes but still require creative contributions from those involved. From research in the finance sector in Australia, Doug Stace and Dexter Dunphy (2001) developed a contingency model based on scale of change (from fine-tuning to corporate transformation) and style of change (from collaborative to coercive). They argue that collaborative strategies are time-consuming as they expose conflicting views that are difficult to reconcile. Where organizational survival depends on rapid and strategic change, they conclude, dictatorial transformation is more appropriate. Veronica Hope Hailey and Julia Balogun (2002; Balogun 2006) similarly advocate context sensitive approaches to change design and implementation. Their framework identifies a number of contextual features in what they call 'the change kaleidoscope', including the necessary speed of change, the scope of the change agenda, the need to maintain continuity on some dimensions, diversity of attitudes and values among those affected, individual change capabilities and organizational capacity for change, readiness for change, and the power of the change agent. These context features, they argue, should influence decisions concerning the starting point and path of change, the implementation style, specific change levers and mechanisms, and the nature of change roles (top down, bottom up, dispersed).

These recipes and contingency models are 'high-level' guides and not detailed 'best practice' roadmaps. They can be useful in practice as long as they are used in that way, although academic critics may sometimes complain of their atheoretical nature. Change agents resorting to these models have to 'fill in the blanks' themselves, with an appropriate blend of local knowledge, informed judgement, and creative flair.

AVOID WHEEL REINVENTION

> That it [the stethoscope] will ever come into general use, not withstanding its value, I am extremely doubtful; because its beneficial application requires much time, and it gives a good deal of trouble both to the patient and practitioner, and because its whole hue and character is foreign, and opposed to all our habits and associations.

> It must be confessed that there is something ludicrous in the picture of a grave physician formally listening through a long tube applied to a patient's thorax, as if the disease within were a living being that could communicate its condition to the sense without. (Forbes, 1821)

Conventional wisdom assumes that the best way to disseminate new ideas in an organization is to copy them from one unit or division to another. For example, Gabriel Szulanski and Sidney Winter (2002) describe a 'copy exact' model for this purpose, arguing that 'wheel reinvention' is slow and costly. As with 'best practice' with regard to change implementation guidance, this is nonsense. What worked for unit A may not apply to unit B. For their examples, Szulanski and Winter chose simple operations that were easy to codify; more complex changes in working practices and operating procedures are much more difficult—usually impossible—to transfer in this way. Attempts to impose inappropriate solutions generate resistance, reduce performance, and increase costs.

The problem in taking a good idea from one part of the organization and applying it to another is known as 'the best practices puzzle'. If it worked for A division, why would B division turn it down? Don Berwick (2003) notes that the treatment for scurvy, first identified in 1601, did not become standard practice in the British navy until 1865, over 260 years later. Why the delay? There is now a considerable body of research evidence which shows, first, that this delay and others like it is not surprising and, second, that this is hardly a puzzle.

One of the leading commentators in this area, Everett Rogers (2003), argues that an innovation is more likely to spread, or diffuse, if it has the following features. *Advantageous*: it should be seen as better than what we currently have. *Compatible*: it should fit with existing systems and values. *Simple*: the necessary changes should be straightforward to implement. *Testable*: new ideas should be checked before commitment to adoption. *Observable*: the change and its impact can be seen beforehand by those who are going to be affected. *Adaptable*: what is being proposed can be customized to fit local conditions.

The features identified by Rogers are relatively easy to establish with new products, because you can touch them and see them working. However, there are problems in applying his diffusion test to changes in working practices or organization structures and systems. In contrast to product innovations, *operational* innovations are often relatively complex, and they can neither be tested nor observed before they are implemented. We are therefore going to have to wait to find out just how advantageous and compatible they will be.

There is now a considerable body of research and evidence concerning the range of factors that can affect the diffusion of operational innovations. Trisha Greenhalgh et al. (2004) conducted a comprehensive review of this work, drawing on eleven research traditions. They found that the adoption of innovations depends on a number of related factors. These include the nature of the idea, the willingness to change of potential adopters, how the innovation is communicated, and who is driving it, organization culture and 'readiness for change', and external pressures (social, economic, political, regulatory). Organizational receptiveness to change (Pettigrew et al., 1992) and individual readiness to change (Rafferty et al., 2013) are themselves multifaceted and can be difficult to establish. Adoption of innovations can be a complex process, which can take time to unfold.

Organization politics can also interfere in the following manner, as Richard Walton (1975) explained. The original inventors or designers get credit for new ideas, and if those ideas fail, they may still be praised as risk takers. However, those who would then copy their ideas get less praise, even if they are successful, too. And if those who follow fail in their efforts, they damage their reputations. Another problem is that innovators often get involved in arguments with superiors and staff groups, where they have to defend their plans aggressively, damaging their reputations as a result. Watching this, other managers want to avoid a similar fate and to not readily try to copy their ideas. It is therefore politically advantageous to avoid new ideas, such as innovative working practices, that are generated by others, even if they are successful, and to develop your own novel approaches.

One of the main conclusions from diffusion research is that new ideas are more likely to be implemented where they can be adapted, refined, or modified to fit local needs and circumstances (Greenhalgh et al., 2004, p.14). In addition, when unit B takes the time that is necessary to learn about and to adapt new ideas, then changes are more likely to be effective and to be sustained. Buchanan et al. (2007, p.250) argue that adaptation of multifaceted changes can take as long as the initial development.

In other words, when spreading new working practices from one part of the business to another, 'wheel reinvention' is necessary and desirable, in most instances, for at least three reasons: First, to establish commitment to the changes from those who have to implement and to work with them; second, to ensure that new working practices are tailored to local conditions; and third, to increase the probability that the changes will be sustained.

CHANGE AGENTS MUST BE SQUEAKY CLEAN

Conventional wisdom says that change leaders must not 'play politics' but should be 'squeaky clean' and avoid these time-wasting and unproductive games. This is nonsense. Organizations are political systems, and change is a politicized process. The change agent who is not willing to play politics will fail, sooner or later, and probably sooner.

In a survey of 250 middle and senior managers in Britain, 83 per cent agreed that 'politics is played at all organizational levels', 84 per cent agreed that 'I am prepared to play politics when necessary', 87 per cent agreed that

9 per cent agreed that	'change agents who avoid organization politics are more likely to succeed in their roles'
24 per cent agreed that	'major changes must be free from organization politics if they are to be effective'
60 per cent agreed that	'politics become more important as organizational change becomes more complex'
79 per cent agreed that	'politics can be used to initiate and drive useful change initiatives'
81 per cent agreed that	'major changes need to be "steered" through the organization politics'
93 per cent agreed that	'politics can be used to slow down and block useful change initiatives'

'politics is a natural part of the management job', and 93 per cent agreed that 'most managers, if they want to succeed, have to play politics at least part of the time' (Buchanan, 2008). The importance of skill in using political behaviour in change appeared to be widely acknowledged:

However, despite the significance of this topic, around 80 per cent of the managers surveyed said that they had no training in dealing with organization politics. Arguing that political skill is increasingly important to management career success, Gerald Ferris et al. (2000, p.30) offer the following definition:

We define political skill as an interpersonal style construct that combines social astuteness with the ability to relate well, and otherwise demonstrate situationally appropriate behaviour in a disarmingly charming and engaging manner that inspires confidence, trust, sincerity, and genuineness. We suggest that people high in political skill not only know precisely what to do in different/social situations at work, but they know exactly how to do it in a sincere manner that disguises any potentially manipulative motives and renders the influence attempt successful.

Political behaviour is not to be equated solely with 'dirty tricks'. David Buchanan and Richard Badham (2008) describe a range of other political tactics including impression management, information games, structure games, scapegoating, alliances and networks, compromise, rule games, and positioning. Jeffrey Pfeffer (2010) offers similar advice with regard to 'forms of leverage'. These include rewarding those who help and punishing (symbolically) those who get in the way, making the first move and catching your opponents off guard, removing your rivals (nicely if possible) through 'strategic outplacement', using 'the personal touch' and working with people face to face, and being persistent—wear the opposition down. Pfeffer also advises making use of your 'discretionary control over resources', to do favours for others and to generate reciprocity. He cites what he calls 'the new golden rule' which is that 'the person with the gold gets to make the rules' (Pfeffer, 2010, p.87).

Pfeffer notes that, when implementing cross-functional projects in complex organizations, change leaders may have significant responsibility but no line management authority to direct anyone to do anything. He concludes that,

> The effective use of power is becoming increasingly important. Yes, we have flatter organizations and more cross-functional teams than we had in the past. But getting things done in a less-hierarchical system requires *more* influence. And as strategies become more complicated, the importance and difficulty of effective execution increase accordingly. (Pfeffer, 2010, p.87)

His parting advice (p.92) is:

> So, welcome to the real world. It may not be the world we want, but it's the world we have. You won't get far, and neither will your strategic plans, if you can't build and use power. Some of the people competing for advancement or standing in the way of your organization's agenda will bend the rules of fair play or ignore them entirely. Don't bother complaining about this or wishing things were different. Part of your job is to know how to prevail in the political battles you will face.

This view of organization politics is not universally shared. Abraham Zaleznik (1979) distinguishes between 'psychopolitics' and 'real work', arguing that managers should stick to the latter. The problem with this argument is that, 'psychopolitics' are a key—and unavoidable—part of the day job (assuming that one wants to be seen to be doing that job well). Most, if not all, managers get their jobs, and get promoted, because they are going to bring new ideas that will change and improve things. You will rarely be hired or promoted for consenting to keep things just the way they are and do exactly what you are told to do.

At any given time, there are more ideas for change, improvement, and development circulating than the organization has the time and resources to implement. Those ideas are in competition with each other. As a manager, your job—the job that you were hired to do—is to ensure that your ideas have the best chance of being implemented. This competition is almost always healthy and can prevent weak ideas from progressing. Occasionally, however, a poor idea is accepted, because the person promoting it was good at 'selling' the issue. There is little to be gained from complaining about this, because that can damage the reputation of the person doing the complaining. The more effective response in the long term is to develop your own 'issue selling' capabilities (Dutton et al., 2001).

It appears, therefore, that the effectiveness of organizational change is dependent, to a large extent, on the political skills of change agents, managers, and leaders. Being 'squeaky clean' may be a recipe for failure. And if one does decide to take that moral high ground, one has to do so in the knowledge that most of one's colleagues think differently. The main rule, therefore, is: play or be sidelined by your colleagues. Or, as Lois Frankel (2004, p.19) says, 'if you don't play, you can't win'.

A REASSURING NARRATIVE?

These eight assumptions about change management are the basis of a reassuring narrative, which says that we understand the problems, and we know how to solve them. The story goes like this:

> In the current economic climate, with the pace of change accelerating, we need leaders, not managers, and we need transformational leaders in particular to drive rapid and radical change, for which accountability must be clear. Bureaucratic organizations are rigid and slow, and they have to change. Fortunately, 'the best practice recipe' for change is well known, and once new ideas are established, they can be shared quickly and easily across and between organizations without the need to 'reinvent the wheel'. Change leaders must not waste time on organization politics, leaving those games to others, while focusing on the task.

This chapter has argued that this narrative is wrong. Most estimates put the failure rate of planned organizational change at around 60 to 70 per cent (Rafferty et al., 2013). Could this dismal record be explained, at least in part, by practice that is based on false assumptions?

REFERENCES

Abrahamson, E. (2000) 'Change without pain', *Harvard Business Review*, 78 (4): 75–9.
Abrahamson, E. (2004) *Change Without Pain: How Managers Can Overcome Initiative Overload, Organizational Chaos, and Employee Burnout*. Boston, MA: Harvard Business School Press.
Badaracco, J.L. (2001) 'We don't need another hero', *Harvard Business Review*, 79 (8): 121–6.
Badaracco, J.L. (2002) *Leading Quietly: An Unorthodox Guide to Doing the Right Thing*. Boston, MA: Harvard Business School Press.
Balogun, J. (2006) 'Managing change: steering a course between intended strategies and unanticipated outcomes', *Long Range Planning*, 39 (1): 29–49.

Berwick, D.M. (2003) 'Disseminating innovations in health care', *Journal of the American Medical Association*, 289(15): 1969–75.

Briscoe, F. (2007) 'From iron cage to iron shield?: how bureaucracy enables temporal flexibility for professional service workers', *Organization Science*, 18 (2): 297–314.

Brooks, I. (1996) 'Leadership of a cultural change process', *Leadership and Organization Development Journal*, 17 (5): 31–7.

Bruch, H. and Menges, J.I. (2010) 'The acceleration trap', *Harvard Business Review*, 88 (4): 80–86.

Buchanan, D.A. (2008) 'You stab my back, I'll stab yours: management experience and perceptions of organization politics', *British Journal of Management*, 19 (1): 49–64.

Buchanan, D.A. and Badham, R. (2008) *Power, Politics, and Organizational Change: Winning the Turf Game*. London: Sage Publications, (second edn).

Buchanan, D.A. and Macaulay, S. (2014) 'How to be a successful change leader', *Training Journal*, January, pp. 45–48.

Buchanan, D.A., Fitzgerald, L. and Ketley, D. (eds) (2007) *The Sustainability and Spread of Organizational Change: Modernizing Healthcare*. London: Routledge.

Buchholz, T.G. (2011) *Rush: Why You Need and Love the Rat Race*. Hudson Street Press: New York.

Burns, J.M. (1978) *Leadership*. New York: Harper & Row.

Collins, J.C. and Porras, J.I. (1995) *Built to Last: Successful Habits of Visionary Companies*. London: Century Books.

Deloitte. (2013) *Organization Acceleration: The New Science of Moving Organizations Forward*. London: Deloitte Touch Tohmatsu Limited.Denis, J.-L., Lamothe, L. and Langley, A. (2001) 'The dynamics of collective leadership and strategic change in pluralistic organizations', *Academy of Management Journal*, 44 (4): 809–37.

Denis, J.-L., Langley, A. and Cazale, L. (1996) 'Leadership and strategic change under uncertainty', *Organization Studies*, 17 (4): 673–99.

Denis, J.-L., Langley, A. and Sergi, V. (2012) 'Leadership in the plural', *Academy of Management Annals*, 6 (1): 1–73.

Donaldson, L. (2000) *An Organization with a Memory*. London: Department of Health/The Stationery Office.

Dutton, J.E., Ashford, S.J., O'Neill, R.M. and Lawrence, K.A. (2001) 'Moves that matter: issue selling and organizational change', *Academy of Management Journal*, 44 (4): 716–36.

Ferris, G.R., Perrewé, P.L., Anthony, W.P. and Gilmore, D.C. (2000) 'Political skill at work', *Organizational Dynamics*, 28 (4): 25–37.

Forbes, J. trans. (1821) *De L'Auscultation Mediate ou Traite du Diagnostic des Maladies des Poumons et du Coeur* [A Treatise on Diseases of the Chest and on Mediate Auscultation], R.T.H. Laennec. London: T &G Underwood.

Frankel, L.P. (2004) *Nice Girls Don't Get the Corner Office: Unconscious Mistakes Women Make That Sabotage Their Careers*. New York: Warner Business Books.

Fraser, S.W. (2002) *Accelerating the Spread of Good Practice: A Workbook for Health Care*. Chichester, West Sussex: Kingsham Press.

Ghislanzoni, G., Heidari-Robinson, S. and Jermiin, M. (2010) *Taking Organizational Redesign from Plan to Practice*. London: McKinsey & Company.

Greenhalgh, T., Robert, G., Bate, P., Kyriakidou, O., Macfarlane, F. and Peacock, R. (2004) *How to Spread Good Ideas: A Systematic Review of the Literature on Diffusion, Dissemination and Sustainability of Innovations in Health Service Delivery and Organization*. London: University College London, and NHS Service Delivery and Organization Research Programme.

Gronn, P. (2002) 'Distributed leadership as a unit of analysis', *Leadership Quarterly*, 13 (4): 423–51.

Gronn, P. (2011) 'Hybrid configurations of leadership', in Alan Bryman, David Collinson, Keith Grint, Brad Jackson and Mary Uhl-Bien (eds), *The Sage Handbook of Leadership*. London: Sage Publications, pp. 437–54.

Hiatt, J. (2006) *ADKAR: A Model for Change in Business, Government, and Our Community*. Loveland, CO: Prosci.

Hope Hailey, V. and Balogun, J. (2002) 'Devising context sensitive approaches to change: the example of Glaxo Wellcome', *Long Range Planning*, 35 (2): 153–78.

Keller, S., Meaney, M. and Pung, C. (2010) *What Successful Transformations Share*. Chicago and London: McKinsey & Company.

Khurana, R. (2002) 'The curse of the superstar CEO', *Harvard Business Review*, 80 (9): 60–6.

Kotter, J.P. (1995) 'Leading change: why transformation efforts fail', *Harvard Business Review*, 73 (2): 59–67.

Kotter, J.P. (2008) *A Sense of Urgency*. Boston, MA: Harvard Business School Press.

Kotter, J.P. (2012a) 'Accelerate!', *Harvard Business Review*, 90 (11): 44–52.

Kotter, J.P. (2012b) *Leading Change*. Boston, MA: Harvard University Press, (second edn).

Leavitt, H.J. (2003) 'Why hierarchies thrive', *Harvard Business Review*, 81 (3): 96–102.

Meyerson, D.E. (2001a) 'Radical change, the quiet way', *Harvard Business Review*, 79 (9): 92–100.

Meyerson, D.E. (2001b) *Tempered Radicals: How People Use Difference to Inspire Change at Work*. Boston, MA: Harvard Business School Press.

Mintzberg, H. (2000) *The Rise and Fall of Strategic Planning*. Harlow: FT Prentice Hall.

Mintzberg, H. (2009) *Managing*. Harlow, Essex: Financial Times Prentice Hall.

Moore, C. and Buchanan, D.A. (2013) 'Sweat the small stuff: minor problems, rapid fixes, major gains', *Health Services Management Research*, 26 (1): 9–17.

Ogburn, W.F. (1922) *Social Change: With Respect to Culture and Original Nature*. New York: B.W. Huebsch.

Olsen, J.P. (2006) 'Maybe it is time to rediscover bureaucracy', *Journal of Public Administration Research and Theory*, 16(1): 1–24.

Pettigrew, A.M., Ferlie, E. and McKee, L. (1992) *Shaping Strategic Change: Making Change in Large Organizations—The Case of the National Health Service*. London: Sage Publications.

Pfeffer, J. (2010) 'Power play', *Harvard Business Review*, 88 (7/8): 84–92.

Rafferty, A.E., Jimmieson, N.L. and Armenakis, A.A. (2013) 'Change readiness: a multilevel review', *Journal of Management*, 39 (1): 110–35.

Rod, M., Ashill, N. and Saunders, S. (2009) 'Considering implementing major strategic change?: lessons from joint venture in the UK health technology sector', *International Journal of Pharmaceutical and Healthcare Marketing*, 3 (3): 258–78.

Rogers, E. (2003) *The Diffusion of Innovation*. New York: Free Press, (fifth edn).

Sirkin, H.J., Keenan, P. and Jackson, A. (2005) 'The hard side of change management', *Harvard Business Review*, 83 (10): 108–18.

Stace, D. and Dunphy, D. (2001) *Beyond the Boundaries: Leading and Re-creating the Successful Enterprise*. Sydney: McGraw Hill.

Szulanski, G. and Winter, S. (2002) 'Getting it right the second time', *Harvard Business Review*, 80 (1): 62–9.

Toffler, A. (1970) *Future Shock*. London: Pan Books.

Walton, R.E. (1975) 'The diffusion of new work structures: explaining why success didn't take', *Organizational Dynamics*, 3 (3): 3–22.

Weber, M. (1947) *The Theory of Social and Economic Organization* (A.M. Henderson and T. Parsons, Trans.) Oxford: Oxford University Press.

Worley, C.G. and Lawler, E.E. (2009) 'Building a change capability at Capital One Financial', *Organizational Dynamics*, 38 (4): 245–51.

Zaleznik, A. (1997) 'Real work', *Harvard Business Review*, 75 (6): 53–63 (first published 1989).

2 Fostering Awareness of Fractal Patterns in Organizations

David M. Boje and Tonya L. Henderson

How can we become more attuned to the patterns of human interaction that impact our organizations? The answer lies in a multi-level attunement called fractal relationality. Fractals are scalable, self-similar patterns that repeat with varying amplitude and timing.[1] By increasing our awareness of these kinds of patterns, we can improve our understanding of organization development and improve the quality of our decisions. This model is well suited to today's organizations and operating environments, where the boundaries of systems are unclear and constantly shifting; the competitive environment is anything but static, both externally and internally; and social capital is every bit as powerful as formal authority.

DIFFERENT PATHS TOWARD COMMON UNDERSTANDING

This approach was developed from the findings of Tonya's doctoral dissertation, for which David was her mentor. The study explored the significance and underlying meaning in fractal patterns observed through storytelling in a network of nonprofit executives. Perhaps the most poignant finding was the discovery of *relational introspection*, a concept we later expanded and renamed *fractal relationality,* as a mode of conscious, ontological Being among successful leaders. For us, openness to this way of viewing the world was the product of several influences along our individual life paths.

As a girl, Tonya was always curious about human interaction and how groups of people came together. Studying political science as a midshipman at the US Naval Academy, she gravitated toward systemic views of power dynamics and change, preferring the big picture to specifics. She happily served the US Navy in various leadership roles, earning her master's degree in space systems operations, but ultimately resigning as a lieutenant commander after her youngest child took his first steps with a caregiver. As a naval officer and later a defense contractor, she worked on systems integration problems, fostering intra-organizational cooperation to address technical issues. While the work required a lot of sequential thinking, Tonya learned to use her more global perspective to see and better explain the interconnectedness of various systems and organizations.

Unbeknownst to her, she was working with scalable, self-similar patterns of human systems' unfolding self-organization. During that time, Tonya started her doctoral work in organization development and change, exploring the social side of collaboration and group behaviors with a complexity lens.

When Tonya met David, he had already published several books on complexity and was happy to chair her doctoral committee, encouraging a deeper, ontologically focused exploration. In ontology, one tries to get below the surface narratives and counter-narratives, because these oftentimes leave out the details, develop generalities, and dismiss what David calls the living stories of day-to-day working and Being-in-the-world. This bent was consistent with his past writings on antenarrative processes, tying together Grand Narratives (often stuck in the past) with living story particularities, stuck in the situation at hand. Antenarrative means those processes of communication and action that are '*before*' a grand narrative coheres into a resolute structure of plot, characters, themes, and generalities. The second meaning is 'bets' on the future that can be 'moments of vision' or anticipations of what are possible to achieve (Heidegger, 1962). David has been working on two new aspects of antenarrative: 'beneath' and 'between.' There is caring for the beneath, those conceptions that help things along, and the between, caring about the structuring that makes things go not just smoothly but with sustainability for generations to come.

David arrived at his current mode of thought through many years of study, teaching, writing, and practice. As a blacksmith artist and someone who works with horses on a daily basis, experiencing and co-creating with the agency of material things within the context of the desert ecosystem are a part of his daily practice. A visit to his home in Las Cruces is not complete without a tour of the workshop, complete with firing up the forge and reshaping a piece of metal—all undertaken with a deep ontological perspective and rich discussion of the meaning, implications, and true essence of every action as emergence and dissipation of patterned ways of Being. He shares these concepts with veterans hoping to restory past tragedies and create positive futures through equine therapy and Material Storytelling workshops.

He calls it 'Embodied Restorying Process' (ERP) to get at ways veterans and family members can re-embody the Self they left behind when they adopted the military-Self or spouse-of or child-of a service member Self. Often veterans return from deployment in a disembodied state, seeking to distance themselves from family, friends, and any Situation reminding them of combat. The spouse has often heard from the military to not burden the deployed soldier with problems, to put on the happy face. The spouse becomes self-reliant and now has to move over to let the veteran once again have their empowered role. A child of the military family has to cope with the challenges military-Self roles place on their parents and cope with the adjustments before, during, and after deployment. Help is often not an option. The soldier is told to not seek help, to never go to therapy, to not admit to things like PTSD or he or she will risk losing his or her career, not be promoted, be discharged, or be confined to Wounded Warrior camps and not go home for months. There is another Self that society, with the help of the media, lays on the military family. There is a stigma, a stereotype, embedded in the Rambo character, its narrative of flashbacks, rage out-bursts, and lack of Self-control.

Participants relate to themselves, others, and their environments through Anete Strands 'Material Storytelling' methods of sandplay and other modes of embodied storytelling, such as Equine Assisted Growth and Learning Association (EGALA) groundwork with horses. The work with horses helps the veteran to be embodied, to see the reaction in the horse-body to their own stress and anxiety moods. A horse is a mirror to how you come across and to your emotional well-being. A horse shies away from anger and stress and will often approach someone feeling down or depressed. This is followed up with Material Storytelling, the use of objects to depict a story in a sandtray.

Veterans are notorious for not wanting to ever share their stories of deployment, the concussions, the death, their role in it. The use of mate-rial objects, such as toy guns, human-like and animal figures, etc. allows veterans to tell their past without words. They resonate with each object they choose to tell their stories and lay them out in a spatial landscape and in a temporality all their own. David adds to Material Storytelling, the ERP, rounds of embodying the telling in the object relations and then restorying to retell with a sense of greater and greater empowerment and Self-agency. This means countering the military and societal Grand Narratives of what a solder is with the living stories, recalling little wow moments of excep-tion to those dominant narratives, and using them to create a 'New' story of their future, if you will, a new 'bet' on the future made form antenarra-tives of 'before' the Grand Narratives took over and adding the 'beneath' and the 'between' to get a greater sense of care for the Self, for Others, and greater Awareness of the Ecosystem (putting life story into the context of the ecology, Nature, how the Self is already a part of Being-in-the-world). They arrive at a more generative and embodied sense of Being present and fostering their own success in new bets on the future possibilities. The work with veterans is especially meaningful to David, because he served in the US Army in his youth, completing a tour of duty in Vietnam while hostilities were ongoing.

The original concept of relational introspection resonated with David, in part, because if its fractal nature and because the model explains a way of Being and working that were consistent with his life and work. Whether meditating for personal growth, engaging with students, horses, or con-sulting clients, or contextualizing situations through active observation, he operates this way consistently.

TODAY'S ORGANIZATIONS: SYSTEMICITY
AS THE NEW NORMAL

Human systems are complex adaptive systems (CAS). They are seldom truly stable, even if the rate of change slows sufficiently to make them appear static. Managing change is not something leaders can simply take a seminar on when they find time; change is the stuff of everyday life. One cannot step into and out of Heraclitus's river at will, deciding one day to create systemic change as if it were not already ongoing. We are all neck-deep in the deluge, whether we like it or not. The choice in each moment is not whether to embark on a journey of change, but whether we swim with the current, take action to affect the river's course, or desperately cling to the rocks.

Even more daunting is the notion that the vessels (organizations) we seek to pilot are not clearly defined themselves. Our boats are not exactly water-tight. So we find ourselves in white water, steering Swiss cheese vessels that often prove seaworthy in spite of themselves. Picking up moss and deadfall from the deluge, we assemble what we can and take on the rapids. We add and subtract from the substance of our organizations, lashing ourselves to others (joint ventures?) and separating as needed when the river forks or a waterfall looms ahead. It is what a pilot friend of ours, Phil Brown, calls "building the airplane while flying it."

Such a system is not easily defined as it morphs, emerges, and dissipates at will. It exhibits what Boje (2008) calls systemicity, as a third-order cybernetic system (D. Boje & Arkoubi, 2005; D. Boje & Wakefield, 2011; Wakefield, 2012). By systemicity we mean the intra-activity of materialism(s) with storytelling. Storytelling is a domain of discourse, a triadic relation of grander narratives, webs of living stories, and antenarrative between these genres. Only through storytelling can we get at the true nature of such an organization in order to foster its sustainability through adaptation.

Such patterns of unruly emergence are difficult to analyze using traditional methods. They cannot be described as either flexible or rigid, for they can be (and are) both, adapting in co-creative intra-action with their environments. They defy reductionist modes of analysis. One cannot bound and dissect them to understand the whole through its parts. Instead we turn to storytelling to explore patterns of behavior and associated operating principles, which are far more stable than shifting organizational structures. In storytelling work, David focuses on how living stories are in-the-middle of becoming and without being stuck on particular origins and not yet accomplished. We cannot always trace the river to its source. A better approach is to dive in at the first inviting point of entry instead of wasting too much time seeking out the perfect beach to test the waters from. If we wait too long, the nature of the system could change drastically while we debate how to approach it.

Leaders of all kinds—those imbued with formal power and those with grassroots level influence—must see themselves as part of the living, breathing attractor state that is the human organization. One cannot simply draw a box around it and say, "The company ends here and I have done nothing to alter it through my attention to it." The observer and observed are entangled, as the researcher attempts to define the phenomenon, and the phenomenon, in turn, redefines the researcher through the experience (Barad, 2007; Latour, 1999, 2005; Strand, 2012). The observer effect is both human and posthuman, tangible and quantum (D. Boje & Henderson, 2014; Roethlisberger, 1941). Much like Latour's discussion of the undefinable boundary between the forest and savanna, where each encroaches on the other (Latour, 1999), organizations of all kinds have runners and roots that extend far beyond the recognizable entity that is given a name and an artificially defined boundary (D. Boje, 2008, 2011). The boundary shifts as the living story web of its stakeholders pulsates with news and emergent relationships, co-creating fleeting glimpses of socially constructed and material realities. This is not the positivist's cold, hard reality—reminiscent of the fictitious Joe Friday's, "Just the facts, ma'am." Instead, our human reality is nothing more than the snapshot of a single, momentary perspective—one among many at any given time. It is bounded in timespacemattering only if we, the observers, choose to make it so.

BINDING THE UNBOUNDED SYSTEM

This choice is, in and of itself, doing violence to the organization in its living, breathing act of becoming. We step in with good intentions, the quest for knowledge and some sort of improvement. Then, with every intention of helping, we examine the patient as a doctor might, consultants seeking out organizational ailments and offering treatments (Schein, 1999). We bound the problem, define the system under study, and then look at it piece by piece in reductionist fashion. We draw a box, agree to look no further, and in doing so blind ourselves and those we support to exploring those runners and root systems that extend beyond our fence. Worse yet, we simply chop them off without regard for their importance or unintended consequences.

Drawing boundaries may be a necessary evil, however, as we try to seek out a reality that works for as many stakeholders as possible. It is sometimes necessary as a coping mechanism. Our intellectual limits as human beings may render us unable to completely grasp the multifaceted unfolding of organizational life. It may also be a matter of avoiding scope-creep, as we help an organization to remain in alignment with its mission statement. The point is not that bounding systems is to be avoided at all costs but that doing so must be a conscious choice, undertaken with full cognizance of the limitations thus created. Boundaries must serve a purpose and should not be arbitrary.

Bounding a system under study not only bounds a problem, but in a way it "binds" the system by limiting the scope of what it might become. We cut off avenues of potential growth and expansion/contraction, because we simply can't wrap our heads around the dynamics of a living, breathing, emergent system. Bounding . . . binding . . . We risk interrupting the natural migration paths and external associations of those elements not considered in our accounting of the firm, those acknowledged superficially, and those considered "other." This is where stakeholder theory can be helpful, although one cannot hope to fully address the complete spectrum of affected parties in most cases. Not unlike artificial political boundaries separating families, tribes, cornfields, and grazing herds, the lines we draw around the firm may blind us to the real story.

In seeking to understand the relational unfolding of aggregate human interaction, we attempt to characterize the river as it flows, to unveil truths faster than they dissipate to be replaced with newer realities. Yesterday's beautiful possibility may be rendered moot by a careless act or a thoughtless statement as actions unfold in what our friend Phil Brown calls the "messiness of human contact." Yet we persist in our efforts to unveil and characterize what Wiener (1954) termed "temporary islands of decreasing entropy" (p. 36). In a complex adaptive system, this amounts to spotting familiar patterns, as fractal occurrences are the only thing even approaching the concept of stable ground.

FRACTAL RELATIONALITY: A LENS FOR VIEWING EMERGENCE

Fractal relationality was conceived through a study exploring these kinds of fractal patterns through storytelling (Wakefield, 2012). It was further developed over the next two years and applied in different settings, including greening efforts at New Mexico State University (Henderson, 2013, 2014; Wakefield, 2013). The original concept, termed relational introspection, is defined as "the threefold, dynamic exercise of self-awareness, regard for others, and ecosystem knowledge" (Wakefield, 2012, p. 114). "It means knowing one's authentic self and at the same time, being aware of one's place in the current situation, one's relationship to others, and what possibilities exist" (Wakefield, 2012, p. 114)

Boje (2014b) expanded the concept into what we now call 'fractal relationality,' illustrated in Figure 2.1. We consider it fractal because the concept is applicable at multiple scales of analysis in self-similar ways. For example, as an individual I may be attuned to my own innermost self, my family members, and our household: self, others, ecosystem. My organization may be self-similarly attuned to its mission and other governance elements (self), competitors and collaborators (others), and the competitive environment within the community and the industry (ecosystem).

In the move to this newer view of fractal relationality, we extend the model to show how we move from one level of analysis to another, generating more extensive, scalable repetitions of relational introspection patterns through active movement, involvement, and participation with ourselves,

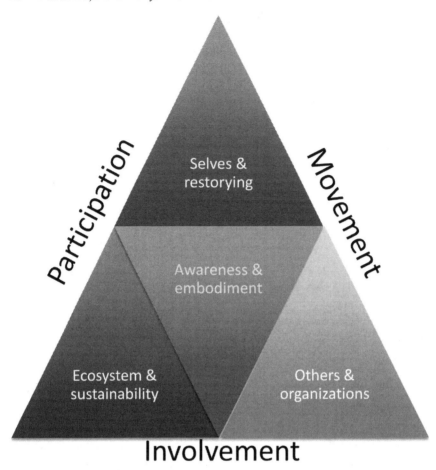

Figure 2.1   Fractal Relationality

others, and the world around us. We also add embodied practices to awareness, which is more than just a cerebral matter. By zooming in and out, we
consider multiple levels of analysis, enabling us to see certain patterns of
behavior as self-similar and scalable.

SELF

The role of the 'Self' in organization development has been explored from
many different angles. In the Hindu and yogic traditions, self-study is considered an important part of spiritual growth (*The Bhagavad Gita*, 2007;
Carrera, 2011). Western philosophers have touted self-knowledge as an
antidote to nihilism, for example, Heidegger (1962). Modern leadership

scholars continue to explore authenticity and self-knowledge as keys to influencing others (Cashman, 2008) and self-as-instrument is an important concept for organization development consultants and facilitators (C. Seashore, Shawver, Thompson, & Mattare, 2004; E. Seashore, Seashore, & Livingston, 2010). Despite societal calls for selfless service and countering egoic individualism, self-knowledge is widely accepted as a necessary element of mental health and effective interactions with others. The premise is that only a whole person, one with self-awareness and self-respect is well equipped to support others.

Self-knowledge can help take us from a state where transactional relationships are the norm, into a more relational state wherein helping another is seen as beneficial to us as well. Boje (2014b) deepens the concept of awareness originally considered to suggest the practices of meditation and restorying as means of moving between perspectives. Among individuals, self-awareness appears as a mixture of individual decisions, emotional reactions, and relationships with others, specifically "understanding one's own choices, history, emotional state, and personal values" (Wakefield, 2012, p. 117). Examples include how the generationally poor lack awareness of their personal spending (Payne, 2001) and a preacher's efforts to master the stagecraft aspects of delivering a sermon.

Attunement to one's own emotional state is also important. For example, leaders may experience discomfort while serving on a dysfunctional board of directors. Whether reacting to specific circumstances or considering more mundane matters, the concept calls for individuals to monitor their own current state at any given time (Wakefield, 2012). Restorying work often serves to help individuals cope with emotions in a constructive way, shifting patterns of behavior into more constructive modes of Being. Boje (2014b) expands on this idea in his work with veterans suffering from post-traumatic stress disorder.

"In restorying work, we do not relive the trauma event, rather we take an embodied and mindful approach to reclaim parts of the Self that have been forgotten or dismissed by the 'Big stories' others have that characterize who we are." (D. M. Boje, 2014b)

Through equine therapy and Material Storytelling influenced by the work of Anete Strand (2012), veterans learn to cope with past traumas in healthy ways. The 'big stories' posited by media stereotypes and others' judgments are supplanted by healthier perspectives that come from inside the individual. This work seems to help veterans cement healthy perspectives about who they are instead of accepting externally derived stereotypes.

In organizations, mission knowledge and adherence support an aggregate sense of self-awareness. Here we consider mission-based behavior and organizational limitations, along with specific systemic weaknesses. Principle-based behaviors characterize organizations. For example, egalitarianism as a unifying organizational principle is apparent in one leader's description of his nonprofit as "middle class people rolling cans of green beans down a tilted table at the needy amid a more egalitarian vision," (Wakefield, 2012, p. 128). Mission fit dictates that all proposed activities be carefully aligned with an organization's mission statement. What we do as an organization has to be consistent with who we are.

OTHERS

Agurre et al. (2013) state, "the concept of being-with-one-another is an essential consideration in an authentic heart of care," (p. 18), tying it to what Heidegger (1962) calls the authentic self. Awareness of others at an individual level is sometimes expressed in terms of similarities and differences between one's own perspective and others'. For example, one subject described how different people experience joy. He explained that people of different walks of life experience joy differently but that no one expression is better than any other. For the destitute, he said, "it may be as simple as a fresh cupcake" (Wakefield, 2012, p. 121).

This sense of Being with others[2] is also apparent at the organizational and community levels. At an organizational level, collaborative efforts stress honesty between organizations about constraints based on funding lines, etc. Such limitations and/or ties to slow, bureaucratic organizations often interfere with collaboration among nonprofits. Between individuals and organizations, attunement to others involves valuing all feedback—even that which is not particularly useful—in order to establish trust and keep communication channels open. At the community level, organizations' missions are viewed in terms of benefit to the community as a whole and clarity about how each fits into the bigger picture. In each case, this kind of Being with others suggests a relational mode of interconnected co-creation (Wakefield, 2012).

ECOSYSTEM

At an individual level, ecosystem awareness requires intense listening, often going back and asking for clarification, especially if we were preoccupied while another person was speaking (Wakefield, 2012). Boje's (2014b) work with veterans suggests meditation as a pathway to greater ecosystem awareness, as one turns inward while simultaneously grounding oneself with respect to the earth, a perspective that has long been shared by practitioners of yoga (Carrera, 2011). "Our body is in constant communication with the ecosystem, and that contact is fundamental to our sustainability, the balance of our body with its environs" (D. M. Boje, 2014b). This path to greater awareness and interconnectedness is an expression of ecosacredness.

In this posthumanist approach to sustainability, all living things are interconnected as they engage in the formation of living story webs. Humans and non-human beings, as well as mountains, streams, and the earth itself . . . Each has a living story all its own. In a posthumanist ontology (way of Being-in-the-world), humans are one of many species, and species are one among many elements of living matter. Posthumanists argue with transhumanists. A transhumanist wants to let technology be the hub of life and is not focused on Being-in-Nature or an ecosystem. Their contention is that life has evolved from the natural world, with science and technology, to be about virtual communities, techno-societies that make their own worlds.

Between individuals and organizations, ecosystem awareness appears as attunement to the operating environment. Seasonal trends and changes related to natural disasters and other community-wide events necessitate attunement with the environment. The perils of poor ecosystem awareness are apparent in the ill-advised but common practice of starting up new nonprofits without first examining community needs. The resulting duplication of efforts increases the competition for finite donor resources and threatening the survival of many nonprofits (Wakefield, 2012). Individuals' ecosystem awareness must be brought to the organization so that external complexity can be matched by internal complexity according to Ashby's (1958) law of requisite variety. We take this notion a step further, blurring the lines between the organization and the environment, considering the organization itself as a pattern of emergent order within the greater context of the ecosystem.

At an organizational level, ecosystem awareness contextualizes the earlier consideration of alignment to one's mission. This kind of awareness requires checking to see what else is going on in the community before starting a new venture. For example, once an immigration-focused organization was considering hosting an event. Instead they joined forces with a larger organization hosting a similar event in the same time frame, improving their effectiveness. Organizations must attend not only to their own missions, collaborators, and competitors but also to what is going on in the larger community.

PRACTICAL APPLICATIONS

Having cultivated this scalable way of knowing, how does one use it practically? NMSU's greening effort is a good example. "[The] model of relationality is about the involvement of our living Body (= Selves + Awareness) with Ecosystem and Others. As a fractal the relationality triangle is connected to Others and to Ecosystems through participation, moving, and involvement" (D. M. Boje, 2014b). This means moving away from just a humanist understanding of "recycle, reduce, and reuse." Rather, it's about how humans can cut back on overuse of the life resources of the planet. David drives a Prius and a motorcycle, and his house is powered by photovoltaic energy of the sun. Yet he knows his footprint (use of carbon) is higher than the average citizen on the planet. Through restorying at all levels of analysis using embodied practices, greening efforts become a lasting part of individual and organizational identities.

Awareness of the self is applied self-similarly at all levels as the university makes greening a part of its identity, involving each department, class, faculty member, and student. At an individual level, greening requires awareness of one's own actions, demonstrating awareness of the self. Students and faculty must evolve from the mindless littering and wasteful disposal methods of past generations toward a more conscious mode of interaction. Recycling containers must be used. Refillable water bottles replace disposable ones as people on campus self-police for the greater good. The campaign is complemented by the existence of an undergraduate sustainability minor. At the individual level, department level, and university level, sustainability is becoming part of one's identity, the concept of self (D. M. Boje, 2014a).

Engagement with others is also apparent in the way these efforts were promoted by the initial core group of enthusiasts until the greening movement affected the organization as a whole. For example, use of the green leaf symbol provided a means of visually engaging with others to spread the message. A teaching academy event was used to convince more people to seek funding and getting the effort off the ground. Formal proposals and presentations followed, educating and co-opting leadership in support of the sustainability minor. Detailed implementation plans were put into place and meetings with individual departments were held, leading to execution of those plans. In each case there were deliberate efforts to engage with others to foster agreement about the way ahead (D. M. Boje, 2014a).

In the New Mexico State (NMSU) greening effort, we see this awareness taken to a more ontological extent, as material and epistemic conditions intermingle with the onto-ethical concept of the heart of care through deep ecology-ecosystem engagement. Ontologically,

> deep ecology . . . proposes that a lack of care is actually symptomatic of a deeper problem of the human self, in which we as human beings are accepted as the dominant force over nature. In order to find the heart of care, the human being must essentially be reprogrammed in such a way that it seeks to live in harmony with nature. (Agurre et al., 2013, p. 17)

Again, levels of analysis are transcended as man's relationship with the ecosystem is related back to man's relationship with himself.

David's role is to be past chair of the NMSU Sustainability Council, co-writing an assessment that brought first a Bronze Star, then a Gold Star from a national accrediting body. Now David is coordinator of an initiative called 'Greening the Curriculum.' The objectives of NMSU's greening effort are to develop minors and majors at the undergraduate and graduate level in all six colleges in sustainability. Because each college, and departments even within the same college, defines sustainability quite differently, the program has to be flexible. An example of the Greening Initiative is working the fundraisers of the university to create sustainability scholarships in each college, working with Career Services (David has a Greening NMSU booth at career fairs), so students can find the sustainability courses, recruiters can find students trained in sustainability, and hopefully close the loop so those selfsame companies hiring students will donate to the scholarships and that can recruit even more dedicated students to greening.

It may sound simple to get agreement from a university to have a minor or a major in sustainability. Believe us, it's not! For example, to get a Graduate Certificate in Sustainability, David had to get buy-in from his department, the graduate committee of his college (where advising would happen), the college committee of deans, and department heads. That is not all. This Certificate also requires approval of the associate Deans Advisory Council, the Dean's Academic Council, the Graduate School and its Committee on Graduate Studies, a memorial from the Faculty Senate, and then agreement from the Provost to send a letter to the New Mexico State Legislature asking for final approval. That is not all; a record of all the approvals is carried by David to the Registrar's Office so that a computer identifier number can be selected and attached to it, and then the Graduate Certificate in Sustainability begins to show up in the Star Audit (a program advisers and students use to sort out what minors and certificates are available to them, in what combinations of electives and required course options, etc.). It is a complicated process.

The NMSU greening effort can be seen as a series of fractal relational triangles, with individuals, departments, and the organization engaging in threefold awareness of the Self, Others, and Ecosystem vis-à-vis efforts to be more sustainable. From a fractal perspective, we are looking at how a multiplicity of fractals exists in various degrees of resolution, such as from each department of the university, with differing understandings of just what sustainability means. For example, to Engineering departments it's about sustainable design, to Economics it's about the market for energy, for Philosophy it's about equity and justice, and for Education it's about sustainability literacy. We can see light in certain wave fluctuations, we experience time in various sequences of events, but there are also in-between smaller events that we can focus in on. Here we apply fractals to management science. Organizations and their environments form fractal relationships of "irregular and/or fragmented scales," to use Mandelbrot's words (Nottalle, 2011, 44). Fractal Management is a methodology for observing and changing scalability attunement in organizations. The organization exists as a pocket of emergent order in relation to its environment.

We can zoom in and zoom out in our observations of the relationships among organizations and environments. But does the manager see them all? Many people have distinct preferences for the strategic or tactical level, based on their organizational roles, but this kind of awareness requires movement among levels, as we consider ourselves and our co-creative (or competitive) intra-action with others contextually. A manager can get stuck in one zoom-scale, understanding only a constricted or very dilated view.

The important question becomes, "To what extent are managers attuned to fractal scalability?" Most managers, we assume, have developed position dependent scale-dependence. This means managing an awareness and action orientation attuned to one specific zoom-scale, for example, with the very local Situation of the organization. With training and experience, the manager can learn to be attuned to alternative zoom scales, thereby getting better at recognizing significant patterns of interaction.

The real challenge is to get people to think in these terms. For many organizations and business people, awareness does not seem important. There's not a return-on-awareness ratio you can put on a balance sheet. Yet we know this works. In our own worlds, we find that writing, teaching, and working with organizations improves with cultivated, scalable awareness. For example, Tonya once worked with a civic organization whose problems can be explained in terms of relational introspection. The board was composed of optimistic, dedicated volunteers balancing numerous interconnected interests. Each member had specific business and personal considerations, history, and concerns. They came to the table cognizant of their own positions (self), those of their peers and the staff (others), and the external community and government agency perspectives affecting their collaborative efforts (ecosystem). Zooming out, one can view things this way. The organization's need for a coherent brand statement grounded in its mission was discussed at length (self). Informal relationships and formal agreements with other organizations that shaped their strategic planning at a tactical level were examined (others). The community itself and its position among similar cities were explored (ecosystem). In many productive board retreats we see these kinds of multi-level awarenesses.

As a consultant, the trick is to be aware of that and notice what is missing. Oftentimes in strategic planning and change processes, groups become sidetracked by individual agendas. There are several tools we use to redirect the meeting in such cases. One of our favorites is rationalization of conflict (Emery & Purser, 1996). In this technique, the facilitator keeps a list, in plain sight, of issues needing more time and attention than the group can give them in the current session. These topics are included in the meeting notes to ensure they are not forgotten. The process validates the concerns of those in disagreement without derailing the group. Once the concern is recorded, it is easier to resume the planned agenda or to help the group consciously modify it as appropriate. We consistently notice how the group is addressing self, others, and ecosystem at multiple levels of analysis; try to prevent one perspective from dominating the meeting; and ask probing questions if any aspect appears forgotten or disregarded.

CONCLUSION

This awareness opens the door to understanding organizational complexity and, subsequently, coming to know the self-similar patterns of aggregate behavior that characterize any system of interest. Fractal relationality can be leveraged to improve risk management and consider efforts to influence the expected patterns going forward. In some cases, it may be possible to affect antenarrative potential at multiple levels of analysis and even instill lasting change. Fractal relationality opens the door to the kind of multi-level, multifaceted knowing that enables leaders and organizations to understand patterned behaviors and instill change through embodied practices.

When individuals and organizations begin to practice multi-level attunement to themselves, others, and their environments, they can begin to better understand the unfolding patterns that characterize third-order cybernetic systems. Such awareness is important as we seek to navigate the rough waters of Heraclitus's river in the age of computers and globalism. Here disparate entities are connected in unseen ways and the unfolding systemicity of organizations as material-spiritual unfoldings in the quantum field of potential necessitates heightened awareness and a more complex approach.

NOTES

1. Benoit Mandelbrot coined the term fractals, described as: "irregular and/or fragmented at all scales" (Nottalle, 2011: 44).
2. Note: Our use of the term "other" is not intended to imply alienation or separation as the term is used in much of the feminist literature.

REFERENCES

Agurre, G., Boje, D. M., Cast, M., Conner, S. L., Helmuth, C., Mittal, R., . . . Yan, T. Q. (2013). University sustainability and system ontology. *International Journal of Organization Theory and Behavior, 15*(4), 577–618.

Ashby, W. R. (1958). Requisite variety and its implications for the control of complex systems. *Cybernetica, 1*(2), 83–99.

Barad, K. (2007). *Meeting the universe halfway: Quantum physics and the entanglement of matter and meaning.* Durham, NC: Duke University Press.

The Bhagavad Gita. (2007). (E. Easwaran, Trans., & E. Easwaran, Ed.). Tomales, CA: Nilgiri Press.

Boje, D. M. (2008). *Storytelling organizations.* Los Angeles: SAGE Publications.

Boje, D. M. (2011). Introduction to agential narratives that shape the future of organizations. In D. Boje (Ed.), *Storytelling and the future of organizations: An antenarrative handbook* (pp. 1–15). New York, NY: Routledge.

Boje, D. M. (2014a). *Greening the curriculum.* Retrieved 23 October 2014, from http://greening.nmsu.edu/, http://greening.nmsu.edu/about-the-project/history-of-sustainability-at-nmsu/

Boje, D. M. (2014b, 26 August 2014). *Restorying stress and sustainability.* Retrieved 3 September, 2014, from http://www.peaceaware.com/

Boje, D. M., & Arkoubi, K. (2005). Third cybernetic revolution: Beyond open to dialogic system theories. *Tamara: Journal of Critical Postmodern Organization Science, 4*(1/2), 138.

Boje, D. M., & Henderson, T. (Eds.). (2014). *Being quantum: Ontological storytelling in the age of antenarrative.* Newcastle upon Tyne, UK: Cambridge Scholars Publishing.

Boje, D. M., & Wakefield, T. (2011). Storytelling in systemicity and emergence: A third order cybernetic. In D. Boje, B. Burnes & J. Hassard (Eds.), *The Routledge companion to organizational change* (pp. 171–182). London: Routledge.

Carrera, J. (2011). *Inside the Yoga Sutras.* Buckingham, VA: Integral Yoga Publications.

Cashman, K. (2008). *Leadership from the inside out* (2nd ed.). San Francisco, CA: Berrett-Koehler Publishers.

Emery, M., & Purser, R. E. (1996). *The search conference* (1st ed.). San Francisco, CA: Jossey-Bass.

Heidegger, M. (1962). *Being and time* (R. Mahnheim, Trans., 7th ed.). New York: Harper & Rowe Publishers.

Henderson, T. L. (2013). *Fractals & relational introspection.* Paper presented at the 3rd Annual Quantum Storytelling Conference, Las Cruces, NM.

Henderson, T. L. (2014). *Spotting patterns in work and life: Awareness and reinvention.* Paper presented at the FEBE (For Entrepreneurs By Entrepreneurs) Superwoman Leadership Conference, Colorado Springs, CO.

Latour, B. (1999). *Pandora's hope: essays on the reality of science studies.* Cambridge, MA: Harvard University Press.

Latour, B. (2005). *Reassembling the social: An introduction to actor-network theory.* Oxford: Oxford University Press.

Nottale, L. (2011). *Scale Relativity and Fractal Space-Time: A new approach to Unifying Relativity and Quantum Mechanics.* London: Imperial College Press.

Payne, R. K. (2001). *Bridges out of poverty.* Highlands, TX: aha! Process.

Roethlisberger, F. J. (1941). The Hawthorne experiments. In W. E. Natemeyer & P. Herssey (Ed.), *Classics of organizational management* (3rd ed., pp. 29–40). Long Grove, IL: Waveland Press.

Schein, E. H. (1999). *Process consultation revisited.* Reading, MA: Addison-Wesley.

Seashore, C., Shawver, M. N., Thompson, G., & Mattare, M. (2004). Doing good by knowing who you are: the instrumental self as an agent of change. *OD Practitioner, 36*(3), 42–46.

Seashore, E., Seashore, C., & Livingston, R. (2010). *Workshop on intentional use of self.* Workshop materials, Colorado Technical University. Colorado Springs, CO.

Strand, A. M. C. (2012). *The between: On dis/continuous intra-active becoming of/through an apparatus of material storytelling.* (Doctoral Program in Human Centered Communication and Informatics [HCCI]), Aalborg University, Aaulborg, Denmark.

Wakefield, T. H. (2012). *An ontology of storytelling systemicity: Management, fractals and the Waldo Canyon fire.* (Doctorate of Management Doctoral dissertation), Colorado Technical University, Colorado Springs, CO.

Wakefield, T. H. (2013). *Fractal management theory.* Paper presented at the Academy of Management, Orlando, FL.

Wiener, N. (1954). *The human use of human beings.* Boston, MA: Da Capo Press.

3 Reflections on Change

Robert MacIntosh and Nic Beech

INTRODUCTION

Change is now a topic that has reached a stage where scholars are beginning to draw breath through retrospective reviews, whilst looking to establish future directions (Todnem et al., 2014). We are told that change is the constant experience of organizational life in the modern era. The confluence of the Internet, globalization, deregulation, new public management, the global financial crisis, and dramatic shifts in the nature, production, and distribution of high-value and mass market products and services may have created a period of unprecedented turbulence. It is worth contemplating the possibility that future generations will study current circumstances in much the same way that our generation studies the Industrial Revolution. Quite what a tech-savvy generation of employees attached to Wi-Fi from birth and accustomed to instant information everywhere will make of our efforts to build organizations that are fit for purpose, only time will tell. In this chapter, we adopt a retrospective stance, sharing six insights from our own work on the management of change and reflecting on some of the experiences that have generated our take on how best to approach change.

STARTING POINTS

We begin by acknowledging that we are persuaded by the argument that organizations are more helpfully understood as being in process rather than being discussed as nouns with the implication that they are 'finished objects'. In that sense, we sit within a community of processual researchers (e.g. Chia, 1995; Marshak, 2009; Tsoukas and Chia, 2002). Further, we have adopted practices as researchers that interpret both organization and organizing in ways that tend to problematize simple and singular accounts of what is going on at any point in time. As researchers, we pay attention to backstory and our own is important here. We found our way into organizational change from very different root disciplines (engineering and social anthropology/philosophy), and we operate in related but separate domains (strategy and organizational studies). These differences caused us to think carefully about our own starting assumptions in relation to change. We can therefore say with some conviction that twin assumptions underpin our work. First, is the recognition of key events, processually linked in organizational narratives. In terms of decisions and events, we believe that there are certain anchor points, such as the merger of two units or the introduction of new processes. The second assumption that informs our research practice may seem somewhat at odds with the first in that we are also interested in the ways in which accounts of these anchor points are created, interpreted, manipulated, and retold over time, because these are the processes by which change (and not changing) are justified. Everyday organizational experience tells us that different people may be involved in the same set of work practices but can offer quite different accounts of what is or has been happening (Buchanan and Dawson, 2007). For us, this is what makes the job of managing change intensely complicated. Actions are open to interpretation and reinterpretation; good intentions can go awry. What started out as a clear communication can become translated so many times that it takes on new meanings (Oswick et al., 2010) and ambiguity pervades the field of change. Yet this complexity may not necessarily be negative. Constant change, ambiguity, and a multiplicity of meaning can be problematic if the aim of management is to control everything that happens. Yet we have worked with many managers and management teams where the intention was less to control than to facilitate and lead (Currie and Lockett, 2007) in such a way that creative action can be recognized and built upon the ongoing flow of activities which can present an opportunity to enable change.

Insight #1: To study change, we find it helpful to consider the relationship between key decisions/events and the ways in which those anchor points are used to create stories, agendas, and positions by those in and around the organization.

The relationship described in our first insight is of central importance in our own research. We describe the form of engaged dialogue (Beech et al., 2010) which flows as those engaged in organizing practices recognize differences and agreements and develop practical steps that move things along (MacIntosh et al., 2012), even when the 'perfect answer' cannot be found. Our focus on dialogue—not merely communication, but a process through which the self is challenged and changes because of arresting moments of contact with the other, not because the other tried to change the self— reflects our personal experience of working together for many years. We close this opening section by affirming that our own research is informed by a felt sense of obligation to be practical. In what follows, we will set out the ways in which we try to be realistic about the complexity of organizational contexts whilst being serious about engaging with theories of organization that enable a thoughtful-action-oriented approach.

APPROACHING CHANGE

Over a decade and more, we have had several privileged opportunities to work with management teams attempting to deliver complex change agendas within a range of public and private organizations. We adopted a simple habit of asking those involved what their approach to change was. Unsurprisingly, the answers we've received to this question have varied widely. Two examples help make the point:

Example 1 (Board Member, FTSE 100 Business)

INT.   How do you approach change?
MGR   Simple really. Bish, bash, bosh. Job done, next.

Example 2 (Founder, Large Private Organization)

INT.   How do you approach change?
MGR   I think of it like the way in which a shepherd uses a sheep dog to move their sheep. The objective is to have the minimum of fuss. You don't actually want the dog in contact with the sheep. It's an indirect thing. If I put the dog here, the sheep will divert over there. In practice, it gets messier than that but the underlying assumption is the gentleness of trying to avoid any big corrections by thinking ahead.

Both individuals held important positions within their organizations, both had stellar CVs, both had successfully overseen a series of complex mergers involving structural, cultural, and geographic change. Yet each interpreted what had gone on in fundamentally different ways. Inevitably, those working with, for, or around these leaders were affected by their attitudes to change. In example A, the organization concerned adopted a highly structured form of project management when approaching new changes. Project plans, milestones, risk registers, and the like were a regular feature of life as was the undercurrent that this particular change was one in a longer series of changes. Getting the job done, imperfectly but on time, would facilitate attention being paid to the next change in the sequence. In example B, the organization also used risk registers and project plans but these same artefacts were treated as important context setting devices for conversations about underlying drivers and blockers of change. Narrative played a much more important part in the organization's attempts to make sense of why things were unfolding in a particular way. Here the sequence of individual change initiatives blurred into a continuum with the emphasis placed on getting the long game right despite short-term setbacks. Both approaches produced what appeared to be successful change outcomes, at least in terms of the objectives set for the change. Yet both individuals regarded other approaches as inherently naïve. The manager in example A also said in an interview with us that s/he didn't "believe in let's just make it happen approaches to change" which in his or her opinion "might work in a web start-up in Silicon Valley but definitely wouldn't work on a wet Monday morning in Stoke-on-Trent." Equally, the manager in example B offered the view that "people who approach change in a formulaic way miss the point, miss the subtlety, miss the nuances and miss the opportunities."

Insight #2: Attitudes to change vary enormously and carry consequences for what is seen as appropriate (let alone best) practice.

From our second insight, we would not go so far as to label these very different approaches to change as right/wrong. Rather, we would point to the need for a deep appreciation of, and sensitivity to, context. Attempting to operate with the two different worldviews set out in examples A and B coexisting would be fraught with opportunities for misinterpretation, confusion, and frustration, even in the face of supposedly successful outcomes. Yet this is often the daily experience of change given that key actors in the situation hold dear to their own personal views of right/wrong.

RESEARCHING CHANGE

Like any other topic, change is researched using the full spectrum of research methods. Our own approach has tended to favour what is variously described as 'engaged research' (Van de Ven, 2007), Mode 2 (MacLean et al., 2002; Tranfield and Starkey, 1998) or action research (see MacIntosh and Bonnet, 2007). Given our introductory comments, it seems unsurprising that we have eschewed the pretence of an objective, detached stance, favouring instead a longitudinal commitment to working within organizational processes and interactions in an attempt to 'understand from the inside' (Alvesson and Deetz, 2000). A consequence of this approach is that we typically establish a subjective connection to the participants in the research settings that we study. This connection generates influence which operates in both directions (Spradley, 1980). We would acknowledge the influence of key collaborators both during and long after research projects conclude.

The following exchange is reproduced almost verbatim and is typical of the kind of conversation which might lead to one of the research projects on which we find ourselves working.

> NB So what can we do for you?
> MGR Well, we've been asked by the regulator to integrate these four separate organizations.
> RMACI Calibrate us; how many people, how much time?
> MGR By Christmas (the conversation took place in September).
> RMACI And how many people are involved?
> MGR Quite a few (the actual answer was over 40,000).

This was the start to what became a three-year project working with the management team of a large organization undergoing significant change. The project was designed at the outset to cover the four-month period September to December. It ended up lasting significantly longer because our relationship with the management team developed. Over time, we realized that our understanding of the change we were studying was shaping some degree of personal change in us as we grew attached to individuals and objectives within the organization. This blending of researcher and researched (Geertz, 1983) is intrinsic to the way in which we study change. Indeed, we have reflected elsewhere on the need to establish a sense of rapport or friendship (see Beech et al., 2010). So-called insider action research (Coughlan and Coghlan, 2002), where the researcher takes on aspects of a managerial role (Coghlan, 2001), has been true of our experience in both this and other cases. As researchers, we thus adopt hybrid roles—both inside the organizational setting and doing theoretical work outside. At its best, this research relationship becomes embedded in subjective connections to the communities of practice inside the organization and in the academic world. We regard it as badge of honour that we have co-published with members of the organizations that we study. We have attended academic conferences with them in an effort to engage them fully as we attempt to theorize from the organizational experience in which they are embedded. Equally, we have attended management boards, contributed to briefing sessions, facilitated workshops, written reports for specific audiences, acted in a mentoring capacity to staff within organizations and many other forms of engagement. The resultant depth of knowledge, and the consequent ability to theorise from the experience, relies on being able to genuinely 'be part of the experience' rather than being detached from it.

Our experience has been that gaining access relies on a level of reciprocity. The German philosopher Friedrich Nietzche uses the metaphor of two boats to suggest that, for a time, two boats might share the same destination (1977). Whilst this contiguity exists, those in each boat may celebrate and feast together; but at some point, their tasks will take them in different directions. For Nietzsche, friendships persist whilst they are helpful to both people either in assisting towards a shared task or fulfilling a social function such as joint celebration or fun, this is somewhat transitory. This is clearly an instrumental view of friendship; one based on exchange and mutual gain. Whilst this occurs in the work/research setting on many occasions, in our experience, genuine and long-term friendships can also occur. Often the non-instrumental friendships, ironically, are the ones which produce the greatest openness and insight and, consequently, the greatest input to research.

As researchers, status, access, and support are all involved in developing research activities and insights. These are not always sought for altruistic reasons. Alongside the genuinely shared interests implied by the co-production of knowledge, there are also times when access is earned through the offering of advice and support where pre-existing expertise is available. Beyond the initiation of a research relationship, we have encountered several rites of passage or auditions where our continued presence in a research project has to be (re)negotiated. Our prior experience played a significant role in moving beyond initial 'gatekeepers' who may have facilitated access (Chikudate, 1999). Presenting findings, preparing reports, offering advice, or facilitating workshops are each examples of the kinds of audition that we have been subjected to in renewing our right to participate. Understandably, these momentary auditions (Beech et al., 2010) hold the possibility that we may fail to secure ongoing access. Hence our third insight relates to access.

> *Insight #3: Securing and maintaining access to study change requires that you pass at least one audition, or more likely a frequently recurring set of 'momentary auditions', with critical groups of stakeholders.*

Once complete, the audition fades, at least for a time, and your presence in the change process is welcomed/accepted/tolerated by both gatekeepers and other participants. Mode 2 research in particular stresses the co-production of knowledge (see Tranfield and Starkey, 1998), suggesting that research is anti-hierarchical because 'empirical settings' are conceived neither as places for 'transferring knowledge' to practitioners nor as sites for experimental data gathering (Van Aken, 2002). We would contend that there is an implied hierarchy in place in as much as members of the organization hold the right to withdraw from the research. However, if practitioners and researchers jointly define problems and issues to be explored, the likelihood of withdrawal is lessened. Further, both parties bring skills and knowledge to the process; and reflection and feedback on the work occurs within the setting, as well as being written up for academic consumption (MacLean et al., 2002). Early in our joint research on change, we perhaps aimed toward parity on both the academic and the practitioner fronts. Whilst we would now acknowledge that role distinctions between practitioner and researcher are blurred, and that both can take on activities and purposes that would traditionally (i.e. in Mode 1 research) be the preserve of the other, our position now would recognize the different drivers associated with the delivery of organizational outcomes and theoretical contributions. Some of those that we have worked with have gone on to pursue doctoral-level qualifications that require them to write extensively in an academic idiom. Most practising managers, even those interested in reading about change, tend not to write about change.

> *Insight #4: It is helpful to recognize and appreciate the difference between collaborating to produce meaningful change in an organizational setting and theorizing about that change.*

DIALOGIC ENCOUNTERS

Having drawn attention to differences between practitioners and academic researchers, we now move on to consider how research about change has operated in our own experience. Clearly it would be dangerous to generalize, because others may have their own counter examples. Our purpose here is simply to set out how our own thinking about change has been shaped by the research we have conducted. From insight #4, we would suggest that it is worth refining our understanding of how practitioner–academic dialogues of co-production occur. In summary, our proposition is that longitudinal research relationships should not be expected to be consistently and fully dialogical (Beech et al., 2010: 1361). Rather, the relationship is punctuated by intense generative *dialogic encounters* which achieve some knowledge co-production in the moment but which also generate a new basis for ongoing productive activities. Such generative dialogic encounters differ from the theoretical ideal in the extant literature in that they can incorporate disagreement and frustration along with mutuality, and they do not necessarily result in 'completed' co-production of either practical or theoretical outcomes. Yet our research contains a handful of particularly vibrant dialogic encounters which continue to be particularly useful in challenging our understanding of what was going on in a particular situation. In our writing practice, we will regularly find ourselves revisiting these dialogic encounters to see them afresh in light of some new theory or empirical experience. Part of our analytical process involves looking across a repertoire of change experiences and asking "How would [name] deal with this situation?" or "How does this situation compare to the circumstances facing [name]?" This leads us to our fifth insight:

Insight #5: Some dialogic encounters become a resource, acting as reference points or test cases when working in new settings.

ETHNOGRAPHY

Having studied change using the highly engaged approach to research set out earlier, recent years have seen an unexpected branch of our work develop. Both independently and jointly we have assumed senior management responsibilities within our own organizations. Like other forms of professional service organizations or adhocracies (Bennis and Slater, 1968), academic organizations feature self-management through temporary roles such as head of department, dean, etc. We have now experienced, and in in some cases led, significant change processes in four different universities. These experiences have afforded us the opportunity to examine the contradictory nature of change in professional settings (Randall and Munro, 2010). It would be fair to say that this auto-ethnographic opportunity to practice what we preach has also coloured our thinking about change.

Auto-ethnography is a version of ethnography in which the researcher researches practices that they perform, or which are adjacent to them, in a culture in which they live. Van Maanen (1988) placed a particular emphasis on auto-ethnography as a foundational part of engaged research of cultures and change. He argued that more detached methods, such as pure observation, could misconstrue people, their practices, and the context, especially when they seek to derive a singular version of events. Van Maanen regards all 'truths' in ethnography as contestable and hence participating in direct experience is a potentially valuable way of disrupting apparent certainties or overly solid conclusions. Humphreys (2005) has argued that auto-ethnographic approaches which apply the same level of rigour as standard ethnography to situations of the self, have the strengths of providing greater insight into the subtleties, negotiated realities, and (re)constructed versions of change management. Of course, it is also possible that auto-ethnography can produce the very thing it seeks to avoid if the practitioner comes to believe their own version of events too soon and with too great confidence. Hence, in addition to individual auto-ethnography, it is helpful to have research relationships with others who can dispute or offer alternative interpretations. This entails quite a degree of trust and is more easily established over time.

Insight #6: The experience of managing change enriches one's ability to theorise about change.

THE ENQUIRY-ACTION FRAMEWORK

There are already a number of models, frameworks, and processes which set out advice on how to manage change. In developing the six insights set out earlier, we are aware that the matter of best practice in change management is a contentious one. Having criticized extant claims to best practice, we are aware that we are entering disputed territory. First, what we mean by the word 'theory' is the attempt to explain and generalize from one instance to another. For example, research might be conducted that examines many cases for their strengths and weaknesses and then concludes with a generalized list of things to do (and actions to avoid). However, many people operating in practice also produce their own theories of change. Working on the basis of previous experience, or on received practical wisdom, people develop a preferred way of acting. This is a local theory in the sense that it generalizes from what has worked (or is perceived to have worked) in the past to what should be done in the future. Our purpose in offering our own framework is to help people improve their theorizing such that as they make judgements about what to do next, they do so on a considered basis and draw from as wide a range of ideas and experiences as is appropriate for the change at hand. To grapple with situations and make actionable judgements promptly, we suggest that you need to understand the situation from multiple perspectives. The Enquiry-Action Framework sets out three key areas of practice which change managers undertake, and we suggest that there are choices available within each of these three practice areas. The Enquiry-Action Framework focuses on questioning and understanding the context, content, and process of change (see Pettigrew, 1978), as well as developing a repertoire of alternative ways of enacting change. We are mindful of the dangers of separating enquiry and action, because action is part of our enquiry process and, equally, enquiring is a form of action. Indeed we would suggest that although it can be helpful to separate these focal areas analytically, in practice they are integrated as aspects of change management practice. Figure 3.1 represents the relationship between these activities within the framework.

On first reading, there is a natural ordering to the themes in the Enquiry-Action Framework, but we would not regard them as following a strictly linear sequence. Each of the three focal areas (diagnosing, enacting, and explaining) incorporates a number of possibilities that provide ways of enacting that aspect of change. For example, activities within diagnosis could focus on understanding the current and desired states of the organization. Diagnosis can be about setting a clear purpose, but on other occasions

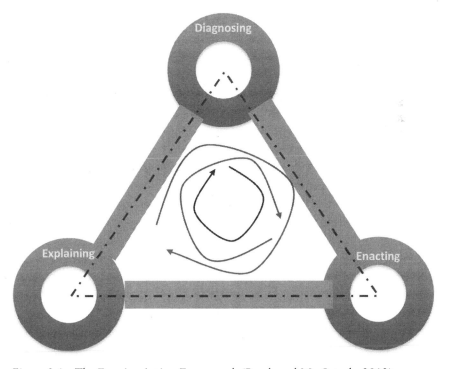

Figure 3.1   The Enquiry-Action Framework (Beech and MacIntosh, 2012)

it can be about understanding the different interpretations that people make of the purpose and recognizing the consequences (both positive and negative) of such ambiguity. It can concentrate on how far people are (potentially) engaged with a change or the state of play politically and whether stakeholders are aligned or not. Equally, diagnosis may need to uncover the cultural context of change, people's established habits and ways of thinking, in order to recognize where it is possible and desirable to introduce innovations. Depending on the requirements of the change being proposed and the context of the change, diagnosis might need to be an extensive area of activity with several variations being worked through, or it could be a light touch diagnosis in which the aim is to act with speed. This principle holds for each of the three focal areas in the framework. We would advise at least some activity in each area, but the actions chosen and the time and effort expended will vary with the nature and importance of the change and its context.

In enacting change, it is rarely the case that one form of action will work well for all aspects of the change and all those who are involved, so it is important to establish a repertoire of options for action. This means embarking on change with a combination of options and enough flexibility to be able to cope with the unexpected events, tensions, and paradoxes that arise. Hence the second focal area entails the change agent and other participants making informed choices about a set of interventions which can involve different foci. The choices include: changing the structure or the organization; exploring and engaging with the identity aspects of change, that is who we are as a group and what we see ourselves doing as a result of who we are; choosing customers and competitors; changing processes; aligning people and their activities; fostering learning and development; and, finally, developing change through dialogue. Of course, the specific circumstances of any change situation may require a blend of more than one set of actions and the diagnostic work previously undertaken might highlight complementary courses of action.

The next focal area involves a switch in emphasis from enactment to explaining. Communication is often cited as being central to organizational life in general and to change in particular (one expression of this is Kotter's observation that we under-communicate "by a factor of ten" in change situations, 1996). Our argument is that communication is too often considered as the mono-directional transfer of instructions or explanation of the change typically from senior figures to more junior members of the organization. Similarly, the idea of piloting a new process in one area and then 'rolling it out' across the organization can be experienced by those who receive the rollout as a hierarchical imposition. This style of communication, however well intended, is likely to elicit some degree of resistance and so alternative styles of communication are generally worth considering. A specific literature explores relationships between different managerial levels (e.g. in the context of strategy development, see Floyd and Wooldridge, 2000), and our focus here is on the nature of dialogue within the organization and across its boundaries. Dialogues often incorporate narrative structures as participants, recipients, and leaders of the change create stories in which the change process is made meaningful in the lived reality of everyday organizational life. Such dialogues and narratives offer opportunities to understand leadership behaviours, political positioning, and cultural norms (Alvesson and Karreman, 2000; Bebbington, et al., 2007). As such, we see them as central to attempts to introduce and sustain change.

No change effort, indeed no managerial or organizational act, can ever be fully understood in isolation (Marshak, 2009). Rather, the ways in which people respond to the intended change have an impact on the future nature of the organization and the actions that become regarded as normal. In developing the Enquiry-Action Framework, our intention was to help attune those managing change to both signals and reactions by developing and interpreting evidence. Although we would contest an overly simplistic sense in which 'evidence' proves that change is working, we believe that reflexivity on the part of those leading and enacting change is significant (Nutley, et al., 2006). With all the abundant complexity of organizational life, taking the time and effort to reflect on the ways in which the change process was enacted offers the best hope of developing an attitude of inquiry within the organization.

In some circumstances, there is a natural ordering to these three focal areas: from diagnosis via enactment to explanation. However, the diagram seeks to indicate that change can start in any of the areas. In some cases, enactment is underway and it is helpful to explain what is going on and then to diagnose, because the change is having unintended consequences. Alternatively, it is possible to start by explaining things and in so doing to recognize the need to analyse and then act in a new way. Equally, the sequence can reverse and explanation can lead to a realization that a particular line of action is needed.

CONCLUSIONS

Change may provide management opportunities but equally it can produce challenges which overwhelm the tasks of normal performance. For example, a structural change may be a way of introducing cultural change in which organizational members come to emphasize certain values and ways of being; but equally, such change is sometimes regarded as near impossible. Change is both personal and social, and what may be a considerable challenge for one person may be a simple step for others. Groups can operate such that they embrace a change with infectious enthusiasm or can reinforce shared views that the proposed change is the wrong way to go. Although the insights we have described focus on enabling change, it is also worth saying that sometimes change is not the right thing to do. It may be the case that costs outweigh benefits, that the politics of the change, even if successful, could have long-term damaging effects, or that the organization is suffering from 'change fatigue' (MacIntosh, et al., 2007) and however effective the change would be in theory, it may be one too many for organizational members to cope with.

Therefore, we are not advocating change in all circumstances. Notwithstanding our observations at the outset of this chapter on the amount of change in the business and organizational contexts of today, sometimes consolidation is the appropriate course of action. Even when undertaking change, careful consideration needs to be given to veering towards an incremental or radical step change. Hence, in the insights we have offered, there is always a balance (or tension) to aid consideration and judgement. Our first insight was to understand the balance between anchor points and narratives of change—incorporating both so that both those who are change enthusiasts and those who are change averse have aspects of the processes that are comfortable and other parts which are a challenge. Our second insight concerned the contested value of change practice and our view is that, in general, it is best to bring out some of the contestation into public so that people can become involved in dialogue that may not reach total agreement, but may reach sufficient agreement/understanding of the other for action to occur (insight #5). Researching change entails not only an agreement to access, often when managers are in a potentially vulnerable position, but also that the researchers provide something of worth. We have typified this as a series of auditions, which it helps to be aware of, as they are often unstated and tacit, but real nonetheless (insight #3). The dialogical approach also applied to the co-production of change practice and knowledge and insight #4 seeks to capture a process of difference coming together for a purpose, not researchers or practitioners substituting for each other. Lastly, in insight #6, we have argued that auto-ethnographic experience, as long as subjected to rigour and criticism, can be intensively helpful in unpacking the nuances and emotional experiences of change.

DO

- Listen to the stories that people (re)tell . . . they usually contain key insights
- Challenge yourself to explain what is going on at any given point in time, write these explanations down, and reflect over time on how and why your explanations change
- Draw on your repertoire of other change stories, situations, and individuals in order to characterize similarities and differences to the current situation
- Try to make a positive difference in the situation that you are studying

DON'T

- Rush to snap judgements about complex situations
- Assume that the generation of new insights about a given situation will end when you depart the scene
- Feel awkward about changing your own story about what is happening, why, and what *you* would do about it . . . if these were fixed you are likely not engaged in the production of new insights

REFERENCES

Alvesson, M. and Karreman, D. (2000) Taking the Linguistic turn in Organizational Research. *Journal of Applied Behaviour Science* 36(2): 136–158.

Bebbington, J., Brown, J., Frame, B. and Thomson, I. (2007) Theorizing Engagement: The Potential of a Critical Dialogical Approach. *Accounting, Auditing and Accountability Journal* 20(3): 356–381.

Beech, N. and MacIntosh, R. (2012) *Managing Change: Enquiry and Action.* Cambridge University Press, Cambridge, UK.

Beech, N., Hibbert, P., MacIntosh, R., & McInnes, P. (2009) But I Thought We Were Friends?, in S. Ybema, D. Yanow, H. Wels and F. Kamsteeg (eds), *Organizational Ethnography: Studying the Complexities of Everyday Life,* London: Sage pp. 196–214.

Beech, N., MacIntosh, R. & MacLean, D. (2010) Dialogues between Academics and Practitioners: The Role of Generative Dialogic Encounters. *Organization Studies* 31(9): 1341–1367.

Bennis, W. and Slater, P. (1968). *The Temporary Society.* New York: Harper and Row.

Buchanan, D. and Dawson, P.M. (2007) Discourse and Audience: Organizational Change as Multi-Story Process. *Journal of Management Studies,* 44(5): 669–686.

Chia, R. (1995) From Modern to Postmodern Organizational Analysis. *Organization Studies* 16(4): 579–604.

Chikudate, N. (1999) Generating Reflexivity from Partnership Formation: A Phenomenological Reasoning on the Partnership Between a Japanese Pharmaceutical Corporation and Western Laboratories. *The Journal of Applied Behavioral Science* 35(3): 287–305.

Coghlan, D. (2001) Insider Action Research: Implications for Practising Managers. *Management Learning* 32(1): 49–60.

Coughlan, P. and Coghlan, D. (2002) Action Research for Operations Management. *International Journal of Operations and Production Management* 22(2): 220–240.

Currie, G. and Lockett, A. (2007) A Critique of Transformational Leadership. *Human Relations* 60(2): 341–370.

Geertz, C. (1983) *Local Knowledge: Further Essays in Interpretive Sociology.* New York, NY: Basic Books.

Humphreys, M. (2005) Getting Personal: Reflexivity and Autoethnographic Vignettes. *Qualitative Inquiry* 11(6): 840–860.

Floyd, S.W. and Wooldridge, B. (2000). *Building Strategy from the Middle: Reconceptualizing Strategy Process (Foundations for Organizational Science).* London: Sage Publications.

Kotter, J.P. (1996) *Leading Change.* Boston, MA: Harvard Business School Press.

Nutley, S.M., Walter, I. and Davies, H.T.O. (2006) *Evidence Use: How Research Can Inform Public Services*. Bristol: Polity Press.

MacIntosh, R. and Bonnet, M. (2007) International Perspectives on Action Research: Introduction to the Special Issue. *Management Research News* 30(5): 321–324.

MacIntosh, R., Beech, N. and Martin, G. (2012, February) Dialogues and Dialetics: Limits to Clinician—Manager Interaction in Healthcare Organizations. *Social Science and Medicine* 74(3): 332–339.

MacLean, D., MacIntosh, R., & Grant, S. (2002) Mode 2 Management Research. *British Journal of Management* 13(3): 189–207.

Marshak, R. (2009) *Organizational Change: Views from the Edge*. Bethel, Maine: The Lewin Center.

Oswick, C., Grant, D., Marshak, R. and Wolfram-Cox, J. (2010) Organizational Discourse and Change: Positions, Perspectives, Progress and Prospects. *Journal of Applied Behavioural Science* 46(1): 8–15.

Pettigrew, A.M. (1978) Context and Transformation of the Firm. *Journal of Management Studies* 24(6): 565–593.

Randall, J. and Munro, I. (2010) Institutional Logics and Contradictions: Competing and Collaborating Logics in a Forum of Medical and Voluntary Practitioners. *Journal of Change Management* 10(1): 23–39.

Spradley, J. P. (1980) *Participant Observation*. Belmont, CA: Wadsworth.

Todnem, R., Oswick, C. and Burnes, B. (2014) Looking Back and Looking Forward: Some Reflections on Journal Development and Trends in Organizational Change Discourse. *Journal of Change Management* 14(1): 1–7.

Tranfield, D. & Starkey, K. (1998) The Nature, Social Organization and Promotion of Management Research: Towards Policy. *British Journal of Management* 9(4): 341–353.

Tsoukas, H. and Chia, R. (2002) On Organizational Becoming: Rethinking Organizational Change. *Organization Science* September/October: 567–582.

Van Aken, J. E. (2004) Management Research Based on the Paradigm of the Design Sciences: The Quest for Field-Tested and Grounded Technological Rules. *Journal of Management Studies* 41(2): 219–246.

Van de Ven, A H. 2007. *Engaged Scholarship: A Guide for Organizational and Social Research*. Oxford University Press.

Van Maanen, J. (1988) *Tales of the Field: On Writing Ethnography*. University of Chicago Press.

4 Change Bites
Stories from the Field

Patrick Dawson

INTRODUCTION

In studying processes of change for over 30 years, there are many anecdotes and stories that spring to mind around what occurs in practice and
what drives change management strategies, plans, and interventions. There
is certainly a lot of hype and attention around how to successfully manage
change, and there are plenty of recipe-type approaches on the 'dos' and
'don'ts' of change, and yet there is often a failure to address fundamental
features of change. For example, in moving from some current state to a
future desired state, the unforeseen will happen, and whilst we can plan for
contingencies, the unexpected character, scope, and nature of these future
occurrences never fails to catch us unawares. Change can easily become
contested and derailed, it often fails to deliver promised results, and the
uncertainties and ambiguities of change are often masked and hidden by
those seeking to present a narrative of 'success'. There are a host of issues
and aspects of change that are often swept under the carpet in post hoc
reconstructions of 'how change happened' that provide dubious materials
from which people extract knowledge and lessons on the practical management of successful change. In this chapter, a number of anecdotes and stories
are drawn from incidences that occurred in organizations during processes
of implementation that aim to highlight some of these problems, fallacies,
and myths that often undermine intervention practices that they purport to
support. From these stories, a number of insights and heuristics are distilled
that question whether there can ever be universal prescriptive lessons on
what is an inevitably open-ended and indeterminate future change.

AUTOBIOGRAPHICAL JOURNEY IN STUDYING
CHANGE IN ORGANIZATIONS

From 1980 onwards, I have been involved in a number of research projects examining the social, material, and organizational effects of change
interventions. During my formative years (1980–1986) I investigated the

effects of Computer-Aided Design (CAD) on skilled engineering draughts-men and draughtswomen in the British Aerospace Industry, and in 1983, I embarked on a three-year research project into the effects of computer technology on freight operations in British Rail. Fieldwork was conducted over an 18-month period involving a detailed programme of observation in five high-capacity marshalling yards in three British Rail Regions. A series of semi-structured interviews were conducted with over 80 employees, ranging from members of the British Railways Board through to local managers, freight supervisors, and shunting yard staff (Dawson, 1987). During 1985–1986, I was involved in setting up and running a two-phase longitudinal study of the public requirements of a computerised system of welfare benefit advice (Dawson, Buckland & Gilbert, 1990) which was followed by a study (1987–1988) on the process of organizational change in an electronic instrument corporation located in Scotland (Dawson & Webb, 1989). The research comprised interviews with production and operations managers, observation of staff activities, informal discussions, and the use of documentary material.

In migrating to Australia in 1988, my attention turned to a number of longitudinal studies in manufacturing companies in the white goods industry and to a range of organizations associated with the automotive industry, including a mirror manufacturer, a seat manufacturer, and a study on the uptake of cellular manufacturing at General Motors (Dawson, 1994). Larger collaborative studies followed in examining the uptake of quality management in a range of Australian and New Zealand organizations—including banking, optometry, cable manufacture, and mining (Dawson & Palmer, 1995)—as well as studies on technological change and the uptake of lean and best practice techniques in, for example, a bakery, an oil refinery, and a global pharmaceutical company (Dawson, 2003). Over the last three years, I have been studying change in the transitioning of the intellectually disabled into aged care, in the uptake of a performance management system at a colliery in Australia, and in the proposed uptake of RFID at an electronics company in Sydney (see, Dawson & McLean, 2013; Dawson, Sykes, McLean, Zanko, & Marciano, 2014). Essentially, I have studied the unfolding of change in a range of industries, including companies such as LG Electronics, Pirelli Cables, BHP Billiton, Royal Dutch Shell, British Rail, Aberdeen Asset Management, British Aerospace, Laubman and Pank, General Motors, Hewlett Packard, Central Linen Services, State Bank of South Australia, Illawarra Retirement Trust, TNT, and the CSIRO.

BUILDING A PROCESSUAL PERSPECTIVE: RESEARCH AND EXPLANATION OF NON-LINEAR CHANGE

Underpinning my research and theoretical development has been the refinement and elaboration of a process approach to understanding change. This perspective originally formulated in my 1994 book, *Organizational Change: A Processual Approach*, promotes the importance of viewing change as a non-linear dynamic rather than as a simple progressive series of stages commonly advocated in the mainstream literature. The approach stresses the importance of examining movements as they occur from a current position (when possible at the initial conception of a need to change) through processes of change (the planning and implementation of change) to a period of review and evaluation (a post-change period). Change in all its facets (recognising that linen gets dirty through activities) is central in building knowledge (warts and all) of change interventions rather than approaches that focus on after-the-event accounts (where the linen is cleaned, dried, and folded for public display). Data are collected throughout this process from all hierarchical levels (janitor to managing director) and examined within a broader contextual frame that takes account of the past (historical and retrospective analyses) and the future (analyses of future expectation before and after the event), as well as the current ongoing processes of change (Dawson, 2013: 252). It is based on the assumption that change is complex and at times chaotic (Alvesson & Sveningsson, 2008). It recognizes that the unplanned, unforeseen, and unexpected will occur and that, consequently, organizational change should not be reduced to a list of simple sequential steps (Dawson, 1994).

This processual perspective highlights the importance of temporality and context (the history and culture of organizations), political processes, power plays, and decision-making that engage people in negotiations, in communications that may be misinterpreted or reinterpreted in various ways that create further uncertainties, ambiguities, and confusion (Dawson & Andriopoulos, 2014: 188–221). It spotlights how forms of 'equivocality' (where multiple interpretations exists) may be progressively resolved through collective sensemaking processes (Langley & Tsoukas, 2010: 4), whilst also sustaining conflicting interpretations between different groups that may be further reinforced through the processes of change (Buchanan & Badham, 1999, 2008). Fine-grained processual accounts (often in the form of in-depth longitudinal case studies) are used to capture these processes in which there is no attempt to resolve 'deviant' data in working data towards forms of generalizability, but rather the aim is to provide narrative accounts of the continuously developing and complex dynamic of people in organizations (Dawson, 1997). As such, complexity is not sidestepped but embraced as the processual researcher sets out to catch the unfolding of change as it happens, collecting and interpreting data on individual and group behaviour, changing practices and the way that people give and make temporal sense to their experiences through observations, interviewing, documentary analyses, informal gatherings inside and outside the workplace, and through individual and group discussions. In adopting a longitudinal qualitative research approach in collecting retrospective and real time data through multiple techniques, attention is given to the temporal reconstitution of practices (management strategy, change interventions, and workplace reconfigurations) and how people give and make sense of the way social and material processes, activities and actions unfold over time (Dawson, 2014). In short, change is viewed as a complex, dynamic, non-linear, temporal process (Dawson, 2012).

CHANGE BITES FROM THE FIELD

In reflecting on decades of studying change in organizations, there are a host of potential stories and anecdotes that can be relayed on how the practice of change differs from the prescriptive guides that often over simplify what is essentially a dynamic and complex process. In limiting these stories from the field to fit the space provided, the final selection aims to spotlight the following needs:

1. An open and flexible approach that is able to accommodate the unexpected and the unforeseen ramifications from well-intended actions.
2. That change interventions and redesign are based on a sound understanding of what the current position is rather than what it should be or is assumed to be.
3. Awareness of the importance of context and the pitfalls of trying to transplant wholesale change management programmes from one organization to another.
4. That communication by itself is not a panacea for change—more communication does not produce better change, lowering resistance and promoting participation that underlines success.
5. To know when a change intervention is not going to bring the benefits expected and should be terminated before creating intractable positions of conflict and resistance that ultimately undermines the purpose of change.
6. To recognize that stories are powerful vehicles during times of change (in terms of sensemaking and sensegiving for individuals and groups), and they can be used to support change, to resist change, and to engage multiple stakeholders in opportunities for new pathways to change innovations or to curtail change initiatives.

The Story of Percy

This is a story taken from my early experience of researching change in which Percy, a freight yard supervisor, took me under his wing as a young student from Southampton University trying to collect data for completion of a doctoral dissertation. Percy took on the role of elder statesmen of freight yard operations; he was the longest serving staff member in the yard, and he had worked his entire life on the railways. In studying changes in freight yard operations and in particular the changing role of supervisors and supervision, I spent 12-hour shifts in the yard observing and shadowing the work of supervisors and shunting yard gangs. After ten days of observational work, I started to arrange a series of interviews with shunting staff and Percy, the yard supervisor. Percy took a very formal stance and insisted that 'we' get this right so that my supervisor (at the university) would be impressed by the detail of the information recorded and level of knowledge that I had acquired from my period of study at the yard. When I asked Percy about his job—duties and responsibilities—he asked me to switch off the tape (the interviews were being tape recorded) and proceeded to get out his job description. He then asked me to start recording again and he read out—verbatim—his detailed job description. Although we both knew that this was not actually what he did in his job, but rather a formal description of what the designers of the job thought it should be, he felt that it was important for him to describe his job as per the formal job description. Similarly with guidelines on change management, a lot of these outline how change *should* be rather than how it *actually* is.

As I followed Percy around the yard and further afield in dealing with breakdowns and other human and technical contingencies, he was happy to convey the real substance of his work and the challenges that he faced in trying to ensure the smooth working of the yard. It soon became evident that the skills and knowledge required in performing tasks (other than those neatly scripted in the job description) involved heuristic problem solving in which Percy drew on pervious instances and experiences in assessing probable best courses of action. However, even working with this wealth of tacit knowledge and experience, there are combinations of factors that occur in a changing context that bring unanticipated responses and outcomes that necessitate further action(s). Percy would explain these situations by claiming that it is generally far easier to know what should not be done (that is, if you are knowledgeable and aware of procedures then you can often assess what is likely to achieve nothing or make matters worse) than it is in identifying the best course of action in an emergency situation (noting that there are always plenty of procedures for dealing with incidents after the event). Not unlike change management, the ability to accommodate and adapt to a changing context in which the ramifications of a well-intended action may precipitate other potential issues and problems highlights the importance of an open and flexible approach to dealing with changing contextual conditions and the unexpected ramification of well-intended actions.

In collecting the views of managers and shunters on the main role and job tasks of yard supervisors, it soon became apparent that the job was viewed very differently from those positioned hierarchically both above and below Percy. Two implications stemming from this were: first, local area managers would request training programmes for their supervisors who often ignored key elements of their work (training programmes were often misaligned with the needs of those attending) and second, that people involved in managing change often focus on how to move from a current position (changing practices of staff for example) before they fully understand what staff actually do under current operations. Paradoxically, change agents are quick to assume that they know what people do in practice and then try to implement changes derived from unfounded assumptions. In short, change interventions are often based on false understanding(s) of current position(s).

The Story of Bruce

In a more recent study of the introduction of a performance review system in an Australian colliery, an attempt was made to impose a system taken from a very different organizational context. The change intervention that was placed on a mining operation without due regard for the nature of work tasks and the jobs of miners proved unsuccessful. In this example, the change management initiative was the 'brain child' of a senior manager who was the friend of another senior manager from another company who had indicated how well a performance review system had worked for them and how it was a tried and tested system for increasing efficiencies and individual productivity. However, attempts to implement the system at an Australian colliery brought about unexpected and vehement resistance to what on the face of it appeared to be a fairly innocuous change. Essentially, the new performance management system assigned ratings that were at odds with individual and group expectations and demonstrated little understanding of the occupational culture and shared work practices of miners. Miners were offended at being brought into a review meeting where pre-set scores were placed before them. Raters had received instructions that they were not to negotiate over scores, and as a result, heated arguments broke out over the ratings; but at the end of the day, the miners were excluded from influencing the final score. This they deeply resented and many of the stories that emerged positioned miners as the victims of a long history of managerial injustice. They used stories to reassert their identity of what it means to be a miner and to resist this change intervention imposed by management.

Interestingly, what could be seen as an orthodox change intervention resulted in a contested terrain that worsened relations between management (above ground) and miners (below ground), resulting in a decline in efficiencies, individual and group productivity, and general morale at the colliery. Managers failed to understand the importance of work practices and culture in creating and sustaining miner identities. In other words, these managerially imposed performance ratings severely violated miners' pre-existing occupational identity. Transgressions against miners' identities set off a complex set of reactions in which miners' stories of the appraisal process provide us with insights into their emotional states and the coping mechanisms they brought into service to defend their identities from the unwelcome interventions of management. Stories became a powerful vehicle of resistance, and although they did not change the sensemaking of managers, they served to undermine the change and acted as the bedrock of worker resistance to management's bureaucratic attack on their self-evaluation of what it means to be a miner. In this example, managerial persistence to pursue change in the face of vehement resistance and obstacles made them lose sight of the reasons and purpose of change (that is, to improve productivity and efficiencies at the colliery). Instead they engaged in a battle of power management getting caught up in their own sense of worth and the belief that they were defending their managerial prerogative of the right to manage change. As such, this change was no longer about change for the good of the organization but about winning a confrontation that could and should have been avoided through a more thorough evaluation of the strategies and reasons for change.

The Story of Helen

Whilst our last example highlighted the problem of insensitive, blunt change strategies that engender distrust, anger, and resistance that further impedes change, this example illustrates how stories can be used to pull people together in a more empathetic understanding that can open up new pathways to change. In our case, Helen is an intellectually disabled resident of an aged care facility who gained admission due to the incapacity of her aged mother. However, following the death of her mother, some of the other residents became resentful of her continued presence in the facility. Helen had no other options; the residential care unit was her home. She was suffering the bereavement of her mother, the smells, corridors, daily routines, staff, and other residents all formed part of her existence and provided some familial comfort. The potential distress and dislocation of being exiled from her familiar environment was readily acknowledge by local staff and here is where the story first emerged in embryonic form and was later relayed, refashioned, and replayed to capture the hearts and minds of a wider audience. The 'problem' of adequately resolving this tension was complicated by existing legislation, residential criteria for aged care, funding arrangements (at the state and federal level in Australia), and the differing vested interests of separate organizations (for clients with intellectual disabilities or those requiring aged care). The situation was seen to present an unsolvable problem (referred to as a wicked problem) that prevented meaningful change. Nevertheless, through using stories to engage clients and staff in the 'problem' and through initiating a pilot in which the intellectually disabled were allowed to make day visits to aged care units, the two groups started to spend time with each other. Regular scheduled time allowed both parties to engage co-jointly in collective leisure activities (local news, music, conversations) after which barriers previously entrenched became loosened and redefined. This process promoted new research stories that were used to facilitate an ongoing dialogue among senior managers and staff in the two organizations and resulted in the submission for collaborative funds to develop a new building that could further a radical change scenario that enabled the possibility for the smooth transitioning of people with intellectual disabilities into aged care facilities (at a time other than that dictated by chronological age). Stories in this setting moved beyond the sending and receiving of information (monologic communication) to sensemaking and sensegiving in which open dialogue enabled the translation and reformulation of ideas and agendas in alleviating previously contested terrains and supporting novel change opportunities that sought new solutions to longstanding intractable problems. In this example, stories proved powerful devices for creating bridges towards new opportunities for change through engaging disparate stakeholders along pathways that had previously been viewed as impossible. This example highlights that it is not communication in simply the medium, message, or amount or, for that matter, simply participation and involvement (that may in turn simply reinforce conventional barriers or create new divisions and concerns), but a dialogue that goes beyond an understanding of the present or a projected future underlined by current conditions (barriers of funding or policy constraints) in reconstituting interpretative frames through the process of a dialogue that starts with a common understanding of what is important and what ideally would be achievable discounting current barriers and working assumptions. In this scenario, new change pathway do not wait for policy change in a reactive way but are proactive in demonstrating—through a small pilot initiative—a potential model from which policy change may later result.

The Story of Tim

Tim, the managing director of a bank, acted as leader and figurehead during a major change programme involving the implementation of service quality initiative that comprised a culture and development programme, an assessment and measurement change (that sought to identify 'internal' and 'external' customers' requirements and then to design measures for evaluating delivery of requirements), an analysis of all internal processes to support continual process development, and a communication programme to facilitate a cascade change strategy. During the early stages of this transformation, the processes were lauded and extolled, receiving wide publicity. Through the social networking activities of senior business managers, other companies soon followed suit in the uptake of service quality. The adulation and praise of others served to reinforce the power and status of the senior banking group, who turned their attention to even greater grand schemes in seeking to extend banking services overseas (as well as collecting expensive pieces of artwork to adorn their offices as the successful champions of change). These stories of success masked problems of change and rendered senior management 'deaf' to the voices from below. Not unlike Enron—a company at one stage seen to be leading the revolution of business change (see, Hamel, 2000)—the unravelling of the bank turned into a major debacle that caused considerable financial grief for the government, which had underwritten the bank (also costing billions for tax payers of the state). What was interesting—in doing a longitudinal study of the change processes at the time—is the way that 'success', power, and hierarchy curtailed upward communication in preventing the concerns of staff lower down in the organization in being heard. Whilst these concerns were voiced in interviews by staff and lower level managers—who indicated concerns over the lack of controls on decision-making around the expansion of the bank's loan portfolio—the attention of the senior management group remained aloof in being caught up in their own grand designs for success. The two main points that can be drawn from this are: first, that 'successful' senior managers can often become convinced by their own invulnerability (reinforced by past achievements) that prevent them from listening to voices or paying heed to signs in the present that highlight potential future problems (the old adage that the seeds of destruction are often sown during the pinnacles of success); second, that companies are often too quick to imitate other companies in joining a wave of assumed change management success. This latter tendency can amplify the consequences of poor strategic decision-making from being organization specific to creating wider industry problems.

The Story of Steve and Stephanie

In reflecting on those on the receiving end of change, the story of Steve and Stephanie springs to mind. Steve and Stephanie work in a cable company undergoing change; whilst Steve has worked his entire life at the cable manufacturing plant, Stephanie has only been working for a few years at the cable processing plant. The two plants are adjacent to each other and on the same site. A change strategy had been tried and developed at another site prior to the roll-out of change at this particular site. The change management team is the same for both plants, and a similar change process is embarked upon. The intention is to identify and bring about enhancement that can reduce costs and improve plant performance.

Steve is signed up as part of a team that is expected to find solutions to the high levels of scrap and rework currently associated with some of the machine operations in the plant. During a brainstorming session (that was observed as part of the research), it soon became apparent that the supervisor was going to manage the event. Although there were a number of suggestions made by operating staff, the evaluation and decision-making on the suggestions was hierarchically based. Shop floor employees identified problems with the age and maintenance procedures for machines as well as problems caused through the lack of training of new staff on how to operate the machinery. As it turned out, all the requests to do things differently came from supervisory and managerial levels with the main suggestions from operating staff being ignored. Although employees did adjust their job activities to meet the requirements and suggestions of management, scrap and rework remained high at the plant. Over time, tensions increased between managers and operators, with employees complaining in interviews that the managers were the main cause of scrap through ignoring their suggestions and insisting that a machine runs at a certain prescribed pace. In short, the initiative within the cable manufacturing plant was deemed 'a dismal failure'.

In contrast, Stephanie joined a team within the cable processing plant with the aim of improving the performance (and reducing breakdowns) of the cutting and stripping machines. The dynamics of the initial brainstorming and subsequent meetings were markedly different with more open communication and wider attention to the suggestions of operators. Material requests were made to management and suggested changes were supported. Employees continued to discuss and debate issues; and over a period of time, significant improvements were recorded. This success was applauded by management—a memo was sent around the site boosting the morale of this particular team. Steve and his fellow operators were informed that this is how teams should work, and if they were any good, they could also make things work—casting blame and further heightening tensions in the plant. In the following months, plant performance further declined in an environment of worsening employee relations. There are a number of issues arising from this in which people management is clearly evident, but the two worth noting here are: first, the same change intervention and strategy, whilst common at a broader level, did not achieve the same results due to the differences experienced within the local context of the manufacturing and processing plant (local context and use in practice is important); second, that equal attention should be given to why something 'fails' and not to assume that those associated with 'failure' should be blamed or reprimanded. Although celebrating 'success' is appropriate as it does raise morale for those associated with the change, it should not be used as a stick against others who have not performed as well, and care should be taken to ensure that it does not direct attention away from the lessons to be learned from other changes that may not have fared so well.

The Story of Prince

Prince is a pseudonym for a politically astute manager who was appointed to lead a change initiative in a company that manufactures washing machines. His remit was to introduce cellular manufacturing with the aim of reducing costs and increasing plant productivity. The newly appointed manager had considerable experience introducing this change in other manufacturing companies, and he was well aware of the need to gain stakeholder support. At the outset, Prince involved the trade unions, indicating that if the changes were supported then productivity would increase and employees would be awarded pay increases. He also informed them of his intention to involve staff in the change process. Prince clearly communicated his intentions to all employees, indicating that change was going to happen, and they were all encouraged to get involved.

A new design for the plant layout was circulated, and whilst a platform for consultation was provided, no responses were forthcoming from employees. Once the changes started to be implemented, employee concerns were raised, but Prince held a hard line in being aware that he had followed the process agreed upon with the union. Nevertheless, conflict and tensions led employees to seek support and help from their union. Surprisingly (from an employee point of view), they were blamed for not taking a more active role and were told to get involved in steering the change process. Although some involvement eventuated, there was fierce resistance from the machine shop to any changes, and this became a highly contested area. After a series of angry arguments between management and employees in the machine shop and following several discussions between management, union officials and employees, the changes were implemented. Considerable tension remained, and a barbeque arranged to celebrate completion of the change was not only blacklisted by a core of five machine shop employees; but this group also aggressively warned others that if they attended they would be 'blackballed' and given a particularly hard time. In a third interview with Prince, he relayed how he and his other managers had identified the five key 'culprits' and that they would set about redeploying them to low-skilled demeaning jobs—justifying this as part of the overall restructuring. In making these changes, the intention was to worsen the employment conditions of these employees, taking away the positions they held from long-term service, whilst purposively maintaining their salaries to limit the possibilities of grievance procedures being supported by the union. For Prince, it was payback time for defiant and rebellious employees who had not only sought to undermine change but also boycotted a celebratory barbeque. He was hoping that this move would hasten their 'voluntary' departure from the company.

In this example, Prince used his political skill and acumen in ensuring the support from powerful stakeholders, for example, union officials, and in then tackling persistent resistance by a group of machine shop employees who were earmarked and then reassigned to repetitive boring jobs. This highlights the political nature of change, the importance of gaining the commitment of powerful stakeholders, and raises questions over the line between ethically acceptable and unacceptable behaviour in relation to both employees and management during times of change.

CONCLUSION: INSIGHTS AND HEURISTICS ON CHANGE IN PRACTICE

These short stories and anecdotes of human behaviour in study processes of change in organizations spotlight a number of heuristics or insights on the practice of management change; they also highlight a number of don'ts of change management—five of these are listed below for further consideration and reflection.

1. Do not underestimate the powers of stories to influence sensemaking and sensegiving at an individual and group level or the ability for those on the receiving end of change to see beyond token strategies of participation that ultimately views communication and decision-making as a cascade process.
2. Do not assume that there is a full and unambiguous understanding of what employees do under present operating conditions. Designing change strategies and implementing change on unfounded assumptions is not recommended. Take time to understand the present before designing change strategies for the future.
3. Do not simply adopt a change initiative tried and tested in a different operating environment and assume that there will be no problems of local adaptation and implementation. Be careful of getting on bandwagons of change that have yet to prove their worth over time.
4. Do not circumvent the need for careful search, selection, and assessment of change options. Always ensure a thorough evaluation of the appropriateness of proposed change in moving from some present state to a future desired state that meets the strategic objectives of the organization.
5. Do not pursue a change initiative regardless of the concerns of others or simply ignore the signs that something is wrong in the belief that all will turn out fine in the end. Aim to learn as much about change from failure and do not become 'success' obsessed.

Change interventions unfold in particular contexts over time and are marked by both similarities and differences (there is a uniqueness to each change initiative). Local contextual variation and reconfiguration in use as well as the occurrence of the unexpected and unforeseen all warrant the futility of trying to identify universal laws for best practice change management. It is hoped, however, that the insights provided in this short piece provide material that will aid those actively involved in managing change as well as those on the receiving end of company change initiatives.

REFERENCES

Alvesson, M., & Sveningsson, S. (2008). *Changing Organizational Culture: Cultural Change Work in Progress*. London: Routledge.

Buchanan, D.A., & Badham, R.J. (1999). Politics of organizational change: the lived experience. *Human Relations, 52*, 609–629.

Buchanan, D.A., & Badham, R.J. (2008). *Power, Politics, and Organizational Change. Winning the Turf Game.* (2nd ed.). London: Sage.

Dawson, P. (1987). Computer technology and the job of the first-line supervisor. *New Technology, Work and Employment, 2*(1), 47–60.

Dawson, P. (1994). *Organizational Change: A Processual Approach*. London: Paul Chapman Publishing.

Dawson, P. (1997). In at the deep end: conducting processual research on organisational change. *Scandinavian Journal of Management, 13*(4), 389–405.

Dawson, P. (2003). *Understanding Organizational Change: The Contemporary Experience of People at Work*. London: Sage.

Dawson, P. (2012). The contribution of the processual approach to the theory and practice of organizational change. In D. M. Boje, B. Burnes, & J. Hassard (Eds.), *The Routledge Companion to Organizational Change* (pp. 119–132). London: Routledge.

Dawson, P. (2013). The use of time in the design, conduct and write-up of longitudinal processual case study research. In M. E. Hassett & E. Paavilainen-Mäntymäki (Eds.), *Handbook of Longitudinal Research Methods: Studying Organizations* (pp. 249–268). Cheltenham: Edward Elgar.

Dawson, P. (2014). Temporal practices: Time and ethnographic research in changing organizations. *Journal of Organizational Ethnography, 3*(2), 130–151.

Dawson, P., & Andriopoulos, C. (2014). *Managing Change, Creativity and Innovation* (2nd ed.). London: Sage.

Dawson, P., Buckland, S., & Gilbert, N. (1990). Expert systems and the public provision of welfare benefit advice. *Policy and Politics, 18*(1), 43–54.

Dawson, P., & McLean, P. (2013). Miner's tales: Stories and the storying process for understanding the collective sensemaking of employees during contested change. *Group & Organization Management: An International Journal, 38*(2), 198–229.

Dawson, P., & Palmer, G. (1995). *Quality Management: The Theory and Practice of Implementing Change*. Melbourne: Longman.

Dawson, P., Sykes, C., McLean, P., Zanko, M., & Marciano, H. (2014). Stories affording new pathways in changing organizations. *Journal of Organizational Change Management, 27*(5), 819–838. doi: 101.1108/JOCM-12-2013-0245

Dawson, P., & Webb, J. (1989). New production arrangements: the totally flexible cage? *Work, Employment and Society, 3*(2), 221–238.

Hamel, G. (2000). *Leading the Revolution*. Boston, MA: Harvard Business School Press.

Langley, A., & Tsoukas, H. (2010). Introducing "perspectives on process organization studies". In T. Hernes & S. Maitlis (Eds.), *Process, Sensemaking, and Organizing* (pp. 1–26). Oxford: Oxford University Press.

5   Change in Practice
Surprise and Sense Making

Stephen Procter and Julian Randall

We came to the management of change separately and found ourselves working together at the same university. Each of us has worked in departments in the Civil Service for a number of years, and recently we began to address the issues arising from imposed change programmes during the 1990s when governments around the world started to introduce what was referred to then as New Public Management.

Working as a consultant in an organization gives ready access to people impacted by change, and it was thus that our work examining the impact of change in civil servants began. Our research focused on staff's perceptions of their jobs, work, careers, and the organization after change in the organization, exploring individuals' responses to enforced change; and this lead eventually to our working together when both departments were amalgamated in 2005.

We have entitled our chapter, 'Change in Practice: Surprise and Sense Making', largely because our own work has been conducted during or shortly after change programmes at work, and the literature suggests that surprise is frequently the response which is triggered in staff affected by imposed change at work. Weick's writing on sense making (1995) has opened up a subject which resonates with Festinger's work on Dissonance (1957). It also draws on the work on job insecurity during the 1980s which, ironically, runs parallel with the emergence of HRM theory, one of whose watchwords were 'people are our most important resource'. Our research suggested that the people affected by imposed change did not always feel that those change initiatives made them feel they were 'the most important resource'.

The advantage of evoking surprise is that it triggers a response from those who experience it. That response may be along the lines of: What is going to happen to me and what can I do about it (Lazarus and Folkman, 1984)? Surprise also indicates something else: that a basic assumption has been disconfirmed. Schein (1985) referred to the three levels of a culture and remarked that basic assumptions are usually taken for granted and are often subconscious and tend to surface only when a person is faced with an external threat. Threatened from the outside, those within respond reactively to defend the status quo and later warn new joiners of the likely dangers which may be faced by similar incursions in the future, thereby alerting the peer group to the danger of further external assaults.

Louis (1980a, 1980b) developed this idea with a series of questions which may be used to surface the basic assumptions that people may have. She suggested that such probes can include:

- What happened that surprised you?
- What didn't happen that surprised you?
- What happened that didn't surprise you?
- What didn't happen that didn't surprise you?

She suggested that surprise thus expressed would often indicate that a basic assumption had been disconfirmed and that lack of surprise, in contrast, might suggest that a basic assumption had been confirmed. Isabella (1990) offers many examples of such narratives and draws out the implications for those researching the effects of change on individuals and groups. Throughout our work, we have found these questions useful to explore the assumptions that underpin individual beliefs about job, work, career, managers, and the organization, and it is this that we have drawn on in this chapter.

Much of our work over the years has been focused on qualitative research in organizations. It has sometimes been described as 'letting people have a voice'. This approach allows research subjects to reflect on change in contrast to the sometimes upbeat accounts of change which PR companies promulgate in the official accounts of change programmes. Czarniawska (1997) suggests that in this way organizations are talked into existence. Narratives allow individuals to evaluate change in their lives and reflect on the impact of imposed change on how they view and evaluate their jobs, work, careers, managers, change events, and the organization and perhaps modify the beliefs they hold about themselves and their future at work. This may also have a significant impact on the culture of the organization in the future, affecting the trust and loyalty which once may have been felt for the organization and sometimes leaving people feeling let down and disillusioned—sometimes referred to as the relational part of the psychological contract (Rousseau, 1998).

SURPRISE AND SENSE MAKING

But surprise and sense making does not only affect the research subject. It also affects the researcher. There have been occasions when we have found the responses we received surprised us: it might have been their vehemence or perhaps their restraint in response to change events. Sometimes the responses indicated that something important and significant had been challenged for the individuals involved, which, if held by significant numbers of staff, might suggest that change is unlikely to be embarked upon without challenge or that one or more of the change outcomes might be detrimental to the future of the organization's growth and development. There can also be times when for individuals the change at work presents an opportunity for self-development—one that they might not have taken if change had not been imposed on them in the way that it was. Emancipation is often referred to in the literature (Alvesson and Willmott, 1992; Ricoeur, 1988) but empirical evidence seems less available that a change event has triggered a previously unlooked for opportunity to take a different path or embark on a new life venture. We will look here at some examples of unusual outcomes that we have come across.

1. Rationalizing the Civil Service

Much of our work has been conducted in the public sector, and both of us have been involved with research into change events over a period of 20 years in two government departments, first separately and then jointly when the respective departments of HM Customs & Excise and Inland Revenue were amalgamated in 2005. We followed subjects through an extended period punctuated by frequent change events and had an opportunity, not always afforded to researchers, to develop an overview of individual reactions to imposed change at work. In our case, such an opportunity was to offer itself over a 12 year period.

To put it into context, governments worldwide have been persuaded by the alleged benefits of privatization of public services (Osborne and Gaebler, 1992). Private—good; public—bad is a mantra that resonates in a society driven by the belief that private provision is more flexible and responsive to the customer (because society does not exist, we are all customers now, etc.). In contrast to this private ideal, the public sector is viewed as hidebound, bureaucratic, and unresponsive to change. Such public services are viewed by many politicians as inflexible and rule-bound, in which the staff cannot exercise the discretion to delight the customer, which, it is alleged, the private sector does much more easily. So the 1990s saw the advent of New Public Management in which the art of government would be exposed to the rigours of the market (Hood, 1998) and the public sector exposed to competition for the work that it had traditionally done by right.

PREPARING THE GROUND

Preparing the ground for privatization meant structural changes to departments. Amalgamation of divisions and departments became the order of the day. In one such example, in 1996 we witnessed two divisions that were amalgamated, meaning that from 2 senior managers one would be retained, from 4 deputies two would remain, and from 22 assistant divisional managers only 8 were retained. Amalgamations had happened before in the department's history but had always been dealt with through natural wastage or movement of staff to other jobs. This was the first time that imposed change led to redundancy for senior managers in the numbers recorded here.

For one senior manager, the way in which he was dismissed after 35 years' service resonated with him deeply:

> I felt cheated. I was boss of a division and I had only just attended the divisional forum and yet I was told on the phone one afternoon, 'We want you to go.' I was told to carry on and to tell no one. It was dreadful. *It was awful. I was bitter and I felt like fighting.*

Interestingly, after redundancy, he set up as a consultant and worked with many of the big companies as an adviser and continued a career as a self-employed consultant. But his expression of grievance at the way change was managed in the department was still palpable.

In many ways, the manner in which such imposed changes are handled could only generate surprise for those working as civil servants at the time. Many of our subjects had been in the organization 35 years and had progressed to the rank of senior civil servant. Their basic assumptions were bounded by the belief that, although they earned less than those working in the private sector at a similar level (they often compared themselves to superintendents in the police or members of Parliament—both of whose salaries had advanced ahead of their own), they had a good pension and the assurance of job security. They expected to progress through the organization with staged incremental rewards and promotion, culminating in retirement with a final salary pension. Their status in the community was thus assured. But now, apparently, none of that seemed to be reliable anymore.

RETAINING THE JOB BUT . . .

One surprise was the vehemence of feeling and loss of goodwill that remained even for those who kept their jobs. For one manager, a reduction of four managers down to two found him remaining in post, whilst his three fellow senior managers were made redundant. But as research on job security found during the 1980s (Hallier and Lyon, 1996), those left behind were not always grateful for the jobs they retained. Regret at the manner in which erstwhile colleagues were treated can continue to rankle even with those who appear to have been successful at retaining the one remaining job. One such senior manager found himself sited in an office across the other side of the country requiring a journey of an hour and half each way by train. His new manager was imposed from outside and had the habit of shouting at everyone in the open office they shared. The whole experience of change lead to him withdrawing goodwill, which took the form of attending work only during core hours, regardless of what else might be going on. So he left his home at his usual time and arrived at the more distant new office at 10.30 a.m. and left at 3.30 p.m. to arrive home at his usual time. He remarked:

> *My experience then was that you could not depend on the organization for any trust. Perhaps I had a rose-tinted view of things up to then in the department. The way Head Office behaved was absolutely appalling . . . It sent out so many damaging messages. For all time organizational perceptions changed dramatically.*

So far, so predictable, we might say. But there was at least one upside to this experience of disappointment in the way change had been imposed which benefited others.

UNEXPECTED SURPRISES

In the earlier example, the manager devoted himself to looking after those who had suffered similarly in the unexpectedly uncongenial change events:

> *I knew from experience I had to become more self-reliant. That and helping others helped me, too. I used to say to others, and myself, 'Let's see how you can restore your self-value.' So, I started to restore more self-belief in myself and those around me . . . I have no desire to go further (in the organization). I would happily take early retirement.*

Like several other colleagues, his belief and trust in the organization collapsed, but the will to help others and find the positive in events motivated him to help others make sense of what each now faced in terms of their careers with the organization. However, the prospect of reengaging his commitment to the future of the organization looked severely constrained, and he spoke openly of early retirement.

So we witnessed here an erosion of trust in the organization and therefore an erosion of the relational side of the psychological contract. As the job security literature suggested in the 1980s, those left behind retaining jobs are in a position of weakened belief in their managers' willingness or ability to uphold the standards that the Civil Service once offered, particularly that of job security in return for loyal service. However, the desire to help others equally affected by change remained strong in life at work for many members of senior management who had felt threatened by change events.

FOR THE HEAD OF PERSONNEL

At this time, the exercise of market testing was set up to explore areas of the service that could be offered to companies outside the service. For a personnel manager, it was the beginning of a feeling that all was not well with the future of employment in the Civil Service she had known. Ironically, she was the head of personnel in the main office responsible for the welfare of other staff:

> *We were always a very proud service and now we were told that the work that we did could be up for grabs by outside contractors and suppliers. I felt very bad about this, I can tell you. I felt utterly betrayed. It was a job for life. But now? I mean they don't really want you. We were being asked to bid for our own jobs totally in the dark. It was so cold-blooded, I couldn't believe it. We had no qualifications recognised by the outside world. We were completely naked.*

Once again the response is one of grievance and betrayal, and her reflection on all this change afterwards was cynical:

> *Don't be bitter with the organization. It's a question of politics. The way we look at things. Learning from this? Privatization and value for money will always be with us. We will always be made examples of. In the Civil Service we are not like teachers and nurses who are an emotive subject. Anyone can have a go at us—we are fair game.*

She reflects then on arranging leaving parties for those who were going to leave the organization:

> *In the old days when there was a retirement do [party] they would be crying. Now, they go with a smile on their faces.*

The imagery is stark here and is reflected by several of the narratives given at that time by female members of staff. The prized career in the Civil Service that they felt they had was exposed to the unremitting gaze of the private sector. The only difference between them and others in the public sector is that they are easy targets, unlike other public servants who may elicit more sympathy from the public. Interestingly, they retained 80 per cent of the business put out to tender. But that did not make any difference to the affront that they felt that their professional position of esteem as civil servants had been threatened.

So imposed change which violates deeply held basic assumptions about their jobs, work, careers, and managers' behaviour triggered loss of trust and loyalty in many senior staff previously untroubled by radical change.

No surprise, there, then—although it is sad that senior managers had come to lose the relational contract that has sustained their commitment to the organization.

CHANGE AS AN OPPORTUNITY

But not all staff members felt quite so daunted by the changes. The youngest female senior manager admitted that the way the organization handled change was 'ham-fisted.' But she went on to say that she had not been surprised by change. Her own view was that the department was good at what they did but not good at negotiating during change—'I think we give too much away.' And her own view of change she put succinctly:

> *It is all about achievement and effort. You have got to deliver. Make sure you do what you say you will do. Confront change and don't shy away from it. Ability may determine how far you will get but attitude is far more important: you must be positive and enthusiastic. You also have to be stable yourself—emotional intelligence is vital . . . My advice would be: don't hang on to negative things.*

She accepted change as a personal challenge which can lead on to rising above temporary setbacks and restoring control in life successfully. She and several other younger members of the staff embarked confidently on a different working life elsewhere within the organization or outside of it.

A TIME FOR PERSONAL CHANGE

Change at work does not always come at a domestically convenient time. For one young training manager, the change came at a time of personal trauma—the loss of her marriage and the care of her six-year-old son. She reflects on the experience that she underwent:

> *I'm very practical and logical. I am always thinking about things. And I thought, 'for 24 years my mother had a miserable marriage. She would have been better off without my Dad.' The the Springboard course (to advance female managers' career progress in C & E) came along and I got a lot out of that. I had to ask myself what I wanted to attain, what were my goals, what was attainable for me. Then I had to plan for a change in my marriage and my job at the same time.*

From training she went into the fraud department. It was different but it enabled her to apply for a job elsewhere and move further down the country. However, as she comments on her experience, she reflects on the implications for the organization:

> *I feel betrayed by the way things turned out in the training department. We did everything the hard way. I thought to myself, 'I won't be here next year.' What I have disliked most is the promotional system. I feel bad just thinking about it. Trust? There are still cuts. I am more loyal than they are. It's a numbers game and it's arbitrary.*

The challenge of change is accepted but there is still a feeling of regret about the way change was imposed and the implication for trust and loyalty is a matter of contrast between her own loyalty and the organization's arbitrary treatment of their staff during change. Life is about learning, and family breakdown can strengthen self-belief while still feeling regret at the way things were done in the organization. Of those interviewed (33) 13, mostly younger staff in their first ten years of service, found new jobs elsewhere. But their regret about the way they had to leave remained after leaving the organization.

MOVING ON TO STRUCTURAL CHANGE, 2003

Seven years later, the department went through a restructuring programme, allocating work sectors to cover large business throughout the UK. We interviewed 20 Band 11 managers (equivalent to the assistant collectors whom we had researched in 1996) who covered the UK and identified three groups with the cohort. We chose to examine our data using the lens of Piderit's (2000) three levels of ambivalence. She suggests that there is a cognitional level—what people think about the change; the emotional level—what they feel about the change; and the intentional level—the level of personal decision making—what people feel they ought to do. So while individuals may acknowledge that change is necessary, they may feel regret about it and determine that they will respond by making a decision about their future as a result of the way the change had been implemented (Randall and Procter, 2008).

We identified three different groups of staff, distinguishable not just in terms of their attitudes to change but also in terms of the basic assumptions about their work that underlay this. The first group was made up largely of the more long-serving managers, some with more than 30 years' experience in HM C & E. Under the traditional system of monitoring companies, junior staff would visit at regular intervals to undertake detailed inspections of company accounts. The intention of the reorganization was that this 'policing' role would give way to an 'educative' or 'supportive' one. Visits to companies would still take place, but it was now the Band 11s themselves who were expected to undertake them, with the intention, as it was expressed, of 'getting tax on the boardroom agenda'—to encourage businesses to learn about the systems they could be using to make it easier for them to monitor and manage their cash flow. For this long-serving group, these visits were reinterpreted to assume the guise of previous management practice. As one older manager described it:

> *So, you are expected to know the minds of the people at your sort of level in industry and anticipate their scams and wheezes business by business and help our policy makers counter them. Because otherwise they would be operating blind in the field.*

The basic assumption of the policing role is restored by older managers who reinterpret new initiatives by restoring the old approach to clients, thus allowing them to feel comfortable with the new regime of visiting companies restoring their authoritative position. The policing role was a basic assumption which underwrote the officers' visits in the past. It is now restored to pre-eminence in the newly established visiting regime.

Our second group of Band 11 staff, younger and less experienced than the first, did not see things in the same way. These were typically staff in their early 30s, with ten or so years' service in the department. Many of them had limited experience of the policing-based system of routinized business visits. What concerned them most of all was whether the restructured organization would continue to offer them the same range and depth of experience that they had enjoyed to that point. Their assumptions concerned not so much their work as the degree to which this was—or was not—reflected in a supported career path. They recognized the importance to themselves of having supportive managers in this position. As one expressed it:

> *One of the most important things is who you work for, not necessarily what you do. You really need someone to invest in you, and maybe put that time and effort in supporting you, developing you, and believing in you.*

The new approach seemed to them to offer less support of the kind they had been used to previously in their formative years, and they expressed the view that such support ought still to be in place.

Our third group of Band 11 staff were those who were new to HM C & E who had been recruited from outside the Civil Service. Concerted attempts to recruit such experienced staff had been made as part of the move to put the new Large Business Group on what might be seen as a more commercial footing. Once having worked in HM C & E for a while, however, many of the staff in this position felt that the Civil Service was failing to recognise and make use of the management expertise they had developed elsewhere. The expertise that they assumed they had been hired for was not, in their view, being put to good use. Thus, said one Band 11, there was an almost direct contradiction between what was expected of them and what had been used to attract them in the first place:

> *One of the things with the civil service is that it is very closed. It only looks at what you do within it: it never looks at what you've done out-side it. It never looks at what you are bringing to it.*

A particular cause for concern on the part of this group of Band 11s was their experience of the departmental assessment centre for senior civil servant (SCS) positions. This seemed to exemplify for them the ambivalent attitude they faced from the Civil Service as a whole. On the one hand, many of them failed the centre's assessment; on the other, this did not seem to hamper their career progression. As one of this group said:

> *I think it is very artificial, to be perfectly honest. And I think the way it is managed as well is, to me, proven to be flawed. What I find really strange is that those who did well in their later career were often those who failed the assessment centre.*

Overall, and in contrast to 1996, it was difficult to identify a single theme to characterise employee attitudes to the reorganization into the Large Business Group (LBG). Employees were divided along different lines apparently determined by previous experience and length of service. We might describe this as a fragmented culture in which newly emergent groups without the long-service experience of past practices had different concerns about their own status in the organization following the reorganization of roles and functions in the LBG (Randall and Procter, 2008). This discrete group of managers view their prospects differently and expressed different concerns about their future prospects in the reorganizing organization.

MERGER WITH INLAND REVENUE 2007

We conclude this section with our most recent set of findings (Procter and Randall, 2014). The context in this case was HM C & E's merger into a single tax assessment and collection body for the UK, the HMRC. The merger was accompanied by plans to rationalise the office structure from 74 to 11 offices and to effect significant reductions in the number of staff employed—12,800 in 2008 and a similar number in 2011. Even by recent standards, the changes envisaged for the (now former) HM C & E staff were significant. As very much the junior partner in the new organization (25,000 against 75,000 in the larger group), our research showed that they faced great change in how they did their work, in their medium- and long-term career prospects, and even in where they might be located geographically.

Despite the two components of the newly merged HMRC performing what from the outside might look like the same basic function, there were important differences in how they went about their work. Officers in HM C & E were accustomed to work being based on regular, physical visits to all companies who fell within their remit, thus relying strongly on direct observation and face-to-face contact with clients. As part of the new HMRC, however, it was the other side's—the Inland Revenue's—methods of working that were destined to prevail. This involved a more 'hands-off' approach, with any direct contact being based on a more considered process of 'risk assessment' and written correspondence rather than visiting clients.

But the concern for these ex-HM C & E staff was not so much the attack on their status and identity as the idea that their effectiveness in the newly merged HMRC would be put at risk:

> *They want us to bring money in and it's quite hard to get the department [HMRC] money if they're not going to let us go out and talk to the people and getting that 'bit' where [our managers] are going to let us go out and talk to people is the bit we're going to find difficult*

The staff in the smaller group also found themselves at a disadvantage when it came to short- and medium-term career prospects. This was a reflection of the imbalance in senior positions in the two departments that had come together to form HMRC. The key qualification in the Inland Revenue had been that of a fully trained inspector of taxes, which was attainable only after a lengthy period of professional training. No equivalent qualification or position had existed in HM C & E. So some C & E people embarked on trying to get past the relevant exams in their own time. However, they were told that they would not necessarily get promotions even if they were successful in gaining those qualifications.

When the HMRC was formed, a new senior management position of customer relationship manager was established, designed to be the main point of contact between the department and their 'client' groups. In the area of the HMRC in which we conducted our research, 21 such positions were created. Of these, just one was filled by a former HM C & E employee.

The impact of these changes in working methods and career prospects were compounded by the uncertainties surrounding the geographical location of offices. In line with the 'client-focused' nature of the new HMRC, the organization was to be based much more on the industrial or business sector with which each part of the department was involved. Thus those with expertise in a particular sector, rather than being dispersed around the country, would be brought together physically in one location. For the individuals involved, this would involve either a major relocation or a move from the sectors in which their expertise had been developed:

> *The worst thing that happened is how slow senior management teams are in making decisions and how little senior managers seem to know*

of the impact of the decisions they are making and how long it was to announce the results of the decisions they were making. That's been the worst part of it for everyone . . . They knew Oil and Gas was moving but we didn't get the announcement till a year later when they had made the decision. As far as this is concerned I don't think they have handled change well. I don't think they have handled it well at all.

Sitting and reflecting on the three interventions that we had made enabled us to reflect on what we had experienced during different change programmes in the organization. What did surprise us was that we encountered in 2007 little sense of the betrayal or anger which we had heard in 1996. While there certainly was a feeling that those formerly employed in HM C & E had not, on the whole, come out well from the merger, this was combined with a matter-of-fact attitude towards the range of changes being experienced; an acceptance that change happens and there is not much that can be done about it except to review personal options and look to take advantage of new opportunities of work.

In some ways we found this disappointing, as it suggested that expectancies of career development among these civil servants might well have been modified to a feeling that it was now just a job for them—and not a very secure one at that. Sad, too, that some of the well-defined best practices of change management had been disregarded as a more politically driven culture removed the direct involvement with clients that had once governed day-to-day experience in the job.

COLLABORATIVE AND EMERGENT CHANGE: A SURPRISING OUTCOME

Not all change is imposed, however, and more positive outcomes can sometimes emerge from informal collaboration between professional groups. There is a tradition that refers to such smaller groups as institutional logics: embedded communities, often professional groups that work together can end up either competing or collaborating during change (Reay and Hinings, 2005, 2009). Some of the most difficult groups are sometimes referred to as bounded communities, one example of which is the medical profession (Nicolini et al. 2008). Such groups will often defend their traditional practices against incursions from others into what they view as their core duties and responsibilities. Reay and Hinings (2009) offer a case study of government initiatives to bring about change among health professionals and reflect that whilst government imposed change initiatives met with eventual collaboration from the doctors, normal practices resumed in what they regarded as their rightful medical practice once the initiative had concluded.

A few years ago, we had the opportunity to look at collaboration within a voluntary forum of practitioners supporting the adult survivors of childhood sexual abuse. Doctors sat down with psychiatric nurses and counsellors voluntarily to review their work and exchange ideas for safety guidelines and practices to do with working with vulnerable clients (Randall and Munro, 2007, 2010). Our research interviews reflected the openness and honesty that working in the forum intended to encourage and support when it was first founded. The doctors seemed much less defensive than the literature sometimes suggested they usually are, and traditional methods of dealing with patients were openly reviewed between them. As one counsellor put it:

> *Psychiatrists are in a state of despair, many of them. You breathe in this philosophy of abnormality, dysfunctional. It's like carbon monoxide poisoning—you don't notice it overcoming you and it kills you. It's reductionist—and the failure becomes you, the patient. You need to use your observation. Human Beings are expressive animals. Patients are denied the opportunity. And then their behaviour reinforces the diagnosis in the mind of the medical practitioner.*

For counsellors the approach is one of trusting the patient, believing the accounts, and accepting that there is a common journey to be made on which they can offer support:

> *I think people know themselves. Even young people, I mean even when I meet a young survivor and I do the initial meetings and assessments if she or he is 14 they have 14 years of being them—I don't know them. You know, how could I, even in half an hour, an hour, ten hours I would not know that person—they know themselves?*

The doctor's themselves had reflected on the comments made about traditional medical interventions and were prepared to question how patients are handled and whether traditional medical treatments are always the best approach. For all of them, the question of the government funding of treatments loomed large and a belief that treatments are often driven by political and budgeting considerations. One senior consultant about to retire after 30 years' practice stated:

> *Many services find themselves having to deal with people with that kind of history, psychiatry probably more than anybody else. But the issue that arises is how well or how badly does the psychiatric services as it's constituted tackle these problems and the answer I think is badly, often counterproductively, through nobody's fault.*

So what exactly was it that was likely to succeed in putting in place the best practice for patients that could be jointly offered? First, they looked at the interference costs of working as they are currently operating again:

> *The indicators in Fife were that in any one year 10–20% of people of the total occupants of acute beds had a history of one degree or another of*

sexual abuse. So it is already costing the Trust if you are wanting to wear
a manager's hat. It's already costing the Trust, but it's money wasted really

Then they questioned what was being done already in medical practice. Cognitive Behaviour Therapy (CBT) is currently a standard treatment. It is cheaper than many other interventions, but how effective is it? Several doctors reflected that quite broad generalizations are often made about such treatment. As one of them stated:

> *we've become I think a little bit self-deluded in thinking we know*
> *what's going on what it's about and that's great, we can go to work*
> *on that. CBT is the treatment of choice for panic disorder which to my*
> *mind leaves a hell of a lot unsaid such as compared to what? It hasn't*
> *been properly compared to anything quite frankly, other than medical*
> *or placebo interventions*

The work of the forum involved all the members addressing the common problems they face and sharing what they knew about good practice. As one doctor put it:

> *One of the common linkages is between most of the people who have*
> *taken this Forum idea forward is the ability to say 'I don't know what*
> *I'm doing, how about you'?*

And the final accolade that medical practitioners have accepted the validity of the work of colleagues in the voluntary sector of counselling? In the words of one senior doctor:

> *I think for individuals who present with issues of childhood trauma*
> *specifically who I don't see as being mentally ill, then I would refer them*
> *to psychology or to K (local counselling service)*

So bounded communities of professionals can sometimes share good practice with beneficial results to all those involved. We were pleasantly surprised that in this case, collaboration continued as the providers worked together to provide the best service according to patient need. In Reay and Hinings' terms, there was collaboration but no competing between the logics that were represented on the forum, which itself became a vehicle of learning and exchange to carry forward the work of both counsellors and doctors in a difficult sector both medically and politically.

THE TEN-YEAR OVERVIEW

So what did surprise us as we listened to the narratives of change?

Well, first that imposed change is still often bedevilled by change managers' failure to appreciate the need to communicate with the staff affected early on—particularly where personal lives and careers are at risk of significant unwelcome change.

Second, we were often impressed by the resilience of individuals to respond to imposed change by addressing the challenge of moving on to different careers.

Third, over the ten-year period, at least in one organization, we noted a tendency of the remaining individuals to be less surprised by imposed change (perhaps because the expectancy of a permanent career anywhere else is now less likely to be apparent).

Then, finally, we noted that emergent change undertaken by those involved in work can be successful. It can overcome traditionally embedded communities of practice and become a vehicle for continuing professional development in a way that preserves traditional autonomy and includes those who would once have been considered as paramedics whose views were not valued by their professional colleagues. All it needed was an effective internal change agent to gather support for change and carry it forward. In the words of such an internal change agent:

> *You take it forward and after a while you find that if it's any good or it offers something different what happens is other people want a bit of that action and hop on board and are really pleased that someone is actually doing something because they're so pissed off and stressed out themselves and someone else has taken the initiative and whilst that's happening the committees are talking at length about what we can do: development and White Papers and Scottish Executive documents— and nothing happens. You get someone who's bright and refreshing and then you get this bow wave effect—that's the way things change—people just do it.*

That sounds about right to us. We need to aim for this in the future. So what about dos and don'ts?

DO

- Listen to people affected by change prior to, during, and after the change programme.
- Reflect on the messages about the feasibility of future strategy (have the lessons of action learning been lost completely?).
- Make decisions that affect people's future in a timely way.
- Show evidence that those embracing change will receive its rewards.
- Conduct exit interviews if you want to evaluate the change programme honestly.

DON'T

- Assume that professionals have no other option than to stay in the organization.
- Assume that they will soon get over ill-thought out and arbitrarily implemented change programmes.
- Assume that normal service will be resumed after the change.
- Ignore the ideas of those affected by change—they often know what is best.
- Forget that those left behind will always resent the way their friends who had to leave were treated.

REFERENCES

Alvesson, M. & H. Willmott (1992) On the Idea of Emancipation in Management and Organization Studies. *Academy of Management Review*, 17:432–464.

Czarniawska, B. (1997) *Narrating the Organization: Dramas of Institutional Identity*. Chicago & London: University of Chicago Press.

Festinger, L. (1957) *A Theory of Cognitive Dissonance*. New York: Harper Row

Hallier, J. & P. Lyon (1996) Job Insecurity and Employee Commitment: Managers' Reaction to the Threat and Outcomes of Redundancy Selection. *British Journal of Management*, 7:107–123.

Hood, C. (1998) *The Art of the State*. Oxford: Clarendon Press.

Isabella, L.A. (1990) Evolving Interpretations as a Change Unfolds: How Managers Construe Key Organizational Events. *Academy of Management Journal*, 33(1):7–41.

Lazarus, R.S. & S. Folkman (1984) *Stress, Appraisal and Coping*. New York: Springer.

Louis, M.R. (1980a) Career Transitions: Varieties and Commonalities. *Academy of Management Review*, 5:329–340.

Louis, M.R. (1980b) Surprise and Sense Making: What Newcomers Experience in Entering Unfamiliar Organizational Settings. *Administrative Science Quarterly*, 25:226–251.

Munro, I. & J. Randall (2007) 'I Don't Know What I'm Doing, How About You?': Discourse and Identity in Practitioners Dealing with the Survivors of Childhood Sexual Abuse. *Organization*, 14(6):887–907.

Nicolini, D., Powell, J., Conville, P. and Martinez-Solano, L. (2008) Managing knowledge in the healthcare sector. A review. *International Journal of Management Reviews*, 10(3): 245–263.

Osborne, D., & T. Gaebler (1992) *Reinventing Government: How the Entrepreneurial Spirit is Transforming the Public Sector*. Reading MA: Addison-Wesley.

Piderit, S.K. (2000) Rethinking Resistance and Recognizing Ambivalence: A Multidimensional View of Attitudes toward an Organizational Change. *Academy of Management Review*, 25(4):783–794.

Procter, S.J. & J.A. Randall (2014) Understanding Employee Attitudes to Change in Longitudinal Perspective: A Study in UK Public Services 1996–2007. *Qualitative Research in Organizations and Management* 38–40.

Randall, J.A. & I. Munro (2010) Institutional Logics and Contradictions: Competing and Collaborating Logics in a Forum of Medical and Voluntary Practitioners. *Journal of Change Management*, 10(1):23–39.

Randall, J.A. & S.J. Procter (2008) Ambiguity and Ambivalence: Senior Managers' Accounts of Organizational Change in a Restructured Government Department. *Journal of Organizational Change Management*, 21(6):686–700.

Reay, T. & C.R. Hinings (2005) The Recomposition of an Organizational Field: Health Care in Alberta. *Organization Studies,* 25(3):351–384.

Reay, T. & C.R. Hinings (2009) Managing the Rivalry of Competing Institutional Logics. *Organization Studies,* 30(6):629–652.

Ricoeur, P. (1988) *Time and Narrative Volume 3*. Chicago and London: The University of Chicago Press.

Rousseau, Denise M. (1998) Why workers still identify with organizations. *Journal of Organizational Behavior*, 19(3): 21.

Schein, E.H. (1985) *Organisational Culture & Leadership*. New York: Jossey Bass.

Weick, K.E. (1995) *Sensemaking in Organizations*. Thousand Oaks: Sage.

6 The Elegant Observer
Engaged Ethnography in a Factory that Time Forgot

Richard J. Badham

Oh! Brave new world that has such people in't.

W. Shakespeare, *The Tempest*

This place is a f . . . . . . circus and that lot up there, they are the head clowns . . . You are good at nuts and bolts, you can be our people person!

Joe, Electrician Cokemaking Oz

If primates have a sense of humor, there is no reason why intellectuals may not share in it.

D. Haraway, The Promises of Monsters

INTRODUCTION

It is a careful dance along a narrow beam, and there is the possibility of much grace in it. But the elegance of the dance probably depends on a fine modulation between talk and action, as well as some administrative consciousness of the meaning of the dance.

J. March, The Way We Talk and the Way We Are, p. 25

There is enough veneer in this place to start a carpentry shop.

Tom, Superintendent, Coke Ovens

If we are to understand and capture the fluid and complex nature of change, then we cannot and should not be blind to its presence or deny its existence in our own experience. The way we research is as subject to the multiplicity, vagaries, and uncertainties as the change processes we observe, document, and talk about. In a twist on the classic action research platitude, we might say that for the change researcher there is no more practical example of the challenges of change than his or her own research practice. We fail to understand, grapple with, and reflect upon this practice at our peril.

The conduct of research is a staged activity. This does not refer to the linear stages so beloved of method bureaucrats but treading the boards of a combined frontstage and backstage performance (Buchanan and Boddy, 1992). Both change researchers and the agents and leaders of change they study act out their own versions of James March's 'careful dance along a narrow beam'. For March, leaders are required to spend a substantial amount of time on symbolic activity, yet are required to deny or deplore such activities for them to be effective. They are required to participate in rhetorics and rituals of rationality, while engaging in a pragmatic and emotive world of realpolitik behind the scenes. This should not be interpreted as a simple instrumental Machiavellianism, however, for not only are we and others brought up to believe in the charade, it may have significant value as a means for guiding cooperative activity. The ambivalent nature and attitudes towards this dance are, however, an indispensable part of modern organizational life. As reflexive researchers, we do well to appreciate, communicate, and explore such issues in our research on change as well as in the change processes themselves.

Entry into and exit from the field, the transitional liminality of the fieldwork experience, the emergent nature of activities and outcomes in contrast to the elegant research plans, the instability and reversibility of results and outcomes, and the institutional demands and personal convictions that drive the legitimation of process and outcomes as a purposeful rational endeavour—in the face of extensive experience and evidence to the contrary—and so on. All of these research experiences exemplify not only the complexity, uncertainty, and lack of control emphasised by process and practice change analysts demonstrate the ignorance, denial, repression, and neglect of such issues in our world of organisations (Perrow, 2002). As March upholds, there *is* an elegance in being able to see through this rhetoric and performance, with an 'ability to look at men and events with an eye at once cold and concerned' (Geertz, 1968: 157). It is an elegance that comes, somewhat ironically, from a recognition of the bumbling muddling through that dominates our experience as change ethnographers as well as the change endeavours of our subjects. It requires a poised ability, as Lanham (1993: 142) puts it, to 'toggle', i.e. to switch with some grace between 'looking through a text' and 'looking at it', in recognition of the necessity, value, and entrapments of both.

Let me briefly illustrate what such a recognition looks like in the field. The first anecdote from Cokemaking Oz, the case study employed in this paper, relates to the uncertainties surrounding our interpretations of meaning, and the insecurities that bedevil any claim that our 'findings' are the reflections of the character of the field rather than the constructions of the observer. As a result of the reflective and amiable relationship that had developed between Joe, an electrician in the plant, and me, I gave him a journal article that I had written on 'Living in the Blender of Change'. The paper was a highly academic theorisation and documentation of the dynamics of one change meeting. After reading it, late at night, Joe scribbled out the following note:

> *Really, really stupid assumptions, the best laid plans of mice and men.*
> *That I know what I am doing*
> *That management knows what it is doing*
> *That the people who make up management know what each other is doing*
> *That all the groups and subgroups that make up Cokemaking Oz have a plan*
> *That at least the people in each group have the same plan as the other people in the same group*
> *That everyone can remember what the plan is*
> *That the plan won't change*
> *That you will be told if the plan changes*
> *That everything can be reconciled*
> *That people believe in what they are saying*
> *Because someone agrees to something the stupidest assumption is that they can be treated as if they agree with it. Reality is that it is still sticking in peoples throats—they've got it down but haven't actually swallowed it—give them something else they don't like and they'll spew everything back eventually.*

Shortly after, the foremost Australian authority on change management at that time, Professor Dexter Dunphy, remarked of this account, 'That is the most perceptive observation of change that I have ever heard in Australia.' But whose observation was this? Was it the product of Joe's wry outlook on organisational life, the result of a researcher biasing data from the field, or an emergent collaborative outcome of two friends engaging with the challenges of change? The outcome was, for me, a delightful elegant turn of phrase(s) and contested interpretations of its source and meaning a source of playful creativity in reflecting on the dance of change.

A second anecdote captures some of the elegance in surfacing the complex and controversial nature of the research relationship. When asked about his relationship with me at an academic workshop on academic-industry partnerships, Garry (the plant manager at the case study site drawn on in this paper) replied, to an intake of breath and gasps of delight from different participants:

> 'Well, you could call it a marriage . . . or prostitution . . . or I could have just done it all by myself'.

In one playful and provocative breath, Garry captured the essence of what Clifford Geertz once described as the 'anthropological irony' of such fieldwork experiences. This is the implicit, and sometimes explicit, awareness of both researchers and subjects of the fictions of the field. These cover the intimate, controversial, inegalitarian, problematic, and often illusory interdependencies of trust and relationships that characterize life in the field and the tales that we tell about it.

What follows in this paper is an attempt to draw on such anecdotes from the field as a somewhat comic mirror in order to help capture and communicate the fallibilities and follies of fieldwork and change and the elegance of its self-recognition.

THE CASE

> *It was the best of times, it was the worst of times. It was the age of wisdom, it was the age of foolishness. It was the epoch of belief, it was the epoch of incredulity, it was the season of Light, it was the season of Darkness. It was the spring of hope, it was the winter of despair, we had everything before us, we had nothing before us, we were all going direct to Heaven, we were all going direct the other way.*
>
> —Charles Dickens, A Tale of Two Cities

> *It is like talking to deadwood, driftwood—even balsawood with 90% floating out of the water and only 10% involvement and contribution. They act holier than thou, but they are up to their elbows in the cream cake, saying easy on the teaspoon.*
>
> —Joe, Cokemaking Electrician

The Plant

When you enter Cokemaking (Oz), the first impression is of one of Blake's 'dark Satanic mills'. The five sets of black, dirty, metallic, and rusty 'batteries' that 'cook' the coal at hundreds of degrees Celsius and turn it into coke rise 100 foot above you. They stand on both sides of the 200-yard-long Battery Road—a road that a number of years ago was hardly visible as the carcinogenic pollution billowed from the plant. 'Hot cars' travel down the outside belching smoke and flames from the burning coke that they are carrying. Overhead, cabined, gigantuan 'rams' spanning a large part of the road move up and down the other side of the batteries, pushing coal in and coke out of the batteries—coke that ends its life burning in the nearby steel furnace. Above the batteries there stands a 200 foot high chimney pouring what looks like smoke but is actually steam high into the atmosphere, and to the side of the plant are large stockpiles of coal being washed and prepared for transport along the large conveyor chutes to the batteries. Attempts to plant and grow a tree at the centre of the works had always failed—the tree never survived.

The conditions for research were the best and worst of all possible worlds. The plant manager, Garry, was a charismatic change leader, renowned throughout the steel company, and seriously and personally committed to a genuine transformation. He was flexible, open, emotive, and accessible, with immense credibility in the company and growing credibility in the plant. Yet the Cokemaking Plant he had been authorized to improve was commonly known as 'the arse end of the Steelworks'. The unions had negotiated an employment clause that no employee could be forced to transfer to the Coke Ovens without their agreement! The environment was dirty, smoggy, and polluted, carcinogenic gases were incompletely contained, health and safety was one of the worst in the overall steel facility, and low-skilled manual work was the norm. When Ezzamell and Willmott entitled their ethnography of 'Northern Factory' as the 'factory that time forgot', the image resonated in my mind.

The Researcher

I first made my entry into this world at Cokemaking Oz as 'Rusty', invited in by Garry, the plant manager, to observe and comment on the cultural transformation they were undergoing. Unknown to me at the time was that this was the beginning of a five-year relationship roller coaster, spending around two days a week in the plant and facilitating the involvement of, at various times, five to ten academic colleagues in a number of research sub-projects on matters ranging from the changing identities of middle managers 'lost in translation' to project-based learning in management teams.

The nickname 'Rusty' was given to me by a colleague, poking fun at my new position as a professor of management in a recently established Steel Institute. As a researcher jointly funded by the company and the university, I was expected to deliver something of value to the management of both institutions. However, as an optimistic partisan for the 'underdog' (or chardonnay socialist, whichever you prefer), I was hoping to draw on a 'sociological Machiavellianism' to help reweave a cultural web that redressed at least some of the cruelties of embedded powerlessness (Berger, 1963). As a critical sociologist, I was expected (and expecting) to unearth the insidious workings of power-discourse and to make an appropriate professionally deconstructive and destructive contribution. What I was *not* prepared for, however, was an environment and experience of such ambiguity, ambivalence, anxiety, humor, and ironic commentary that it undermined these initial demands, expectations, and hopes.

The Tale

It is a standard academic narrative trope to provide a post-ethnography 'confessional' (Van Maanen, 2011). This is not one of them. In the terms of the rhetorician Kenneth Burke, there is a tragic entelechy about the standard confessional, seeking punishment or redemption in a purging process. The reflections provided in this paper take a different form. The present tale is a comic celebration not a tragic confessional.

For many ethnographers, entry into the field is a romantic quest, driven by a Promethean pursuit to remove the veils of Maya, uncover the truth, and provide useful knowledge or informed by a medical model of helping to cure natives or patients of the diseases created by their unhealthy practices. Alternatively, the romance may take the form of a perceived heroic defence of the underdog, opening up communication and dialogue, and helping to liberate those suffering from domination and exploitation. For others, the field, and those entering it, are participants in a tragedy, living out a story of hubris and failed expectations, a Faustian fate of eternal punishment, a Kafkaesque incarceration in an iron cage of disenchanted calculation, or a Foucauldian ensnarement in webs of power and domination that dare not call their name. For others, however, these romantic and tragic visions are little more than grotesque illusions in a world that is far more personal, uncertain, polysemic, and absurdly pragmatic than such perspectives allow (McGhee, 1999). At the start of one of the emotive weekly middle management meetings, one supervisor scrawled 'Confessional' up on the whiteboard. It is a world in which pragmatic intelligence and political nous is a comic ingredient but not a tragic sledgehammer.

In the spirit of Kenneth Burke and Clifford Geertz—and such institutional commentators as James March, Karl Weick, Peter Berger, and Niklas Luhmann—this is a tale in the latter genre—what Northrop Frye (1957) called the 'ironic mode'. It is a narrative 'from beneath' (McGhee (1999). There is, in essence, nothing particularly new or controversial about such a perspective. A bearable lightness of being in regard to our own sensemaking activities is now the stock-in-trade of mindfulness research and behavioural studies (Langer, Weick, Kegan, March). This was not, however, a perspective fully fledged in my mind at the start of this ethnographic experience. It was, at least in part, a view that emerged as a result of my experiences within Cokemaking Oz of the often inept and comic struggles of fallible, frequently deluded, and often ineffective human beings—researchers and others. It was forged in a world in which people appeared 'in' not 'above' (Burke, 1984) society, finding meaning in a context in which, in James March's (2007) terms, 'victory is elusive, and virtue is not reliably rewarded'.

To make observations and write in this vein—particularly about one's own research experience and contributions—is not a popular contemporary genre. Much like Freud's humourless tale of jokes and the unconscious, researchers may analyse the role of humour and irony in organisational life, but the studies are often not funny—or ironic! (Woolgar, 1983). In rhetorical terms, most studies of organisational life adopt a superior view from above, an Apollonian ironic tale of research subjects as mere mortals, as an all-knowing academic author communicates with dramatic irony the unwitting activities of deluded actors to an in-group academic audience. Such authors rarely apply humour and irony, even when they investigate it, to themselves as researchers, nor to the research outcomes or processes that they create. As the English philosopher Anthony Quinton (1998) observed two decades ago, the comic genre is not accepted as serious literature in our late modern age. The same applies to organisational studies. Tragic angst and ironic negativity have traction, but comic delight in self-reflective satire, the parody of the hubris of ourselves as well as others, that is another matter.

This paper is intended, however, to go against the grain, to recount, somewhat ironically, a tale of ethnographic research on change and transformation that provokes and amuses, as a way of gaining traction for an outlook that is more akin to celebrating a comic carnival than confessing a tragic failure. In Kenneth Burke's terms, it is intended to 'help us take delight in the Human Barnyard, with its addiction to the Scramble' (Burke, 1969a: 442). The comic perspective on organizational life that grew gradually in my mind during the ethnography of Cokemaking Oz, and which this paper presumes, deploys and illustrates, regards people, in essence,

> *not as vicious, but as mistaken. When you add that people are necessarily mistaken, that all people are exposed to situations in which they must act as fools, that every insight contains its own special kind of blindness, you complete the comic circle, returning again to the lesson of humility that underlies great tragedy. (Burke, 1984: 41)*

UNDERSTANDING

> *Nor have I ever gotten anywhere near to the bottom of anything I have ever written about, either in the essays below or elsewhere. Cultural analysis is intrinsically incomplete. And, worse than that, the more deeply it goes the less complete it is. It is a strange science whose most telling assertions are its most tremulously based, in which to get somewhere with the matter at hand is to intensify the suspicion, both your own and that of others, that you are not quite getting it right.*
>
> —Geertz, G., *Interpretation of Cultures*, p. 29

> *We are living in the blender of change at the moment, we identify the next Lego blocks that we can handle, but it is a bit hard to structure it. We don't feel empowered, we are in the water trying to achieve change, but someone left 6 sharks in the water—we are in the chaos theory situation.*
>
> —Dennis, Supervisor, Cokemaking Oz

It is difficult, if not impossible, to effectively communicate the full ambivalent experience of anxiety and delight that comes from a recognition that you really don't know 'what is going on'. We are brought up in a Western culture and trained in professions that celebrate knowledge, certainty, and the achievement of intended outcomes through intelligent action. Yet the experience of fieldwork reveals another aspect of life, an ambiguous, messy, uncertain, and contradictory flow of events that we are caught up in and cannot extricate ourselves from. This shows up in the many mistakes we make, the ways we fool ourselves, others fool us, and, in turn, fool themselves. One of the characteristics of symbols is that they are multidimensional, multi-levelled or 'polysemic' in their meaning and significance. This is an idea that it is much easier to record and agree with in the abstract than it is to adhere to and appreciate in practice. Yet it captures a fundamental dimension of our experience in organisations in general and change in particular.

When talking to other academics about having spent three years in the Cokemaking Plant, the frequent comment was that I must now have a really in-depth understanding of what was going on. This made me feel uncomfortable, a discomfort that I began to voice after a while with the phrase:

> 'No, not really. Every week I attend about five meetings, but they hold another 50. So each week, I get more and more ignorant!'

As I became more aware of levels within levels, my scepticism also increased about those processual studies claiming to have captured *the* process of change in a plant, after a short period of observation or a set of repeat interviews (Badham and Garrety, 2003; McLoughlin, Badham and Palmer, 2006). Of course, one may say, here goes the post-modernist again, another tedious series of relativistic narratives within narratives. I have two responses to this, a partial yes, and a partial no. The stance I am taking is not a superior one above the fray, but a reflective appreciation of life within it. This stance is no solution to the problem of knowledge but an approach towards it. Rather than encouraging a superior cynical distance towards the knowledge claims of others, it advocates a sympathetic grappling with an existential dilemma. While the devil lies in the details of such a stance, the trickster (Haraway, 1992) delights in them. Let us begin to explore this issue with an illustration of the multiple, misleading and confusing interpretations of our role in the research process.

You Are a Shrink

An encounter on the pathway from the Coke Ovens at Cokemaking Oz:

GARRY (PLANT MANAGER): *You are in real trouble!*

ME (ETHNOGRAPHER): *Why? What have I done.*

GARRY: *Come into my office and I will tell you.*

(Both of us walk into the admin building and into his office.)

GARRY: *You know the operator you just met who was attending the Cokemaking Redesign Working Party meeting?*

ME: *Yes! I was going to talk to you about him. Really interesting and perceptive guy. When the Working Party asked for any questions from the participants, he said 'Yes, who is the laptop?' Tom (the supervisor) responded 'The laptop is an Apple Mac, the person typing into it is Richard, from the university. And what IS it that you are doing, Richard, writing a book or something? I replied with the usual stuff, writing up the story, feeding back observations to those involved and so on. The operator interrupted me 'Sometimes I see you typing when we speak, and at other times you aren't. How do you decide?' I was impressed, 'That is a really good point . . .', and I rambled a bit about what I was doing. He cut me off again, 'You are a shrink aren't you?' I said, no, there was a big difference between a psychologist and a sociologist . . . He replied, 'I saw you in Shellharbour Hospital with a white coat on!' This took me back, then I responded 'Well, I was there last weekend as my son broke his leg'. At this point, he didn't seem satisfied, but the meeting went on. I thought what an interesting guy!*

GARRY: *I repeat, you ARE in trouble. He is a diagnosed schizophrenic, has to take drugs for his condition, but when he takes the drugs he cannot drink. Well, in order to drink over the weekend, he went off the drugs. He actually DOES think you are a shrink, and there to study him! So be very very careful.*

Within ethnography, as in life (and change!), there are levels within levels of meaning and understanding in even our simplest interactions— with uncertainties that may be personally threatening. 'The secret of life', Oscar Wilde once remarked, 'is to appreciate the pleasure of being terribly terribly deceived.'

Keeping Our Promises

ELISE (FEMALE HR MANAGER): *Any questions before we begin?*

CRAIG: *Yes. Where are the minutes for the last meeting?*

ELISE: *Oh, I am really sorry. I have been frantically busy, and I didn't have time to write them up.*

CRAIG: *Oh! I see! So, when management has a vision statement saying 'We will keep our promises', it only means 'when we aren't too busy!*

ELISE: *Look, I am really sorry. I will get them out this week.*

CRAIG: *I'm not sure this is good enough. Either management is committed to this process or not.*

ELISE (BREAKING   *I have said I will do it, and I will . . . I'm sorry.*
INTO TEARS):   *That's all I can do.*

At this point, people in the room are hushing Craig up with whispers of *'Leave it alone'.*

Then the meeting continues on to address the formal agenda. I type up some comments about the macho aggressiveness from the male craftworker towards the HR manager, the only woman in the plant. In the first coffee break, I go up to Craig:

RICHARD: *How are you feeling?*

CRAIG: *To be honest, really pissed off. I have had this problem with HR before. They say 'give us your opinion', but then when you do, they get you. They have destroyed my career before. And then people hush you up, and say 'Don't be so aggressive. Don't make her cry.' It makes me sick.*

After the session, I wrote down another note about the power hierarchy between HR and operators, the cross-cutting nature of hierarchical authority and gender relationships, and also my capturing of different levels of meaning from two moments in an ethnographic encounter. Two years later, after I had left the plant, I bumped into one of the plant supervisors.

TOM (SUPERVISOR): *Have you heard? Elise and Craig got married, and are expecting their first child!*

I was thrown into another turmoil of re-interpretation. What *had* gone on? Not only are the levels within levels of meaning and understanding, requiring an appreciation of how different contexts and different sets of information can shift how we 'capture' and frame an event, but, just as significantly, as an ethnographer (and human being) we need to be mindful of our leap to judgements, influenced by our intellectual preconceptions and ethical/political stance, and these perspectives and judgements shift in the face of more information or subsequent events.

To Be Honest

Most weeks, I met with Garry for a debrief of the week's activities late on Friday. The meetings took place in his office. The following was one interchange.

> RICHARD: *One thing that confuses me. You have been leading this highly emotive, participatory and 'below the green line' change program, and now here they come with this hierarchical and structural 'requisite organisation' program, that seems to challenge everything that you stand for and have been doing. Yet you appear to be going along with it. Do you believe in it or not?*
>
> GARRY: *Well, yes and no. You see, the leaders, they haven't read the books! I do. I read Elliott Jacques,* Requisite Organisation. *And you know what? He talks about all the cultural, emotional and political dimensions of change, at the same time as he focuses on hierarchy and structure. But the senior management, and the consultants, don't read the books! They just take the structural element. However, I think we can use what Jacques says, and I am trying to push that.*

I write down in my notes about the flexibility and complexity of management fads, the disparities that often exist between the guru originators, the consulting practices, and the implemented programs, and the creativity of Garry in fashioning or refashioning of this interpretive resource. After the chat, Garry asks if I want a lift to the station, and so we go out into the car park. Once he starts driving, he turns around and says

> GARRY: *To be honest. The reason I am going along with this new change program is that they are resourcing it. I get funding for two new people, and I can use them to do the work that we are already doing.*

Later that night, I re-described the incident as illustrating the far from subtle direct political manoeuvring of line managers during change, a far different side to Cohen and March's 'garbage can'. The categories of formal/informal interviews, semi-structured or not, do not capture the fluidity and complexity of interpretation flowing from what are, in Burke's terms, essentially different rhetorical encounters, capturing little more than what Mills termed situational 'vocabularies of motive'. A reflective appreciation of this phenomenon is a key feature, an intellectual lightness, a cognitive and emotive toggling, characteristic of an elegant observer.

CONTRIBUTION

> *The widespread notion that social scientific research consists of an attempt to discover hidden wires with which to manipulate cardboard men should have some doubt cast up on it. It is not just that the wires do not exist and the men are not cardboard; it is that the whole enterprise is directed not toward the impossible task of controlling history but toward the only quixotic one of widening the role of reason in it.*
>
> Clifford Geertz, 'Thinking as a Moral Act', p. 155

> *You don't mean to say you don't recognise that what is going on here is theatre do you?*
>
> Joe Pollard, Electrician (A smiling response to my idea of bringing in a professional organisational theatre company to stimulate discussion and reflection on change.)

Whether or not anthropologists or ethnographers have or should have a specific impact on the cultures they investigate is a long-standing variant of the hoary old social science chestnut—the fact/value debate. At the risk of being oversimplistic, our standpoint here is quite specific: whereas some ethnographers talk of cases of engaged ethnography (Jay, 2013), all ethnographers are inevitably engaged. It is, however, a form of engagement that is complicated, uncertain, and emergent in character. Recognition, communication, and reflection upon this fact is an important part of change ethnographies claiming to be capturing and communicating the complex processual nature of change in general. If we are to make the claim that the changes we are investigating are messy and political, then it is arguably imperative upon us to be open and reflective about, and draw insight from, such features of our own work and impact.

Within organizational studies, a strong case has been made for independent research, informed by the Star Trek 'Prime Directive', to not interfere with the cultures that ethnographers enter into (Barley and Kunda, 2001; Kunda, 2006). There is much to be said for avoiding the ideological blinkers of 'servants of power' research, from the more obvious effects of power in defining problems and restricting and censoring solutions, to the subtler influences of engagement upon focus, perception, and judgement. However, as Geertz remarks, the benefits of this stance should not lead to a lack of critical reflection on the complexities of one's commitments and impact. At one level, if researchers are akin to publication vampires, extracting data from the field to support publications that enhance their career and intellectual community, this is far from being a neutral stance—it advocates the devotion of public resources and the time of everyone in the field for 'disciplinary' ends that are caught up in their own 'imperialistic' webs of power. At another level, involvements and relationships in the field involve a whole range of bargains, favours, trade-offs, and ethical dilemmas, as the researcher strives to obtain access, data, time, and resources, and those observed seek insight, relief, advice, and even material, reputational, or career enhancement. We ignore such phenomena not only at our peril, but at the risk of having highly problematic unintended impacts. Geertz (1968: 156) puts it rather nicely, fearing that

> *Like a eunuch in a harem, a scientist is a functionary with a useful effect; and, like a eunuch, correspondingly dangerous because of an insensibility to subcerebral (often called 'human') concerns.*

A reflective appreciation of the macro and micro dimensions of the power plays is an important dimension of change investigations *and* our understanding of the role of the researcher in capturing them.

Those accepting the active role of an engaged ethnographer often view this role in definite and programmatic terms. For the diagnostic organisational development advocate, it involves action research with a documented and observable impact. For critical ethnographers of a Habermasian ilk, the desired outcome is facilitating increased openness and freedom in communication (c.f. Flybjerg, 1998). For others, of a more Foucauldian persuasion, all forms of communication are imbued with a micro-physics of power, however 'open' and 'free' it is claimed to be, and the ethnographer can do little more than make such processes more transparent—whereas any such 'transparency' process is itself suspect! (Ehn and Badham, 2002; Flybjerg, 1998). In contrast, however, for those with a more ironic perspective on the 'human barnyard' (Burke, 1969a, 1969b), the organizational world and the role of the researcher within it is characterized by a greater degree of chaos, irrationality, and folly than such perspectives suggest. Within such a view, a key role of an ethnographer of change is to highlight the exaggerated faith in human reason embedded in our (overly) rationalized Western culture, deconstructing not only our public and private understandings of change in organisations but also the role of research on these phenomena. As Donna Haraway (1992: 300) puts it, 'revisioning the world as coding trickster with whom we must learn to converse', rather than a more structured, predictable, or systemic view of organisations and the social world.

At the level of public performance, our fieldwork at Cokemaking Oz was involved in a number of activities with diverse outcomes. Studies of the leadership and culture change program resulted in a series of published reflections on the tensions, uncertainties, and ambiguities of change experiences (Badham and Garrety, 2003: McLoughlin, Badham and Palmer, 2006: Badham et al., 2003), the liminal and ironic nature of middle management identities during change (Badham, Claydon and Down, 2012; Down and Reveley, 2009; Garrety, Badham et al., 2003), and the dramaturgical nature of both phenomenon (Badham, Mead and Antocopolou, 2012; Down and Reveley, 2009). Longitudinal studies of the social dynamics of engineering projects, participative technology design, and leadership development resulted in a number of doctoral theses and a series of publication streams on the social construction of technology and project-based learning. (Garrety and Badham, 2004; Garrety, Badham and Robertson, 2004; Sense, 2009; Wotherspoon, 2001). As part of these and other sub-projects, the research prototyped socio-technical software in reshaping the introduction of new technology; established learning forums for project teams; led to corporate-wide changes in procedures for engineering projects; advised on, participated in, and made improvements in communication during change; facilitated transformations and improvements in operations management; and created a number of videos, a series of art works, and a compilation of leadership stories in helping to communicate experiences and challenges of change within the organization.

Backstage was, however, another story. One of the informal features of the relationships established was encouraging and demonstrating a stance of humour, play, and reflexivity; massaging egos under stress; illuminating and surfacing absurdities; giving public voice to critiques of overly rational managerialist pronouncements for those without sufficient authority and confidence to question them (at least in public); and establishing friendships with many of those undergoing change, sympathizing with their pains, and joining in satirical mockery at the Dilbertian stupidities of a world undergoing purportedly 'rational' transformation.

This was, in many ways, part of a strange *Alice in Wonderland* world (Badham, 2013) of closed managerialist university commitments contrasted to open learning experimentation by many line managers and employees, and politically defensive sections of senior and middle management counterposed to university researchers wending their relatively autonomous way through the unpredictable life in the field (c.f. Geertz, 1996).

Let me illustrate. When asked by his superiors, 'What is the value-add of having Richard doing research here?', Garry, the plant manager's immediate response, was:

> '*Every week, I see Richard walking past my window going down to the plant. An hour or so later, I see people coming back with red faces, arguing and clearly upset—and I know he is doing his job!*'

For Garry, the challenge of change was simply to stimulate energy for transformation, 'giving it a go' in what he termed the 'mudpit' of change— to stimulate what one of his managers termed 'do management' rather than participating in the formal ritual of 'change management'. His apparently flippant phrase had a harder edge to its humour, reflecting as it did his contempt for formal methodologies and quantitative performance measures for leadership and change.

In sympathy with this view, I worked closely with Garry, gaining entrée into sensitive meetings and interpretations that would not normally have been accessible. For me, this provided genuine collaborative insight, embedded in a sympathetic understanding that led to me purchasing for him a colourful statue of the Mexican God Kokopelli as a symbol of his managerial style. Kokopelli was a God of fertility, a humpbacked flute player well known as a 'trickster God', spreading innovation, surprises, and stirring up trouble. Garry's Don Quixote style, and defense of the underdog, while committed to institutional change, was something that I both appreciated, identified with, and supported in an emotive way noted, at times appreciatively, by my colleagues (Down, Garrety and Badham, 2006)

For other colleagues, however, the rapport established had all the dangers of 'going native'. One colleague wrote a satirical story for the research team, on myself as 'Ro of Varna'. The reference was to Alison Lurie's famous novel *Imaginary Friends* (1968), in which an ethnographer studying a cult of 'truth seekers' assumes leadership of the group as this superior being from another planet that they were expecting—to the chagrin of his fellow worker. In our research team, the *double entendre* of the word 'collaborator' was a source of ongoing, non-acrimonious, and (at least for me) creative debate.

Within and outside the plant, the political role and context of the research was also a source of frequent observation as well as faulty communication and misunderstanding. Prior to my observation of a series of communication sessions, the shop floor operator and facilitator instructed me to,

'Just explain you are not a spy'.

After my ineffective attempt at justifying my storytelling and feedback role, he butted in,

'All you need to know is that he is not a spy, right?'

At a broader political and strategic level, the top 50 leaders of the Australian steel company and the university met together in the University Board Room towards the end of the program. I raised the issue that university management and company R&D managers were in danger of encouraging 'grant getting' at the expense of implementing change through meaningful collaborative work and dialogue, and I would like to concentrate our efforts on the latter. There was silence in the room.

'Well, if Richard doesn't want money',

said the vice chancellor, in a term laden with sarcasm yet very seriously and deliberately spoken. At which the BHP manager sitting next to me leant across and whispered

'Let me tell you more about the deep structures of power here. Watch out, they will swat you like a fly. We need to talk about this.'

We never did. But in reflecting on the incident, I was reminded of an apt observation by Peter Berger (1963: 185). After noting that

> *sociological understanding . . . can combine compassion, limited com-mitment and a sense of the comic in man's social carnival . . . in which men parade up and down with their gaudy costumes change hats and titles, hit each other with the sticks they have or the ones that they can persuade their fellow actors to believe in.*

Berger continues to emphasize that this

> *does not overlook the fact that non-existent sticks can draw real blood.*

Towards the end of the program, the 'protection' given to the 'lighter' research approach adopted by myself and the research team—by a deputy vice chancellor, pro-vice chancellor research, the CEO of the local steel company, and the head of the company research lab—was weakened by their departures, and after a first formal renewal of the contract, my position was not renewed again.

During the course of the fieldwork at Cokemaking Oz, there were a myriad of political interventions, well-meaning, and with some rationale in support of the 'underdog' (Gouldner, 1970), but often also with curious and unintended consequences.

At one of the weekly day-long work redesign meetings, the various levels of the project team at the plant were in ongoing and continuing conflict. I was asked for my opinion, and I prepared a presentation. Drawing on my academic knowledge of the 'non-contractual' underlying the 'contractual', I decided to raise the issue of their 'implicit' or 'psychological' contracts that were leading to undiscussed tensions. I raised, and illustrated, what Steven Lukes (1992) and John Gaventa (1982) had argued were some of the personal and social problems raised by embedded powerlessness amongst the 'disadvantaged' (fatalism, low self-confidence, conflict amongst themselves, and so on), and the problems that people brought up under such conditions had in participating. I then said I was prepared to work with them in surfacing and resolving the implicit contracts and encouraging cooperation and participation. My intention was—on reflection—to *take the politics out of politics!* After listening understandingly and a brief discussion, a heating operator, Craig, remarked

> '*I don't want him* to tell us his contract, I want to write it *for him*'.

The sessions ended up dropping the intervention, and another organizational development observation and phrase was brought home to me—that not only are some issues undiscussable, but the fact that they are undiscussable is, as Argyris (1980) has aptly pointed out, also undiscussable!

Another illustration of political simplicities and shifts in interpretation concerned our participation in the work redesign team. The project appeared worthy of research support. There was a promise of no redundancies, upskilling of the operators, improving teamwork, increasing base salaries, and improving OHS and environmental emissions. But I was gradually made aware of another point of view in the plant. Many of the employees were older semi-skilled migrants with limited English skills and education. They earned high salaries through extensive overtime and saw themselves as wedded to a 'shit' job in order to secure their family's status by paying off their Australian McMansions and their children's education. Unsure about their capabilities, worried about overtime, and feeling scared and unappreciated, many only gave the work redesign grudging acquiescence, while a sizeable group was directly and vocally opposed.

In the process of this transformation, similar to many other redesigns of this kind, operational teams were heroized and maintenance workers demonized—a perspective that I have to admit was initially my own, with the operators being favoured, yet again, as the 'underdog'. The maintenance team was, in effect, coerced and bullied into participation. As part of the project, for example, the work redesign team regularly fed back their discussions and reflections to the whole workforce in consultative meetings. In one of the first meetings with the maintenance group, the facilitator asked 'Any questions?' A hand went up, and the maintenance operator asked, to laughter, 'Why don't you go away?' 'Any serious questions?', was the facilitators response. In a repeat version, six months later, the facilitator put the same question to the group. A hand went up.

> 'Last time you were here, I said why don't you go away? Why did you come back?'

The 'participative' process was only within limits, and the concerns of maintenance staff about working conditions and relativities were marginalized. As I talked further with the group, they told me about the gradual reductions in their pay and working conditions that had occurred over time as the operators' union improved their relativities. Whereas most of the operators were semi-skilled at most, and the maintenance staff had spent three years at the local TAFE college getting their additional skills, the maintenance team was having its numbers, independence, and pay differences eroded. I felt my sympathies shift and my political allegiances alter in an emergent roller-coaster ride. A part of an elegant ride is, arguably, an ability to understand and reflect on the 'good guy'/'bad guy' identifications embedded in the rhetoric embedded in the purportedly academic frameworks we deploy and the data sets that we selectively employ.

A CONCLUSION OF SORTS

> *If you are out to describe the truth, leave elegance to the tailor.*
>
> —Albert Einstein

As I reflect on these ethnographic experiences, under the title of this piece, my immediate reaction is 'I didn't feel elegant'. Scrambling, insecure, anxious, pressured, confronted are the words that leap immediately to mind—an existence on a perennial edge of disaster, overwhelmed by diverse pressures, unwittingly trampling on sacred cows, and facing a constant threat of withdrawal of cooperation and support. In one team session dedicated to self-confessed weaknesses, Garry proclaimed his 'Don Quixote' tendency to 'tilt at windmills'. I have to make the same confession.

For many, Don Quixote is far from an elegant figure, a misguided fellow, with a head full of illusions, rusty armour, sitting astride a nag with a quest to save the honour of a prostitute. However, in his leadership documentary, *Passion and Discipline*, James March takes an opposing view, celebrating Don Quixote's imagination, persistence, and joy in pursuit of his personal quest. While sympathetic to March's point, I would add a qualifier to this: the requirement for elegance of the capacity for recognizing the symbolic nature of one's thoughts and actions and an understanding of the illusions and limitations of one's own perspective in a 'consciousness of the dance'.

It is tempting now to end on an authoritative statement of the value of such 'toggling' on the part of the researcher on and participant in change, and hence the need for a humble, reflexive, comic sensitivity on the part of ethnographers of change. I want to resist this temptation, at least in part, in preference for an illustrative personal note. There is a danger in such personal notes for, as Geertz aptly observes, there is a tendency for ethnographers to romanticize and exaggerate their significance for those in the field, tempted to see tears in their eyes that are not there! The 'ethnographer/native' relationship is, in many ways, as Geertz illustrates, a lightweight fiction, a set of exchanges of views, trust, and gifts that inevitably founders on the divisions that remain. That said, however, I would like to take the risk and end with a small 'ode to Joe', for it hopefully illustrates one of the points I would like to make—that valuable ethnographies of change are about more than the ability to generate pragmatic understandings, rules, or maxims for change. They are a personal endeavour to further the role of reason and humanity in both our understanding and our actions.

Joe was an electrician in the plant with whom I had, what I would like to see as, an intimate relationship across the void. A year or so after I left the plant, Joe got pancreatic cancer. It was a horrible and painful disease, from which he eventually died. The company helped him out initially, but did not continue the assistance. Hanging over the illness, and its tragedy, was the knowledge that Joe had been working in potentially cancer-inducing conditions. Joe was in his late 40s, overweight, and had been a frequent smoker. He had to make decisions about surgery or special new treatments; he went for the new treatment but didn't have enough money to go to Ireland to have the recommended additional chemotherapy. In the early stages, when he was fit and mobile, I planned to arrange for him to present a paper on his experiences in Europe, to get the university to help pay for the trip. He didn't take the offer that seriously, and at that time we were uncertain whether it was necessary.

Over the time of his sickness, I came to visit him at his home a couple of times. His girlfriend was looking after him, and he was putting on a brave front. His house was a humble bungalow in a steelworks suburb, and a world apart from my country residence only 20 minutes or so away. His girlfriend said that the visits cheered him up and got him energized and told me how important our friendship was to him. I hoped so but still felt guilty. The guilt was not only about not doing more, but the fact that his network and life was not really mine, and I was living a separate privileged existence. There was an overlap, a creative and wonderful synergy of cultural life worlds that existed between us, but it did not have the staying power necessary to extend beyond the shared moments and activities into our routine normalized worlds. When he died, I attended the funeral with his family, friends, and many work colleagues. I was the only one invited back to spend time with the family at his house. I felt privileged, but still a strange insider-outsider.

I took his girlfriend out to dinner afterwards, trying to show that my concern was not just show, but it seemed somehow inappropriate. Again, I felt it was hoped that I would do more, and the guilt returned. When I read Geertz's reflections on the cool caring of the ethnographer and the importance yet strangeness of the part-fictional rapport, it was my relationship with Joe 'in the field' that immediately came to mind. My main hope is that how I handled this exemplified, at least in part, how ethnographers of change should conduct themselves. If how we so conduct ourselves *is*, in a number of ways our main cultural contribution—I hope that my relationship with Joe enabled us both to capture, revel in, and expand our mutual capabilities in dealing with the uncertainties and contradictions of organizational change, to also celebrate the discovery of each other's worlds, the questions these discoveries raised about our own, and the emotional pull of mutual discovery and comradeship, and, finally, to leave behind a contribution and memory in each other's lives and those who knew them, about how to live and work together in difficult and little understood situations. It was like that for me, and I hope also for him.

> the impact of the social sciences upon the character of our lives will finally be determined more by what sort of moral experience they turn out to embody than by their merely technical effects or by how much money they are permitted to spend. As thought is conduct, the results of thought inevitably reflect the quality of the kind of human situation in which they were obtained.
>
> Clifford Geertz, 'Thinking as a Moral Act', p. 140

SOME POINTS FOR REFLECTION

On a personal front, I would have liked to end with Joe. However, the purpose of this book is not only to provide the reader with individual accounts of research-on-change-in- practice but to use these to help further general understanding and reflections. Towards this end, it is helpful to provide some heuristics on what might be learnt from the recounted experiences. A reflective commentator might observe that assumptions about such guidelines are probably what informed and led to the account in the first place. On this matter, however, I would like to take refuge in at least part of Oscar Wilde's advice that 'The only thing to do with good advice is to pass it on. It is never of any use to oneself'. While I am passing this on, I have found the following five 'P' principles useful post hoc reflections for myself—but then I was not advised to take them!

The Process Principle

Many organisational development theorists and practitioners aspire to be process rather than content experts. In a research-based twist on this aspiration, engaged change ethnographers should capture and reflect on the complex processual nature of their own research enterprise. This has a benefit that goes beyond an enhanced understanding of and reflection on the nature and validity of their findings. By reflecting on their own experience, it helps researchers to identify, capture, and empathize with the often chaotic and emergent lived experience of change.

The Performance Principle

One key area in the leadership of change is the balancing of formal 'frontstage' and informal 'backstage' activities. This is an activity that inevitably accompanies ethnographic research on change. It occurs within the field as well as outside, in justifying, reporting, and publishing on research to academic and funding audiences. Reflecting on how this takes place, the ambivalence it creates, and the political and ethical issues that it raises is something that helps give researchers an embodied understanding of the lived experience of change in the field.

The Polysemic Principle

Organisations in general, and change programs and processes in particular, are characterized by multiple levels of meaning, embedded ambiguities, shifting zones of uncertainty, and emergent processes and outcomes. In the course of grappling with this phenomenon, actors' perspectives and views are shaped by the frames they impose, the interpreted experiences that they have had, and knee-jerk, emotive/political judgements embedded in their more or less deeply held vocabularies of motive. A reflexive awareness of such phenomena in their own practice helps change ethnographers to better understand these characteristics of the field as well as enhancing their ability to take this into consideration in the accounts that they create.

The Personal and the Political Principle

Just as organisational change is far from being a unitary rational process, so the change ethnographer's research is also never a purely cognitive and instrumental activity. It is undertaken for and shaped by emotion and politics and has outcomes that are inherently partial and contestable. Whether this involves the personal and political dimensions of life in the field, or the disciplinary strictures or political goals of the research communit(ies) that we are part of, there are always obligations and relationships that structure what we take to be 'good', 'sound', and 'useful' research. Being sensitive to these loyalties and what they are worth, and the ways in which these intertwine with formal research methods and objectives, is part of the requirements of a reflexive researcher and one attuned to exploring the complexities of capturing change goals and evaluating outcomes. How the researcher handles the inevitable trade-offs and intimacies of emotion, relationships, and politics, is, as Geertz emphasizes, a key component of not only who you are as a researcher but the social contribution that your 'research' makes.

The Principle Principle

From the ironic perspective adopted in the account of the research experience at Cokemaking Oz, a key desirable component of all thought and action is learning to take your own views and perspective lightly. To be aware of one's own rationalistic bias; to be ready to expect the fallibility and folly of oneself as well as others; and to experience, despite this intellectual awareness, one's own resistance to ignoring or downplaying one's own rational belief system is a key competency. It is one thing to note the existence of paradoxes of change, regarding issues such as the importance of structure or culture in organisational transformation, or the role of coercion versus participation in the leadership of change. It is quite another thing to appreciate and learn to live with paradoxical tensions within one's own research practice. To learn to cope with, creatively respond to, and even come to enjoy the ironies of research has something to commend it as a research stance and as a shared human endeavour with actors in the field.

REFERENCES

Argyris, C., 1980, Making the Undiscussable and Its Undiscussability Discussable, *Public Administration Review*, May/June, pp. 205–213.

Badham, R., 2013, *Alice in Changeland*, Business Perspectives, Sumy, Ukraine.

Badham, R., Claydon, R. and Down, S., 2012, The Ambivalence Paradox in Cultural Change, in J. Hassard, B. Burnes and D. Boje (Eds) *Routledge Companion on Organizational Change*, Routledge, London, pp. 407–424.

Badham, R., Dawson, P., Garrety, K., Griffiths, A., Morrigan, V. and Zanko, M. 2003, Designer Deviance: Enterprise and Deviance in Organizational Change, *Organization* 10, 4, pp. 651–673.

Badham, R. and Garrety, K., 2003, Living in the Blender of Change: The Carnival of Control in a Culture of Culture, *Tamara*, 2, 4, pp. 22–38.

Badham, R., Garrety, K., & Zanko, M., 2007, Rebels without applause: time, politics and irony in action research. *Management Research News*, 30, 5, pp. 324–334.

Badham, R., Mead, A. and Antocopolou, E., 2012, Performing Change, in J. Hassard, B. Burnes and D. Boje (Eds) *Routledge Companion on Organizational Change*, Routledge, London, 187–205.

Barley, S. and Kunda, G., 2001, Bringing Work Back In, *Organization Science*, 12, 1 Jan–Feb, pp. 76–95.

Berger, P., 1963, *Invitation to Sociology: A Humanistic Perspective*, Anchor, New York.

Buchanan, D. and Boddy, D., 1992, *The Expertise of the Change Agent: Public Performance and Backstage Activity*, Prentice Hall, London.

Burke, K., 1969a, *A Grammar of Motives,* University of California Press, Los Angeles.

Burke, K., 1969b, *A Rhetoric of Motives,* University of California Press, Los Angeles.

Burke, K., 1984, *Attitudes toward History*, University of California Press, Los Angeles; Cambridge University Press, New York.

Down, S. and Reveley, J., 2009, Between Narration and Interaction: Situating First-Line Supervisor Identity Work, *Human Relations*, 62, 3, pp. 379–401.

Down, S., Garrety, K. and Badham, R., 2006, Fear and Loathing in the Field: Emotional Dissonance and Identity Work in Ethnographic Research, *M@n@gement*, 9, 3, pp. 87–107.

Ehn, P. and Badham, R., 2002, *Participatory Design and the Collective Designer*, International Participatory Design Conference, Malmo University, 30 June, pp. 109–116.

Flybjerg, B., 1998, Habermas and Foucault: Thinkers for Civil Society, *The British Journal of Sociology*, 49, 2, pp. 210–233.

Frye N., 1957, *Anatomy of Criticism,* Princeton University Press, Princeton, NJ.

Garrety, K. and Badham, R., 2004, User-Centred Design and the Normative Politics of Technology, *Science, Technology and Human Values*, 29, 2, pp. 191–212.

Garrety, K., Badham, R. and Robertson, P., 2004, Integrating Communities of Practice in Technology Development Projects, *International Journal of Project Management*, 22, 5, July, pp. 351–358.

Gaventa J., 1982, *Power and Powerlessness: Acquiescence and Rebellion in an Appalachian Valley*, University of Illinois Press, Michigan.

Geertz, C., 1968, Thinking as a Moral Act: Ethical Dimensions of Anthropological Fieldwork in the New States, *Antioch Review*, 28, 2, pp. 139–158.

Geertz, C., 1996, *After the Fact: Two Countries, Four Decades, One Anthropologist*, Harvard University Press, Boston.

Gouldner, A., 1970, *The Coming Crisis of Western Sociology*, Basic Books, New York.

Haraway, D., 1992, The Promises of Monsters: A Regenerative Politics for Inappropriate/d Others, in L. Gorssberg, C. Nelson, P. Treihler (Eds), *Cultural Studies,* Routledge: New York, 295–337.

Jay, J., 2013, Navigating Paradox as a Mechanism of Change and Innovation in Hybrid Organizations. *Academy of Management Journal*, 56, 1, pp. 137–159.

Kunda, G., 2006, *Engineering Culture: Control and Commitment in a High-Tech Corporation*, Temple University Press, Philadelphia.

Lanham, R., 1993, *The Electronic Word: Democracy, Technology and the Arts*, University of Chicago Press, London.

Lukes, S., 1992, *Power: A Radical View*, Palgrave/Macmillan, London.

Lurie, A., 1968, *Imaginary Friends*, Avon Books, New York.

March J., 2007, *Management and Don Quixote*, HEC Lecture, 17 September http://www.youtube.com/watch?v=bztgYMoTEjM.

McGhee, R., 1999, *John Wayne: Actor, Artist, Hero*, McFarland and Co, New York.

McLoughlin, I., Badham, R. and Palmer, G., 2006, Cultures of Ambiguity: Design, Emergence and Ambivalence in the Introduction of Normative Control, *Work, Employment and Society*, 19, 1, pp. 67–90.

Perrow, C., 2002, *Organizing America: Wealth, Power and the Origins of Corporate Capitalism*, Princeton University Press: Princeton and Oxford.

Quinton, A., 1998, *From Wodehouse to Wittgenstein*, Palgrave/Macmillan: London.

Sense, A., 2009, *Cultivating the Learning within Projects*, Palgrave/Macmillan, London.

Van Maanen, J., 2011, *Tales of the Field: On Writing Ethnography*, University of Chicago Press, Chicago.

Woolgar, S., 1983, Irony in the Social Study of Science, in K. D. Knorr-Cetina and M. Mulkay (Eds.), *Science Observed: Perspectives on the Social Study of Science*, Sage, London, pp. 239–266.

Wotherspoon, R., 2001, *Janus: The Multiple Faces of Engineering Design*, Unpublished Ph.D, University of Wollongong.

Part II

Consultancy Cares
The Travails of the Change Agent

Julian Randall and Bernard Burnes

What is it that consultants do? Comments about their role in the organization will be as various as there are people who have experienced their work. Perhaps that reflects the many different management briefs that they receive and the different roles that each entails. And then consultancies themselves range from those whose names would be well known to most people to the many thousands of sole proprietors who work singly or on coordination with others. The context they have in common is change, and frequently that is imposed change at work.

Until quite recently there were few specifically designed courses to prepare individuals to become consultants. Perhaps the nearest acknowledged qualification was the trusty MBA degree which alerted potential clients that the consultant was bright, high-stepping, and knowledgeable about most aspects of management (superficially at least). We say this because our contributors in this section of the book are mainly drawn from the small business sector. They have sometimes worked for larger organizations in a training and development role and then found that most of their work centred on change initiatives and supporting clients in training staff in new or different skills or enhancing their knowledge to enable them to undertake more demanding or extended job roles. After that, opportunities arose to focus on change management work with a range of different clients, and they chose to follow a career as external change agents.

Experience as an internal change agent would be a frequent way into consultancy for many people. They found they had an aptitude, gaining experience in one sector they then changed to another sector thus continuing to gather different experiences until they were considered by potential clients as able to apply their knowledge and experience in more general roles. These roles might be quite various:

EXPERT:	providing knowledge to solve a problem defined by the client
DOCTOR:	Identify and solve the problem for the client
FACILITATOR:	Provide a process which the client can use to solve a problem

HIRED HAND: Provide temporary capacity for the client not
                            related to the specific client problem
LEGITIMATOR: Provide legitimacy to a client's solution against
                            which other stakeholders are opposed
POLITICAL WEAPON: Provide arguments for a client's position in a
                            political fight
SCAPEGOAT: Take the blame for the client's solution that is
                            not in the interests of other stakeholders
                            (Baaij, 2014)

All of these are roles which consultants become adept at adopting and adapting to may give the impression of the consultant as chameleon. But functional
flexibility seems to have been the skill most often required by our contributors.

More familiar to students of change management will be the steps which
underlie the step approach to the management of change:

- Identify the problem
- Diagnose the problem
- Develop solutions
- Make a decision
- Implement the chosen decision

All of these helpful lists of desired qualities and sequenced strategies can
make it seem as if the solution is an applied programme of change which someone with experience of applied techniques has come up with for the client. In
some cases, that is still what happens and it may account for the often repeated
mantra that 70 per cent of change programmes fail. In other words, we have
just left one thing out of account: the people on whom the change is visited.

Our authors offer different starting points of their journeys through the
consultancy experience. For Jean Neumann, that journey began in 1972 and
consolidated round her master's degree and experience in Organisational
Development and Change. This she consolidated with work at the Tavistock
Institute of Human Relations. Training Interventions included one-day courses
where she admits to offering uplift to participants, while suspecting that once
the day was over, no attempt would be made by the participants" managers to
continue the work begun by her. Increasingly she became aware that exploration prior to running events and agreement about content and outcomes was
essential if the learning journey was to be undertaken successfully. She outlines
a learning journey as much hers as those she attempted to help.

Our second chapter is written by Phil Jackson, whose experience includes
previous management experience and an involvement in many change programmes as an internal change agent. His experience has reinforced the
need to understand 'mindsets': the basic assumptions which people have
about their jobs, work, careers, managers, and organizations which gov-
ern the expectancies by which they interpret events and ascribe meaning

and value to them. For Phil, change and learning are synonymous, and the means of achieving success is the interaction that comes between all participants in the change.

Less often mentioned by the textbooks on consultancy are the challenges which come to every consultant change agent and which require conscientiousness and a clear view of the ethics of what we are invited to embark on by the client. Elaine Mottram, who writes our third chapter, examines this in detail as she unfolds how she moved across from her role as a physiotherapist to become an internal change agent in the health service. Should we be doing what is being asked? Can I engage successfully with this group? Have I the credibility that will give me acceptance? Am I being fair to all those involved in the change process? These questions she explores with great care.

For many sole proprietors, there can be the option of working across cultural boundaries, and this means a whole new way of looking at identity as a consultant and questioning who am I and what ought I to be? Our fourth chapter writer, Norrie Silvestro offers a detailed and frank account of one assignment which he recently undertook and the outcomes for the client and the consequences for himself and his family.

Finally, there are many internal consultants whose work has focused on one organization, and it is no mischance, given its size that the NHS is that organization. Several of our contributors have worked there and conducted consultancy there. It could be said that the NHS has been subject to so (too?) many change initiatives put in place by governments of all persuasions. They have often focused on performativity (getting more out of people for less outlay). Less often has the care of the patient experience been in the forefront of the change. The impact on the NHS staff has been affected and captures the headlines now on a daily basis as doctors and nurses leave and seek employment elsewhere. Our fifth chapter writer, Tricia Boyle, who has run her own consultancy and now runs an internal consultancy service within the NHS, devotes her chapter to the challenges that this can bring to the internal change agent. She deals with constant change interventions and their effect on the staff and the challenge of continuing to gain commitment from health workers whose jobs are already demanding enough and who may find change programmes an unlooked for extra constraint on their time and attention.

The mantra 'change is normal' is easy to say but not so easy for any of us to do. The challenges that this brings is not only to those who undergo change but also to those who attempt to facilitate it. We hope that in this section we have offered an insight into some of those personal challenges which change agents face in the chapters included in this section.

REFERENCE

Baaji, M.G. (2014) *An Introduction to Management Consultancy*. London: Sage.

7 From Consulting Technique to Methodology to Scholarly Practice

Jean Neumann

INTRODUCTION

I have worked as an organisational development and change (OD&C) consultant since 1972, a researcher in the same area since 1982, and an educator of and consultant to consultants and change agents since 1993. Today, my portfolio of work includes all three. The dates roughly correspond to apparent evolutions in my approach to monitoring and intervening in change.

From 1972, I was preoccupied with learning and applying OD&C techniques. During and immediately after studying for a BA and MA (in USA), I focused on developing myself professionally as an internal change agent and private practitioner. From 1982, I entered a doctoral programme in search of improved capability with practical challenges. I emerged with both a PhD and a much enhanced understanding of theories and methodologies underlying OD&C.

From 1987, I relocated to London (UK) to take up a consulting social scientist post at the Tavistock Institute of Human Relations (TIHR). There I was thrust into a continual process of working within and between theory and practice, for both consulting and action research projects. Eventually, this work was translated into education for OD&C practitioners. By 1997, I understood that I was in the process of becoming a scholarly practitioner.

In 2007, I wrote a paper that experimented with making my approach to consulting explicit (Neumann, 2007b). Based on analysis of two of my action research cases, I found it possible to identify principles. In this chapter, I consider how challenges in practice and education influenced each of my eight principles by tracking them across three broad stages in my professional evolution (i.e. from consulting technique to methodology to scholarly practice).

PRINCIPLE #1: LEARN TOGETHER FOR PROGRESS

Design events for trust formation and experiential development around current and unresolved issues, blending data collection for diagnosis, educational design, and action research.

Technique. I entered the field of organisational development and change (OD&C) from the disciplines of adult development and educational psychology. An undergraduate student at an experimental 'university without walls' programme, I worked as registrar in its management centre. One Saturday, we administrators and managers all gathered for a 'team building and future planning workshop' provided by an external consultant.

I was smitten by this OD&C work and determined to learn more. I began participating in residential workshops and applied my learning within the university as an internal change agent. The first event I attended, 'educational design and programme planning', blended group process with experiential learning. I chose the topic as relevant to my undergraduate dissertation, 'facilitating self-direction in adult learners'.

Indeed, I learned to customize the design and delivery of developmental events, incorporating experiential learning throughout. Combined with other applied behavioural science laboratories in group process and organisational development, I found that educational design technique proved an excellent foundation for building a part-time consultancy practice after graduation. It allowed me to become competent in data feedback and planning, team building, problem solving, and other micro-level, short-term OD&C interventions.

A subsequent MA in adult development and education extended this technique by including curriculum development for training and development programmes. This helped tremendously in my next job as a part-time internal change agent for the Rhode Island Office of Higher Education. Creating developmental events delivered together and separately with a dozen community organisations, universities, and government agencies—for the purpose of implementing social policy—required such technique with a longer time span.

Methodology. I thrived on my initial OD&C work of integrating educational design, experiential learning, and self-directed learning. However, I sometimes felt disappointed and depressed after an apparently successful intervention. There was an uncomfortable element of 'entertainment' in one-day events; sometimes I felt shame at my workshops being used to help people cope with a contested change. A data feedback event comes to mind with a medical practice, staffed mostly by freelance health-care providers. As the day finished, it was clear to me that the senior managers would not follow-through on the excellent start we had made in revealing issues.

The master's degree had opened a door to a wide social science and educational philosophy basis for OD&C. It helped knowing there was a link between my professional development and my academic studies. Even so, I was unprepared professionally for emotional and political difficulties that were somehow related to structural issues. I decided my further development needed to incorporate macro-organisation behaviour.

In 1982, I moved to Ohio as a doctoral student at Case Western Reserve University—a programme created originally to enable established OD&C

practitioners to carry out research. There I read extensively and broadly for nearly five years. An article about strategies for changing human systems pointed towards 'learning for progress' as a methodology.

Chin and Benne (1969: 34) asserted that OD&C can be understood as a 'normative, re-educative strategy' for changing human systems. In reflecting on my consulting experience, I thrilled at this assertion as well as sensed an interrelationship alongside their other two strategies (i.e. power-coercive and rational-empirical). Instead of being an accumulated set of techniques, 'learning together for progress' held a recognised place in the context of a wider OD&C field.

Scholarly Practice. A decade later in London, I directed academic studies for the advanced organisational consultation (AOC) programme for the Tavistock Institute of Human Relations (TIHR). We faced the dual challenge of educating consultants to a high level, as well as designing and delivering a learning environment that embodied the methodologies and approaches that we were teaching. We had noted that OD&C practitioners tended to know some aspects of applied social science, while being ignorant about others. We set out to provide professional development that integrated consulting competence, organisation theory, and systems psychodynamics—thus bringing TIHR schools of thought together with NTL Institute's practice theory (Jones & Brazzel, 2014) and contemporary organisational studies.

It was my job to coordinate this difficult task with an interdisciplinary team of consulting social scientists. We evolved a seven module post-graduate certificate and master's degree. These incorporated five varieties of experiential learning: curriculum and module design, experiential activities and reflection, consultancy experience and reflection, vicarious learning, and institutional reflexivity (Neumann, 2007a). Not only did this practice-based programme enact the principle of 'learning together for progress', but it has proven a source of practical scholarship for organisational consulting.

PRINCIPLE #2: TAKE TIME TO EMBRACE PHASES

Work rigorously, authentically, and professionally through each step of a cycle of planned OD&C; with one or more streams of intervention action, this constitutes a phase; whole systems change requires subsequent, iterative phases.

Technique. I remember first meeting the idea of a 'cycle of planned change' while participating in a residential workshop in organisational development. A careful trawl through my original notebooks, stored on my office shelves, does not support this memory. Maybe it was a figure drawn on a flipchart, but my reliable handwritten notes do not show any such image. What is apparent is that my earliest OD&C training incorporated the concepts of 'contracting', 'intervention', and 'evaluation', while completely neglecting the concepts of 'scouting', 'entry', and 'mutual negotiation of intervention'.

This fact of record surprises me, because I explicitly emphasize some version of 'a cycle of planned change'—with a beginning, middle, and ending. For the first eleven years of practice, I consulted with what I now regard as a paucity of diagnostic technique. A factor in my 'getting by' may have been my client base. Small voluntary organisations and subunits of medium-sized charities were contracting for short-term, one-off projects. My internal work at both the university and state government level was conceptualized as stand-alone 'tasks' and 'projects'.

When I began to attract or retain clients into a second or third round of project work, it became obvious that something more was needed in my technique. Back to my OD&C bookshelves, I used desk-based resources with design ideas to inform areas of work for which I had little specialist development. I combined my 'learning together for progress' principle with content from books written by knowledgeable others.

A project with a theatre company comes to mind, wherein it was possible to work for three rounds of OD&C using data feedback and planning, plus some conflict resolution and interpersonal dialogue techniques. By the end of the third cycle, the theatre company's need to redesign roles emerged but neither client nor consultant had the capacity to do so.

Methodology. I finally read a paper on a cycle of planned change (Kolb & Frohman, 1970) during one of my doctoral courses that focused on OD&C approaches and methodology. I was struck with the familiarity of a stepwise approach to interacting with organisational clients. Through readings and seminar discussions, it was possible for me to draw on my strong client experience to make sense of the theory and connect it with actual practice. The syllabus mirrored a cycle, providing readings for each step.

This was my first experience of writing essays and papers based on my own practice. I learned how to describe and explain what happened in my previous internal change agent and external consultant roles, analysing these experiences from the viewpoint of different theories. I found the 'cycle of planned change' to be particularly useful in describing and explaining actual projects. The writing process, itself, helped me to glean insights about practical challenges I had not understood before.

One paper stands out in particular. After reading a book about failures in OD (Mirvis & Berg, 1978), our assignment was to write about our own experience. I chose a failed contracting process with an international charity, during which I had visited their offices three times without agreeing to a contract. By writing about it, I understood what happened. Basically, under the label of 'contracting', I allowed myself to engage in a type of quickie diagnosis that evolved into two sessions with staff and then with managers—all without payment. In retrospect, I could see that this international charity required a slower, more differentiated walk through the early steps of a 'cycle of planned change'. I determined to behave more methodically and professionally, especially during entry and contracting.

Scholarly Practice. A few years into my working life at the Tavistock Institute of Human Relations (TIHR), I bid for an extensive 'people strategy' project. Four executive directors of a paper company were to make a choice from a shortlist of consultants. By then I rarely agreed to such selection processes. I was better prepared to handle scouting, entry, and contracting in a way that diagnosis was the outcome, followed by a mutual negotiation of intervention before actually acting in the system. Because the CEO explicitly wanted my participation expertise, I agreed to a one-hour conversation with the executives. I wasn't offered the contract, as they decided to do their own teamwork first. I thought this was the wrong approach for what they wanted to achieve. I wrote the CEO a letter along those lines, encouraging them to come back to me when they were ready for the broader project.

They did invite me back. We started a six-month (paid) process of entry, contracting, diagnosis, and negotiating the intervention—32 contacts (telephone, email, letters, lengthy meetings) between me as consultant and the four executives. After that we began OD&C in the wider organisation. I managed to conceptualise what we were doing as a cycle of planned change with just the executives. Theoretically, however, I remained puzzled by this 'difficult beginning' and wrote about it (Neumann, 1994).

Writing helped me move from methodology to scholarly practice in regard to the principle of 'taking time to embrace the phases'. I now appreciate that 'entry and contracting' absolutely starts the OD&C work and echoes repeatedly throughout a project. I ceased conceptualising my initial contract with a client as one complete cycle of OD&C. I find that even short-term, apparently one-off projects tend to have phases. I now work with smaller, more manageable cycles, almost always starting with some version of data feedback and discussion. I take 'mutual negotiation of intervention' very seriously and expect it to come up at each round of OD&C.

PRINCIPLE #3: NEGOTIATE DIAGNOSIS-BASED INTERVENTION

Work with a small group of authorised insiders no later than contracting in order to plan and implement a broader, appropriate entry and diagnosis; evolve this into a 'backstage group' for collaboration, monitoring, and troubleshooting interventions and subsequent phases.

Technique. My earliest OD&C training did not prepare me for diagnosis followed by mutual negotiation of intervention with the client. Instead, my technique with data collection came from two other sources. (1) The educational design process from adult learning theory uses 'gathering interests and needs' as an essential step before proceeding (Knowles, 1970: 79). (2) A well-established practitioner book on 'data feedback and planning' offers several versions of collecting and presenting data (Nadler, 1977: 83). I count myself lucky to have had these sources available.

My OD&C training was heavily oriented towards interpersonal interactions. Trainers normally associated the skill of 'giving and receiving feedback' with an imperative of 'using self as instrument of change'. Relating these ideas to beginning OD with 'contracting' may explain the lack of emphasis on diagnosis, per se. There may well have been a disciplinary bias: authentic disclosure of a consultant's thoughts and feelings—combined with effective listening and feeding back the clients' thoughts and feelings—constitutes contracting.

For my early career, such 'use of self' was necessary for contracting, supplemented by alternative approaches for diagnosis. Designing developmental events required me to 'derive learning objectives' from the interests and needs of clients and participants. The 'data feedback and planning' literature emphasized presentation of data and concerned itself with feedback along the lines of interpersonal effectiveness—i.e. feedback that people are likely to understand and use.

Clients appreciated a careful summary of their interests and needs or a display of a few commonalities and differences that they and their colleagues thought needed attention. In the absence of diagnosis, I recall teaching clients to use 'force-field analysis', and other problem-solving techniques, to participate in coming up with their own recommendations and next steps. A well-selected model or practical theory from my bookshelf often provided a framework for further inspiration.

Methodology. From that technique period, the quality of any reporting process grew in importance to me from an ethical viewpoint. To that end, I effectively used the concept of feedback—to individuals, groups, and the wider organisation. Diagnosis, per se, came into sight at the same time as my doctoral studies challenged me to design and undertake organisationally based research projects.

In reading Argyris (1970), I felt that my external consulting echoed his core point: social scientists entering social systems to intervene required practical and ethical standards for applying theory. I became aware how my practice incorporated both my accumulated knowledge and strong values. My previous client portfolio only included organisations and clients with whom I shared such values. For example, I advertised myself as working with clients who valued participative decision making, provided good services, or made healthy products. Such careful, mutual filtering by values was less possible with larger enterprises and in a different geographical location.

I fundamentally accepted Argyris's three directions for professional diagnosis: valid and useful information, free choice, and internal commitment (ibid: 16–20). About the same time, I also discovered that the fields of anthropology and sociology had much to offer about organisational diagnosis. Subsequently, I selected and used qualitative methodology that worked both for my OD&C role and met academic standards required for my PhD research. This was a wildly exciting time—reading case studies of OD&C, action research, and field experiments. In my part-time OD&C practice, I began to experiment with diagnosis using qualitative methods.

Scholarly Practice. A downside to my doctoral studies was that I tended to take lead responsibility for making sense of a situation in which I was hired to consult. Such an expert stance sometimes contradicted my stated values around participation and involvement. Once I began working for TIHR, I felt even greater responsibility to offer clients carefully researched and worked through data and analysis, culminating in recommendations.

This approach was most evident during a five-year socio-technical system project to redesign jobs for semi-autonomous teams. Throughout we used quarterly review and reporting cycles to track the multiple, simultaneous OD&C projects underway on site. As consulting social scientists, we wrote these reports and fed them back to the management and internal change agent teams. The resources available for such careful evaluation for each cycle allowed us also to feed the results into the next cycle—an exciting action research process.

At the end, the executive and I participated together in a closing conversation. He and his colleagues had been leading change implementation for nearly a year by then. He expressed a wish that 'there hadn't been such big gaps in the review reports'. He felt that the operating managers needed more frequent time with the consultants working out issues. On reflection, I thought our reports were over-elaborate and reflected my anxiety to be an expert in the multiple, simultaneous complexity of such a large Socio-technical system project.

As a result, I now use shorter diagnostic reports offered earlier to clients. I've experimented with flipchart reports, big 'Post-It' rough categories, and less thoroughly considered 'working notes' (Miller, 1995). I have relearned the importance of involving the client in interpreting and deciding how to make sense of their own situation and how to proceed. I also ask each client to form a 'backstage group': an effective blend of theatrical metaphor (Goffman, 1959) and the notion that such small groups become a 'microcosm' of their larger system (Slater, 1966).

For me, a 'backstage group' enacts client and becomes my point of collaboration, review, and routine, working between client system and consultant system. More nimble than a steering committee, a small authorised group of insiders makes it possible to conceptualise and implement the diagnosis. They also help consider how to move through the cycles of planned change so that the methodology can be customised to their timescale and situation. Block's notion of sharing the OD&C work 50/50 (Block, 1981: 67) with the client can be realised with a backstage group, thus releasing the consultant from taking on too much of the reflection and thinking.

PRINCIPLE #4: INCLUDE CHANGE STRATEGY

Concentrate primarily on levels of analysis above individuals and pairs to link with overall change strategy; use tactics whereby people change themselves through the process of changing their collective patterns of behaviour; strategy probably requires multiple, simultaneous, and sequential initiatives.

Technique. Early on, the closest I came to strategy was thinking that interests and needs related somehow to work demands. I asked: What is happening in this organisation that requires participants to learn something or to behave differently? This technique comes from the idea of a 'motivational gap' (Tough, 1971), wherein adults engage in self-directed learning in order to close the gap between what they currently know or do and what they need to know or do.

It is fair to say that I took for granted the changes going on in the wider organisation or its environment. I treated them as unproblematic, accepting the viewpoint of the commissioning clients as to their relevance to OD&C for which I was consulting. In this regard, my consulting might have helped clients to adapt to the wider change or not.

Methodology. Such an approach treats change strategy as little more than an element of context surrounding individuals and groups to which they feel the need to respond. This ignores power and influence going back and forth across boundaries, differences in functional and occupational identities, and complications of representational differences within and between different subsystems and subunits. Without awareness, I was colluding with an attitude that people in organisations are passive subjects (i.e. as if they are only and primarily on the receiving end of others' agency). This contradicts my normative, re-educative values that people change themselves through changing their situation.

An NTL programme for OD&C specialists, focusing on power and influence during strategic changes, helped me think differently. Theoretical inputs and experiential learning both illuminated dynamics between different levels of analysis and addressed how social identities (e.g. gender, ethnicity, nationality, occupation, class) help or hinder individual's capability to participate effectively during change. For example, during an organisational simulation, I unintentionally slowed down one aspect of a change just by playing my roles carefully and without variation. This got my attention!

I began to sense interconnections between different levels of analysis beyond individuals and wider collective activities at the level of groups, inter-groups, departments, hierarchical levels, divisions, etc. Particularly, I was intrigued by the idea of 'conflict at organisational interfaces' (Brown, 1983) and immediately understood how it related to the sectors in which I had been consulting. I could sense that 'in-between space'—the interface—was a promising arena for both organisational design and developmental interventions. A drawing of the 'linking pin' model stuck in my mind (Likert, 1961). I came way confident in the possibility of interfaces for working with influence and power across boundaries in organisations.

Scholarly Practice. This confidence was reinforced when I began to consult with commercial organisations and larger enterprises. During my doctoral studies, theory about open systems thinking and organisational design expanded my awareness of strategic change. Change strategies consistent with my values especially interested me in terms of what worked or didn't at enterprise level (e.g. quality of working life, employee involvement, and participative management).

Once in London, I attended TIHR's Leicester conference on authority relations and organisational behaviour. During this 14-day experiential workshop, participants learn sequentially through five organisational configurations. Distinct learning opportunities in individual, small group, intergroup, and large group study culminate in something called the 'institutional event'—at which point, participants are challenged to integrate learning across all five. I strongly experienced the connection between psychological phenomena and political dynamics, as well as viscerally understood the simultaneous enactment and influence of culture and structure across the different parts of the institution.

After reading a seminal book on systems of organisation (Miller & Rice, 1967), I added 'primary task'—and subsequently 'primary risk' (Hirschhorn, 1999)—to my way of describing and analysing organisations. I accepted the double meanings in much that goes on in real-life workplaces, pursuing a learning process of coming to terms with the central importance of authority relations in everyday organisational life. Thus the necessity to include change strategy came with noticing attitudes towards leaders, interweaving this principle into all my OD&C projects.

PRINCIPLE #5: WORK THROUGH REGRESSION AT BOUNDARIES

Expect and legitimate defensive behaviour, resistance, and other political and psychological dynamics; work with the data that emerges through educational design, process consulting, including working with transference and taking up one's authority in role.

Technique. My first exposure to regression as a legitimate field of study and practical action came when I was required to participate in a group relations event. It was like entering a foreign land: I was unfamiliar with the method (originated at TIHR in the late 1950s). During the small study group, nothing made sense to me: the psychoanalytic language, the figure-it-out-without-help culture, and the role of interpretation enacted by the consultant. I did sense, however, that something important was happening: something to do with social differences, power, compliance, and resistance.

Early in my OD&C career, I think it is fair to characterize my bias as 'progress is always possible if you do it right'. The fact that the group relations weekend was required for certification in applied behavioural science reassured me that this unusual learning opportunity mattered. But the closest I came to accepting 'regression' was to evolve techniques for addressing 'resistance' as a legitimate response to feeling forced into workplace change.

When I attended that two-week NTL programme for OD&C specialists towards the end of my 'technique' period, I was aware of echoes of unprocessed experiences from that earlier group relations weekend. Now I could articulate differences of various kinds and verify that such differences frequently could be mobilised during resistance to change. I understood, but I had no explicit techniques to do anything about it.

Methodology. Thus I entered the doctoral programme with the fresh eyes of a newcomer; albeit, a newcomer recently alive to organisational structure and change strategy, as well as alive to issues of power, resistance, boundaries, and interface. From the position of first year student, there was much stratification to experience and observe. I was thrilled by both the possibilities and the constraints.

The chairman of the department led a group process course during the first year. He combined what I now understand as the progressive theory of group development (originating within the NTL Institute related traditions) with a regressive theory of group relations (originating within the TIHR related traditions). The faculty did more than interpret, they also explained and our readings spanned sociology, anthropology, social psychology, and psychiatry of small groups.

Differences in nationality, age, experience in OD&C or academe, gender, race, and class—all were food for thought in the group process setting. Hierarchical differences between students and faculty mixed with broader departmental issues. Throughout I was holding on to my dominant normative-re-education methodology of 'using participation to get participation'.

Much of my established technique was under challenge and rapid development, but I stuck with my personal and professional commitment to 'employee involvement' and 'participative management' (both fads of the day). Discovering language was easier (through reading and class discussions) than knowing what to do about 'working through regression at boundaries'. My role models were erratic in their own attitudes towards progress or regression. Sometimes regression was treated with respect, often it was taken as evidence of immaturity. Equally, resistance was not okay within the actual workings of the academic department but was encouraged as a topic of study.

Scholarly Practice. In retrospect, I was confused by my reading of two different streams of literature related to the Tavistock Institute of Human Relations. On the one hand, I was dipping into socio-technical systems (STS) thinking about work organisation redesign that incorporated and used the concept of 'boundaries' regularly. To a lesser extent, I was reading recommended articles about group and inter-group dynamics. While I got a better sense of regression and diversity, I was struggling with a making sense of boundaries and authority relations.

Once I arrived in London to work at TIHR, their practice differentiation between STS and group relations was apparent. While it didn't last, it helped me to develop intellectual and practical capability to engage separately with the two theories and their historical and current practice. For several years I found it possible to 'use participation to get participation' by operating simultaneously or sequentially from one orientation or the other.

The points at which they came together were in diagnosis, design, and delivery of cross-boundary interventions (e.g. inter-group meetings, third party consultation, and large group planning and problem-solving meetings). Leading the advanced organisational consultation (AOC) programme for 16 years contributed greatly to the evolution of this principle in my OD&C practice. I found my idea of 'design for progression, consult to regression' made a difference in the working lives of other consultants.

Through the process of teaching experienced practitioners, my ability to encourage self-reflexivity between consultants and change agents increased. This related directly, in my mind, to an integrated awareness of regression, resistance, interfaces, and boundaries. Crucially, I was much influenced by the work on 'resistance as identity formation' (Jermier, Knights, and Nord, 1994). Coincidently, several client-based experiences made it possible to experiment with working through regression at interfaces.

PAUSE IN THE STORY

These five principles bubbled away and developed throughout my career from consulting technique to methodology to scholarly practice. They can be seen as precursors to what follows. These elements and proclivities prepared me to grasp broader schools of thought. The table below offers a shorthand summary of 'what to do' and 'what to avoid' for each principle.

I did not have a 'technique' period with the next three principles. Systems psychodynamics, socio-technical systems, and action research arrived on my TIHR doorstep as substantial, existing methodologies. Each of these has its own detailed set of principles and needs to be understood, thus as of a different quality from OD&C technique. Below, I offer a paragraph about how I was introduced into each methodology and then sketch a case vignette illustrating a moment when I felt able to act from a scholarly practice stance. Then I offer a brief note about how I continue to work within this school of thought.

Table 7.1 Summary of Dos and Don'ts

Principles By Number	Do	Avoid
#1: Learn Together for Progress	• Focus on human development and self-direction by integrating trust formation with experiential learning about change issues. • Blend data collection for the simultaneous needs of diagnosis, educational design, and action research.	• Being used as 'entertainment' for retreats and away days. • Underestimating the amount of time needed to tackle controversial issues and challenging changes.
#2: Take Time to Embrace Phases	• Contain the OD&C work by using a public cycle of planned change, sharing the work of each step with clients. • Begin with a version of 'data feedback and planning' using a representative 'backstage group'.	• Consulting without an agreed contract. • Cramming too much into each phase of change without appropriate review and planning for subsequent phases.
#3: Negotiate Diagnosis-Based Intervention	• Always undertake diagnosis of some sort before planning and undertaking intervention. • Find some way to negotiate the intervention before or, at minimum, early in the first intervention.	• Delivering feedback reports and recommendations for action so tightly prepared that clients feel discouraged in their own interpretations and actions. • Conceptualizing one person as the 'client'.
#4: Include Change Strategy	• Help people to change themselves by changing their situations. • Notice interconnections between different levels of analysis above individuals and groups, especially institutional levels.	• Targeting individuals for change directly on their own. • Ignoring organisational structure and strategy as an important element in the change situation.
#5: Work through Regression at Boundaries	• Use social stratification data as a clue in diagnosis, especially between roles, groups, departments, occupations, etc. • Combine progressive OD&C techniques with approaches to working through regressive emotions.	• Vilifying those who resist the change interventions. • Acting 'as if' the dynamics at the boundaries above, beside, and below the target unit for OD&C do not matter.

(Continued)

Table 7.1 (Continued)

Principles By Number	Do	Avoid
#6: Attend to Systems Psychodynamics	• Design and consult to meetings for the purpose of surfacing strong emotions and opinions and working through politics. • Take an umbrella stance to overall difficulties offering observations and interpretations to help free-up thinking.	• Taking on the role of change manager or leader for the client system. • Treating emotional and political reactions as disembodied from actual experiences relevant to workplace changes.
#7: Think Socio-Technical Systems & Strategic Debates	• Identify the strategic dilemmas being faced by the organisation and develop hypotheses about how those relate to the OD&C. • Depict the organisational systems, flows of work, hierarchical relationships, etc., as they relate to this OD&C.	• Forgetting to name both primary task and primary risk as they relate to this particular OD&C project. • Assuming that your particular OD&C project is the most important one underway in the client system.
#8: Trust Action Research	• Accept that each diagnosis and intervention can only embody partial understandings and imperfect solutions. • Commit to learning with clients by reflecting on iterative rounds of understanding, action, and experience unfolding in real time.	• Promising to offer complete understandings and solutions within unrealistic time frames. • Rushing into the next round of OC&C without review and reflection with the client's representative group.

PRINCIPLE # 6: ATTEND TO SYSTEMS PSYCHODYNAMICS

Avoid being the 'change champion', instead enable and contain organisational members as they work through their own disagreements and strategic debates; work with transference in a way that connects feelings to facts of the change situation.

Methodology into Scholarly Practice. Being both a participant and staff member for TIHR group relations conferences (from 1988–1995) resulted in me becoming aware of the complex literature and practice relevant to applied psychodynamics (Trist & Murray, 1990). I learned to work with transference – particularly as emotions related to tasks and risks of change. In addition, my capabilities were extended during many OD&C projects in which emotionality permeated the roles taken and given during real-life changes.

I began to use the phrase, 'systems psychodynamics', in order to avoid treating emotionality as disembodied from actual experiences in workplaces (Neumann, 1999). For me, adding 'systems' to the phrase calls attention to politics and social differences, stereotyping, and scapegoating and other elements of difficult behaviour during comprehensive changes. An example comes to mind when I felt I was on the road to using this principle in scholarly practice.

In the chemical plant, senior managers disagreed about how to deal with collective bargaining between older operators in the existing plant who worked under one payment system, and the younger operators brought to work the new technology plant under a new arrangement. Three-quarters progress into negotiating the new system, covert political processes were being ignored by leaders of both management and unions. One day, a strike brewed under the surface and gossip spread that the Managing Director was going to give the new operators yet another rise.

I encouraged the senior managers to meet 'informally' that afternoon with a combined gathering of trade union representatives, participants of the various change committees, and implicated line managers. The situation was serious enough that everyone attended. The gist of the meeting was to bring the gossip to the surface, subjecting it to discussion and reality testing. The room vibrated with emotions and politics. A logjam was freed and subsequent collective bargaining and OD&C progressed.

Since that incident, I have gone on to experiment with median groups (De Mare, Piper & Thompson, 1991) to give clients a reliable forum for difficult issues. I openly introduce the concept of uncertainty (Marris, 1996), exploring which OD&C methodologies encourage decreased competition and increased reciprocity. Of central importance is the ability to depersonalize systemic issues, especially anxiety as it relates to environmental pressures and business challenges.

PRINCIPLE #7: THINK SOCIO-TECHNICAL SYSTEMS AND STRATEGIC DEBATES

Conceptualize the whole system, depicting points of possible development and intervention; describe primary task, strategic debates, work clusters and flows, cross-boundary relationships, and consulting related to decision making.

Methodology into Scholarly Practice. I entered socio-technical systems (STS) having idealized QWL (the quality of working life movement). Ironically, the Norwegians hosted the final QWL conference the same year that I entered TIHR. I became enamoured with 1960s–1970s STS (Trist & Murray, 1993), applying it whenever I could. Around that time, my colleagues and I integrated our research on how UK manufacturers were using STS with another TIHR methodology on multiple, simultaneous change initiatives (Neumann, Holti & Standing, 1995).

This had been inspired by the phrase, 'change everything at once', used by many managers in our 40-plus network of workplaces introducing group-based job design and payment. I became preoccupied with how leaders balanced multiple, simultaneous change initiatives, while managing ongoing operations at the same time. USA research on comprehensive change (Mohrman, Mohrman, Ledford, Cummings & Lawler, 1990) reassured me that STS had something to offer service sectors. About the same time, I started to apply non-linear STS (Pava, 1983) to service and project-based enterprises. An example shows a situation in which I found it necessary to apply the principle in scholarly practice.

A religious monastery that specialised in training and development for religious leaders faced numerous changes that all coalesced around the idea that their elected leader was about to retire with no heir apparent. They approached me, asking for organisational process meetings for succession planning. But the principle of 'think socio-technical systems and strategic debates' highlighted the unrecognized undercurrent of the monastery in the context of its current environment and the conditions under which they would survive and thrive in the coming years.

We built an OD&C intervention strategy around their main quarterly decision-making body—called 'chapter'. We used developmental events to diagnosis, analyse, work through, and plan actions to be taken by the monks outside of chapter. From the original diagnosis, they identified six areas of change they needed to make before electing a new leader. Over four years, they clustered their jobs into teams, established a rota for team leadership, ensured each brother had a meaningful spread of tasks, resolved several long-standing complaints, and elected two brothers as leader and deputy leader of their renewed monastery.

Since that project, I have worked extensively with the idea of rotating priorities at decision-taker level. I am currently experimenting with strategic dilemmas (Hampton-Turner, 1990) and management of polarities (Johnson, 1992) as they manifest during organisational redesign and leadership selection processes. Most of my current cases involve some aspect of non-linear STS: for example, mutual adjustment during project-based working within internal OD&C units.

PRINCIPLE #8: TRUST ACTION RESEARCH

Mark the ending of one phase of OD&C and the beginning of another phase with review and planning meetings for normative, re-educative processes; use appropriate involvement and participation throughout, enhancing the client's ability to do the same on their own.

Methodology into Scholarly Practice. For me, action research (e.g. Clark, 1972) summarises and incorporates all the principles that have come before. Yet it has to stand on its own because OD&C projects shorter than three phases tend to limit the range of phenomena available for action. It is not always possible to know if and when OD&C will turn into action research. Sometimes it clearly needs to, but the client already has a consultant for the overall thinking, and I am being invited to do something within a subunit. Since moving to London in 1987, I typically undertake one action research project at any one time. I find it possible to manage two but not more.

As I write this, I have a project that needs action research but my colleague and I never know if the client will contract for the next phase until the end of the one that we are in. An international pharmaceutical firm, they are experts at project management and find it difficult enough to work through their accumulated plans linked to growing and competing in a global market. But they are experiencing challenges related to communicating across geographical boundaries and between different nationalities and languages. Two OD&C purposes have emerged in the midst of a third cycle in 14 months: to introduce conversations within and between existing mechanisms, and to do this without using the culture of project management. OD&C activities take place in two sites: a factory and within a tangle of regional 'interface' relationships.

This project reflects my current action research about interrelating dualities within approaches to OD&C (e.g. planned and emergent approaches, structural and cultural, familiar and experimental). Going slow and covering less ground is a direction for this work. I have been studying Kurt Lewin's original writings for a couple of years now and find his essential principles and concepts especially useful (e.g. Marrow, 1969). At the moment, I am preoccupied with his ideas of 'degrees of freedom', 'atmosphere', and 'total life space'.

GETTING STUCK AND RUNNING INTO PROBLEMS

During action research for organisational change, getting stuck and running into problems is part of the territory. The underlying social science being applied is based on the idea that actions for changing a social system will stimulate 'here and now' data unavailable before action. Research supports and challenges ways of thinking and behaving during continued action. Thus keeping track of what is happening and reflecting on thoughts, feelings, and behaviours are essential to change practice (principle #8).

I keep track by taking notes and keeping copies of archival materials (e.g. agenda, minutes, reports, announcements), filed in a chronological sequence. During my doctoral studies, I learned about a notation system based on field sociology (Schatzman & Strauss, 1973) that still serves my consultancy practice. Observation notes (ON) indicate something actually observed by me or reported to me by someone else (i.e. heard, saw, or felt). Methodological notes (MN) alert me to something I need to know more about or a bit of data still needing to be collected (e.g. a recent policy document, a key stakeholder I haven't met, and a backstage complaint reported to a colleague). Theoretical notes (TN) refer to thoughts, feelings, judgments, and connections to concepts and ideas that I have as the participant observer (i.e. both consultant and social scientist).

This notation system covers most of my reflections on what is happening, what problems are emerging, when something works or does not work, challenging interactions and disagreements. As an in-the-moment prompt, these notes cover most of my needs for thinking and making sense. Some practitioners would call this 'journaling' or simply use a notebook. I find the scientific discipline very practical as it links to my way of collecting and analysing qualitative data during consultancy and action research.

When difficulties do not respond to this process or persist despite repeated interventions, I have two other strings to my bow. Either I engage in a more concentrated type of writing up of the situation or I ask a colleague for a consultation session to help me make sense of what is happening. Writing up usually takes the form of several sessions of free writing about what I am experiencing (this is also called a 'memo' within the natural sociology tradition). The consultation session might be via telephone or Skype or over coffee or in the mode of peer exchange where we each get a turn. I usually select a colleague based on the nature of the problem.

Once I have depersonalised my thoughts and feelings (principle #6), something more useful usually emerges with insight and possible next steps. At that point, I arrange for a working session with my client, often tied to a 'review' step within a phase of work (principle #2). For that session, I would provide some version of a working note (Miller, 1995).

This same process applies with difficulties with my colleagues, although the turnaround might well be faster, because the professional capacity to reflect on our experiences will be well established. Having consulting colleagues usually means I do not need a consultation with someone else. And any writing ends up focused on the client's needs. Known as 'parallel process' within systems psychodynamics (principle #6), tensions we are noticing between colleagues almost always trace to difficulties being experienced by the client system. It is our job to figure that out so we can work with the client better.

CONCLUDING THOUGHTS

My eight principles for change practice serve me well both practically and theoretically. In the table, I offer a snapshot of what to do and what to avoid as a supplement to the longer winded text under each principle. I hope that this chapter indicates the importance of practice challenges, ongoing education, and writing as professional development. Thus a back and forth between theory and practice continues to be an essential process for me as a scholarly practitioner. I feel blessed to have had such a rich career from consulting technique to methodology to scholarly practice.

REFERENCES

Argyris, C. (1970). *Intervention theory and method: A behavioural science view.* MA: Addison-Wesley Publishing Company.
Block, P. (1981). *Flawless consulting: A guide to getting your expertise used.* TX: Learning Concepts.
Brown, L.D. (1983). *Managing conflict at organizational interfaces.* MA: Addison-Wesley Publishing Company.
Chin, R. & Benne, K.D. (1969). General strategies for effecting changes in human systems. In W.G. Bennis, K.D. Benne, R. Chin & K.E. Corey (Eds.), *The planning of change* (3rd ed.) (pp. 22–43). NY: Holt, Rinehart and Winston.
Clark, P.A. (1972). *Action research and organizational change.* London: Harper & Row Publishers.
De Mare, P., Piper, R. & Thompson, S. (1991). *Koinonia: From hate, through dialogue, to culture in the large group.* London: Karnac Books.
Goffman, E. (1959). *The presentation of self in everyday life.* NY: Anchor Books.
Hampton-Turner, C. (1990). *Charting the corporate mind: From dilemmas to strategy.* Oxford: Blackwell Publishers.
Hirschhorn, L. (1999). The primary risk. *Human Relations,* 52(1), 5–23.
Jermier, J.J., Knights, D. & Nord, W.R. (1994). *Resistance and power in organizations:* London: Routledge.
Johnson, B. (1992). *Polarity management: Identifying and managing unsolvable problems.* MA: HRD Press.
Jones, B.B. & Brazzel, M. (Eds.). (2014). *The NTL handbook of organization development and change* (2nd ed.). CA: Wiley.
Knowles, M.S. (1970). *The modern practice of adult education: Andragogy versus pedagogy.* NY: Association Press.
Kolb, D.A. & Frohman, A.L. (1970). An organisation development approach to consulting. *Sloan Management Review,* 12(1), 51–65.
Likert, R. (1961). *New patterns of management.* NY: McGraw-Hill Book Company.
Marrow, A.J. (1969). *The practical theorist: The life and work of Kurt Lewin.* Maryland: BDR Learning Products.
Mohrman, A.M., Jr, Mohrman, S.A., Ledford, G.E., Jr., Cummings, T.G., Lawler, E.E., III. (1990). *Large-scale organizational change.* San Francisco: Jossey-Bass.
Marris, P. (1996). *The politics of uncertainty: Attachment in private and public life.* London: Routledge.
Miller, E.J. (1995). Dialogue with the client system: Use of the 'working note' in organizational consultancy. *Managerial Psychology,* 10(6), 27–30.
Miller, E.J. & Rice, A.K. (1967). *Systems of organization: The control of task and sentient boundaries.* London: Tavistock Publications.
Mirvis, P.H. & Berg, D.N. (1978). *Failures in organization development and change: Cases and essays for learning.* NY: John Wiley & Sons.
Nadler, D.A. (1977). *Feedback and organization development: Using data-based methods.* MA: Addison-Wesley Publishing Company.
Neumann, J.E. (1994). Difficult beginnings: Confrontation between client and consultant. In R. Casemore, G. Dyos, A. Eden, K. Kellner, J. McAuley & S. Moss (Eds.). *What makes consultancy work: Understanding the dynamics* (pp. 13–47). London: South Bank University Press.

Neumann, J.E. (1999). Systems psychodynamics in service of political organizational change. In R. French & R. Vince (Eds.), *Group relations, management and organization* (pp. 54–69). UK: Oxford University Press.

Neumann, J.E. (2007a). Becoming better consultants through varieties of experiential learning. In M. Reynolds & R. Vince (Eds.), *The handbook for experiential learning and management education* (pp. 258–273). UK: Oxford University Press.

Neumann, J.E. (2007b, August). *Applying design rules for whole system intervention.* Paper presented at the annual meeting of the Academy of Management, Philadelphia, PA.

Neumann, J.E., Holti, R. & Standing, H. (1995). *Change everything at once! The Tavistock Institute's guide to developing teamwork in manufacturing.* Didcot, Oxfordshire: Management Books 2000.

Pava, C.H.P. (1983). *Managing new office technology: An organizational strategy.* NY: The Free Press.

Schatzman, L. & Strauss, A.L. (1973). Strategy for recording. *Field research: Strategies for a natural sociology* (pp. 94–107). NJ: Prentice-Hall.

Slater, P.E. (1966). *Microcosm: Structural, psychological and religious evolution in groups.* NY: John Wiley & Sons.

Tough, A. (1971). *The adult's learning projects: A fresh approach to theory and practice in adult learning.* Toronto: The Ontario Institute for Studies in Education.

Trist, E. & Murray, H. (1990). *The social engagement of social science. A Tavistock anthology, volume I: The socio-psychological perspective.* London: Free Association Books.

Trist, E. & Murray, H. (1993). *The social engagement of social science. A Tavistock anthology, volume II: The socio-technical perspective.* PA: University of Pennsylvania Press.

8 Change into Practice
Communicating Change

Phil Jackson

In this chapter, I will focus on the importance of the way change is communicated. If the communication of change is done well, you will gain the overriding enthusiasm and cooperation of those affected; and if the communication is done badly, you will create resistance and opposition.

With the extent and frequency of change now taking place, organisational success increasingly depends on the ability to unlock the potential for people to accept and implement change effectively.

My experience as both giver and receiver of change communications is that there are more cases of bad communication than good in organisations, with the result that most change has to be driven without the supportive flow of the employees affected by it.

It is widely reported that most change projects do not achieve the outcomes expected of them. In fact, several reviews of the change literature indicate that more than two thirds of change projects fail (Burnes, 2014; McKinsey & Company, 2008), and it's my belief that this is in large part due to poor quality communication.

I repeatedly find employees going through change with the mindset of:

- not understanding why the change is happening,
- not knowing what the change will result in,
- feeling that their needs are not being listened to,
- feeling kept in the dark about what was really going on,
- and wishing that none of this was really happening.

These thoughts and feelings are all psychological interference and on the basis that

Performance = Potential–Interference

(Gallwey, 2000)

there are often marked falls in performance during poorly communicated change projects.

This mindset results in the disenfranchised employee. It's also my experience that organisations that communicate change effectively and have greater success in their change projects also have fewer cases of absenteeism due to work-related anxiety and stress. Although this is beyond the scope of this chapter, it is a factor worth considering when assessing the benefits to be gained from making improvements to workplace communication.

WHERE I COME FROM

In terms of where my views come from and how my opinions have formed, I began work in 1979 at the age of 16 as a junior laboratory assistant at Unilever Research in Port Sunlight. I took the 'work your way up from the bottom' route, working full time and studying chemistry part time; and with the help of two Unilever scholarships, I completed my PhD at Liverpool University in 1989.

My Unilever career included:

1985–1990 Participant on Unilever's management training programme
1989–1994 Process Engineering Research Project Manager and then Programme Manager
1994–96 Factory Operations Manager
1996–97 Project Manager—factory new-build including: engineering, operations, and start-up
1997–2000 Head of Quality Assurance—Unilever Detergents Europe
1999–2001 Head of Manufacturing Outsourcing Operations—Unilever Detergents Europe

Throughout this experience, I became really interested in what motivated people, why some groups worked so well and others so appallingly. In 2001, I left Unilever to pursue this interest.

Following two years as sales and marketing director for a small IP software company, I set up as a freelance trainer and coach specialising in individual and organisational change, and I have been doing this ever since.

2004–05 I trained as a coach—a skill I value hugely and one that, until I completed this training, and speaking as a person who previously valued giving advice—I had no idea how counterintuitive it was.
2005–07 I became a Neuro-linguistic programming (NLP) Trainer with the International NLP Trainers Association,
2008–09 I completed an MSc in organisational psychology at Manchester University Business School.

I currently run courses focused on developing communication, self-awareness, and mindfulness.

CHANGE COMMUNICATION IN CONTEXT

I'd like to begin by putting this chapter into context. There are of course
many aspects to organisational change, and I will deal with one of them—
the communication of change and the involvement of people. If you have
been involved in the activities of any organisation over the last five to ten
years, you will no doubt have experienced the organisation going through
some or all of the stages of change, including:

- the identification and assessment of the necessity for change,
- the business case and return on investment,
- the risk assessment,
- the decision-making processes,
- the planning and communication,
- the implementation,
- the integration into 'business-as-usual',
- the follow-up and the review.

And there are of course many reasons for why this change may have happened, for example:

- the rescue package for a failing organisation,
- the forced or cooperative merger or acquisition,
- functional outsourcing,
- new markets,
- new geographical areas,
- new external partners,
- new distribution channels,
- new products and services.

For each of these, I consider there are two key aspects:

- a substantive change, i.e. the list of things that will be structurally different as a result of the change
- a human change at a psychological level, i.e. a new way of thinking, a
  new way of acting and interacting, new behaviours, and the associated
  new or different feelings

It is the second of these, helping people to move with the substantive
change, that is the centre of my training and consultancy work, and it is this
that I will focus on for the remainder of this chapter. I will talk about:

- Mindsets and perceptions of change
- The parallels between change and learning

- Gaining commitment through involvement
- How to make people the driving force for change rather than its obstacle

MINDSETS

If change projects depended on economics alone, more would succeed. It is people that mess things up! The way people, both leaders and followers, respond to the notion of change and the way people think and act causes the greatest challenge during change implementation.

I'd go a step further and say it's just one part of each individual that causes the challenge—the instinctive and emotional part of the brain—that reacts uncontrollably to the communication it receives. If the emotional brain feels that '*You cannot treat me like this*', then the associated feelings and behaviour are likely to be highly disruptive and interfering. However, feelings are largely controllable by thoughts, and effective communication can be delivered so as to create positive thoughts and therefore mitigate potentially negative feelings.

It's all about mindsets.

```
Change  determines  change  determines  employee  determines  employee
Leader  ————>  leader  ————>  mindset  ————>  behaviour
mindset             behaviour                                      ↓
↑_____↓
```

The mindset of change leaders determines their behaviour and the way they communicate, which in turn determines employee mindset and resulting behaviour. If the leader doesn't know what he or she is doing or lacks mindfulness, he or she can be drawn to react to employee behaviour, in which case the leader unwittingly becomes the follower and the disruptive employee now has the lead and your change project is going downhill fast.

One of my key areas of interest is how mindsets are formed, where they come from, and how they can be changed.

I consider mindsets to be a collection of thoughts and feelings that result from a combination of *values*—things that are important to us—and *beliefs*—circumstances that we hold to be true about the world—and we accumulate all of these throughout our life experiences. What is interesting about mindsets is that:

- They are largely unconscious (we are not usually thinking of the values and beliefs that affect our behaviour)
- They are largely responsible for judgements, feeling, and actions
- They form our perception of the world and therefore they appear as our reality
- They don't have to be factually correct to have this effect

THE PERCEPTION OF CHANGE

This brings me to a very important point in the communication of change. It is not the reality of the change that causes the positive or negative response; it is the mindset that is created by the communication that forms the perception of whether the change is bad for us or good for us. This is so crucial I recommend you read the last sentence again.

As a communicator of change, you are managing mindsets, and so it can be very useful to understand them. By way of an introduction, consider the following generalisations in response to change:

- If I'm choosing of my own free will to do something, it's probably good for me
- If someone else is choosing something for me, it's probably good for them
- If someone else is choosing for me, I don't have control and am at risk
- If I don't understand the reason behind their choice, I am in greater risk

The mindset we create leads to our perception of the situation and our decisions and our actions follow accordingly.

By way of example of how to get it wrong, I'll draw from my own personal experience and at the same time illustrate one of the experiences that shaped my own more positive mindset towards change:

> I can clearly recall a number of announcements from throughout my career, delivered through a 'top-down' communication 'cascade process' or at some huge gathering of employees at which a change of some description was communicated. This would be the first time most of those present were made aware that any issue required change, and in more or less the next sentence we would be told what the change would be. No involvement, no perception of choice, and very low ownership.
>
> These announcements were also very effective at starting the natural human worry process of constructing 'what-if' scenarios—redundancies, job losses, uncertainty about the future. Every day that followed would be filled with conversations immersed in fear and speculation, both in and out of work that pervaded the lives of employees and their families. They were often painful times for many, but in most cases, people were unnecessarily distressed as the majority of things they worried about rarely actually came to happen. Worrying comes from lack of being informed.

These were important experiences for me, and I think the lessons I learned at that time had a profound influence on my later approach to managing and leading change where I strive to achieve the opposite effect and communicate change in such a way that employees are involved, grasp the purpose, and run collectively with it.

HOW CHANGE CAN BE PERCEIVED—EXAMPLE

Before I talk about how communication increases the likelihood of getting enthusiastic commitment towards change, I think it would be useful to reflect, by way of an example, on what might be going on in the mind of an employee who is on the receiving end of a poorly communicated change initiative. I'm sure you've been there and that you might relate to some of what follows. I was involved in coaching some of the effected individuals in this example, and I also knew the finance manager on the change-project team.

> Outsourced pension administration—a poor change process that failed.

> Purpose: improve perceived shareholder value
> Objective: a 35 per cent reduction in pension administration operating costs
> Result (two years later): a 10 per cent increase in operating costs and a 'failed' change project

The change involved:

- Three departments of about 130 roles transferred to a third-party service provider
- Geographical relocation of about 20 miles
- Many employees made the move but some couldn't accommodate the relocation
- In the first year over 60 per cent of the transferred employees left

From the employee's perspective, their mindset was the result of:

- They had been sold to another organisation
- They used to work for an organisation they cared about and they thought cared about them, but clearly didn't
- They used to work for an organisation they chose to work for. Some had made this choice because other family members had (and still) worked there
- They had been paying into the company's pension scheme which was now uncertain
- They now felt insecure about the present and the future
- Engagement towards their new organisation was virtually non-existent

So what happened to the cost target and why did the change fail?

The client, i.e. the original organisation, was invoiced on an activity-based-costing basis according to numbers of customer cases and individual customer contacts (letters sent/received and phone calls). The change process failed on cost grounds, because the quality of the customer interactions was so poor that the number of customer contacts had to increase threefold to satisfy each enquiry. The difference can be summarised as follows:

Previously, administrators had been answering queries and processing cases on behalf of employees in their own organisation. They

- had a good long service record and high employee loyalty towards colleagues,
- strong emotional engagement with the process of providing information and services,
- and cared about the quality of what they did because it mattered to them to get it right.

In the new service organisation, they

- left in increasing numbers,
- were replaced with people who had no emotional contract with the organisation they were servicing or its employees,
- worked flexibly and often serviced a number of different customer accounts simultaneously,
- and where performance measured based on quantity of contacts processes rather than quality.

The economic case that justified the decision to outsource this function was undermined by the mindset of its employees and the behaviours that resulted.

This situation is common and yet avoidable. An awareness of the mindset of the affected employees means a communication strategy can be delivered to mitigate the perceived negative effects of the change. The appropriate management style and working culture in the service organisation can further add to this. What I find frustrating is that not only do organisations rarely get this right, but often so engrossed are they in the substantive aspects of the change, they give it nothing other than minimal thought and attention.

The communication strategy I advocate is aimed at creating positive perceptions of change. You can't tell people what to perceive and how to feel, you have to allow them to learn it for themselves.

CHANGE AND LEARNING AND WHY WE DO THESE

I like to work with the idea that change and learning are for the most part synonymous, that they are actually two aspects of the same process; if you are learning something you are changing, and if you are undergoing change you are learning. Even if it's a change you've done before, the experience is teaching you something . . . in the words of Heraclitus, 'No man ever steps in the same river twice, for it's not the same river and he's not the same man'.

On this basis, I have always considered that as a change agent who takes people through a process of change, I am a teacher taking people through a learning experience, and this gives me what I have always found to be an effective mindset.

If change is a learning process, it is useful to consider that learning something new inevitably means moving away from the familiar to the unfamiliar, moving beyond the edges of your comfort zone, and involves accepting a degree of uncertainty about the future. The problem with this is that, for many people, the very idea of 'moving with uncertainty towards the unfamiliar' carries a high risk of personal failure and the fear of (negative) judgement. Questions that typically arise are 'Will I be able to handle the new situation'?, and 'Will I be able to cope'?, or 'Will I fail and let people down or get into trouble or be an embarrassment'? These are not usually voiced, they are rhetorical questions-to-self that don't typically have answers but do result in people's fears escalating. As a result, people often resist change and learning as a means of self-protection.

My reason for drawing the parallel with learning is that learning processes give us a potential solution to this resistance. Kolb's learning cycle or Bernice McCarthy's 4MAT model (based on Kolb) give a good outline of basic concepts of learning sufficient for this discussion, and I recommend anyone involved in communication to familiarise themselves with these concepts. McCarthy describes learning as having four essential stages: Why, What, How, and Where-Else. The most important to pay attention to in the context of communicating change is the first one—often simply referred to as the 'Why' stage. It's the stage in learning that gives us the motivation to put effort and energy into moving towards the unfamiliar, dealing with the uncomfortable feelings of uncertainty, and pressing ahead regardless until we get the hang of our new situation. In our broader lives as human beings, we quite regularly volunteer to put ourselves through change of our own free will. We move houses, we get married, we change jobs, we change careers, we get divorced, we build extensions on our houses, we move to live in different countries, and although we often encounter difficulties and hurdles along the way, we generally remain in pursuit of our goal, because we have a strong enough motive—before we have taken any action we have conceived of a great big Why—and that makes the effort worthwhile. This type of change is also self-initiated—it has a high degree of free choice.

The Why-stage is the stage of communication where you deliver the message that gives rise to support and cooperation from employees and commitment to making the change work. There is a skill to doing this, and it is worth taking the time to learn it.

TWO REASONS WHY CHANGE IS POORLY COMMUNICATED

1. Change leaders' attitudes:

   a) Change leaders are often immersed in the substantive changes being made as they have often been involved from the beginning in problem solving and decision making on the action to be taken. In their enthusiasm, they often forget to slow down and bring employees up to speed using a learning process.

   b) Change leaders become overly self-important. One of the underlying reasons for much change leader attitude is driven by their organisational culture. Change leaders often feel that they have to be seen to have made the clever decisions, come up with the ideas, and put them into practice so they can claim the success as their own and gain the recognition and reward. This attitude makes for poor downward communication. Leaders who are out for recognition don't want to acknowledge ideas and suggestions from the bottom up. Such leaders generally have high self-efficacy, they believe they have the best answers, they sell themselves well, they communicate outwardly and upwardly in the organisation, and build their own status in the eyes of senior decision makers. They are not, in contrast, servant leaders (Greenleaf, 1977, 2003). The servant leader's prime concern is for the well-being of their employees, because high well-being means high quality, high conscientiousness, fewer errors, and greater productivity. Servant leaders see themselves as equal but different and certainly not superior to their employees; they lead with a coaching style. Servant leaders shine the light on their employees and say 'Look how good they are', 'Look what they've created'. Their leadership style creates voluntary followship, and they gain employee commitment through change processes. Ironically, because this leadership style has the effect of keeping a workforce engaged and committed, servant leaders will usually be credited with having led a successful change project. Leaders are usually credited with the collective output of their teams, it's not necessary to claim every idea for themselves. This leadership mindset, probably more than anything else, is the factor that determines effective downwards change communication.

2. The reason for change gets undercommunicated

The Why, i.e. the reason for the change, is something that is usually understood at great depth by the senior team responsible for leading the change but not by the employees it affects. The leadership team spends weeks or months grappling some major issue and, motivated by a clearly understood reason for change, progresses through a problem-solving and decision-making process to arrive at the second stage in the learning process—the 'What'—the decision on 'what' is going to be done. This is the point at which most communication processes begin, and this is the problem. The first thing that most employees who are to be affected by the change get to hear are announcements about 'what' the leadership team have decided is going to happen. They are announcing a solution to people who are not even aware that there is a problem to be solved.

Whenever I consider this situation, I am always reminded of the apparently never-ending stream of school children bemoaning mathematics with comments like, 'Why do I have to learn algebra, when am I ever going to use this in real life'?! This entirely valid question is evidence of poor teaching; if there is no known purpose to making the change, in this case learning algebra, why would anybody bother to commit to it enthusiastically and put in the necessary effort. (Yes, I accept some children take to algebra anyway, but this is for different reasons to do with intrinsic satisfaction, and they are generally far and few in number.). Good teaching has a purpose to the work that gives it relevance.

When the 'What is going to happen' is the first thing that gets communicated, it is perceived as an imposed change—one with a low degree of free choice—and one for which there is no apparent reason, result: zero buy-in.

Therefore, I believe that as a change agent taking people through a change process, it is necessary to convey the purpose, the reason, the 'why' for the change before you get anywhere near descriptions of 'what' the change might involve.

COMMUNICATION KNOW HOW?

This is one of those key points where the distinction between common knowledge and common practice applies. I have discussed the issue of communicating 'Why' before 'What' on many occasions; and generally I find it's something that most people agree with, and yet their behaviour demonstrates the opposite. It seems to be something that everybody knows about but nobody does well enough. I don't think this avoidance is intentional; in fact, most change leaders have a communication process in their plan. I think they understand 'Why' communication is important and 'What' needs to be communicated, but they have not had the opportunity to learn 'How' to do it effectively. The learning cycle affects us all.

Here's a common mistake in communicating change. You deliver the 'Why' message to motivate your workforce. You hope to gain their contribution to possible solutions as input to the management decision-making process to build ownership. However, in the same announcement, the 'Why' is followed by some comment or suggestion that management has already decided on a plan. This eliminates any possibility of any meaningful contribution from the bottom up. It also implies you're not disclosing everything, which damages trust. I have even heard this done in announcements that close with the invitation to 'Please give us any comments or suggestions on what we've said'! The 'why' cannot be delivered quickly, it takes several weeks or months to really communicate the true meaning of the problem that requires the change solution. This is not a one-off announcement but a two-way process of conversation and engagement which should be started earlier.

Whenever I make the point about early involvement of employees in the decision-making process, I usually receive comments from managers about confidentiality and not being able to disclose sensitive information to employees; and yes, of course, I accept this, but that does not mean employees need to be excluded. The exact circumstances can be generalised, a message can be constructed that would allow some early employee involvement to be gained. The confidentiality issue is a convenient argument for leaders who actually don't want employee involvement, and I think this exclusion is more about the leadership mindset I mentioned earlier.

RESTRUCTURING EXAMPLE

Change does not have to be for the benefit of all staff to get active employee participation. I have personally been involved as a consultant in the restructuring of a warehousing operation in which 70 employees would be reduced to just under 50. On face value, you would be reasonable in thinking that you would have to impose that change on that workforce, because they're not going to like it. It would be reasonable to think this, and it would be wrong. So much so that in this example we had members of the employee group coming forward with suggestions on how it might be done. They participated, they cooperated, and they became an active part of the success of the change process.

So how can we influence people in this way? Mindsets result from the way we communicate, the choice of words, the construction of our sentences, our attitude, and our tone of voice. Tone in particular is how we convey emotion when we communicate, and the emotion we convey is the one we have inside us at the time we speak. We are far more transparent than we typically think. It's therefore most important, before beginning to communicate and influence the mindset of others, that we develop the ability to control and construct the right mindset for ourselves. If you have in your mind that you are taking people through a learning experience, you'll communicate in a very different way than if you think you're taking them through a downsizing project!

The high level of engagement achieved during the warehouse restructure was a result of the time taken over the communication process as to 'why' the change was needed. The reason for the change was the strong possibility of the warehouse operation being outsourced to a third-party logistics (3PL) special-ist. Currently, the warehouse was an in-house UK division of a multinational consumer goods organisation that was going through a process of logistics evaluation and had come to the conclusion that its UK distribution operation could be more cost effectively delivered if it were handed to a 3PL operator.

This would have a significant impact on the working lives of everyone involved. Jobs would be lost, they would have a different employer, a differ-ent pension fund, a different work location, and many other areas of uncer-tainty about future work life. But there was an option, because the decision was being made predominantly on cost grounds. If the in-house operation could match the cost model of the 3PL alternative, the operation stood a good chance of staying in-house.

The management team had ideas on how to make cost reductions hap-pen, but these were not included in the initial announcements. To announce this would have been to impose a solution on a group of people who were not yet fully aware of the problem that existed—news of cost cutting and restructuring takes time to sink in, as it does for the various consequences to be realised. Management teams blurting out solutions too early take away the possibility that employees might reach that solution themselves and then own it and work hard to deliver it—these are the principles of coaching that underpin my approach to communication of change.

I'm grateful to the management team of the warehouse organisation for allowing the application of this philosophy in practice. It was fortu-nate timing that the wider organisation had been embracing coaching as a management style, and I had been running coaching workshops in this organisation for a number of years before the warehouse challenge arose. The management team was therefore accustomed to this language and way of thinking.

Following the initial communication sessions of about one-hour dura-tion, which took place with all employees in groups of 10–15, I ran a series of one-day workshops on the ideas of empowerment and involvement and collective cooperation.

The warehouse organisation was evolving, but a lot of old values remained in many employees, and values are a part of the mindset that affects behav-iour. In this context, the idea of workshops on empowerment and involve-ment and collective cooperation would not normally sit comfortably, but the initial communication spelled out the problem and gave no mention of a solution being available. This is an excellent way to create curiosity and engagement in a situation. The workshops were pitched as the beginning of helping the organisation find a solution. Attendance was strongly advised but, in the principle of involvement and empowerment, not compulsory. All but three employees attended the workshops. The workshops used a series of activity-based exercises to demonstrate the principles and benefits of col-lective involvement and contribution, to give the message that the current management wanted suggestions for improvement and other input from its employees, a previously unheard of practice.

The workshops delivered two key messages:

- An understanding of the commercial realities of the world they operated in, which encouraged employees to think about the need for competitiveness
- The value of the active contribution of thoughts, as well as actions from all members of a team, not just top-down

The change journey was supported with additional training in facilitation skills and problem solving and decision making; and over a period of two to three months, gradually suggestions and ideas began to appear, one of which was a system for capturing and evaluating suggestions regardless of where they came from. Easy wins were implemented with much praise and appreciation—behaviour that is praised and appreciated grows and occurs more and more often—and so it went on. What emerged was a Japanese-style continuous improvement programme involving everybody.

After two to three years, substantial cost reductions had been made through process improvements that led to substantial reductions in rework and damages, and gains in order fulfilment and on-time-in-full measures. The overall performance improvement initiative was made publicly visible internally and to customers when they visited. Improvement projects were visibly displayed on whiteboards around the warehouse and operatives, not managers, would willingly run through a quick presentation of their project to any interested visitor.

There were, as there inevitably are, a group of resistant objectors. This group of employees, common to many organisations, are often predicted as being problematic. They are often outspoken and have the ears and respect of the workforce and can do untold damage by bad-mouthing your project. Yet if you understand their motives and coach these people to involve them in what needs to be done differently, they will turn their experience to the change plan and become your strongest advocates and champions.

Gradually over the three years of my involvement in this project, early retirement and natural wastage—many were ready to leave—made a big cost reduction contribution. The offer of voluntary redundancy added to this and resulted in the workforce dropping in number by more than the original target envisaged. With the parallel process and efficiency improvements delivering the same if not greater than previous output with reduced workforce numbers, the project was a marked success, making the distribution centre more competitive than the 3PL competition. So much so that, rather than closure, in 2012 an 80,000 square foot extension to the existing warehouse building was approved to bring third-party 'over-spill' operations in-house and meet growing market demand.

This example is testament to how effective communication in the early stages of a change project can create employee involvement and their collective commitment to maintain successful, profitable operations.

IT ONLY WORKS IF YOU COMMIT TOTALLY, BUT NOT EVERYONE AGREES

There are, of course, many conceptions of leadership and management and not every change leader I speak to agrees with these principles. For me, this is part of an important selection process as I am only prepared to work with organisations if I can be true to my beliefs and values about leadership, and I would politely decline to work with anyone who wanted something else from a consultant/trainer. This discrepancy emerges fairly clearly during initial discussions and is simply a question of being ethical; however, there is a more complicated scenario that's slightly more difficult to deal with. It's the situation were a leader says all the right things about wanting involvement and equality and empowerment, but, as the change process develops, it becomes apparent that their behaviour is inconsistent with their message. I think there are two possible motives for this: a) they are subject to Argyris and Schon's 'espoused-theory' versus 'theory-in-use' (Argyris and Schon, 1978, 1996) in which what we say we do and what we actually do are, without us being aware, quite different to each other—a situation caused by a lack of self-awareness and mindfulness or b) they want their managers to be empowered and to proliferate empowerment but 'not that much empowerment'! In other words, as leaders, they actually want to retain control of most things most of the time; however, they would like their managers and their teams to act independently and with initiative in the face of unusual, out-of-the-ordinary, or crisis situations, or to think creatively in the search for performance improvements. This is an interesting idea and quite common in practice. It's also quite problematic, because it requires two conflicting mindsets: When the leader is in control and available to exert that control, the managers and their teams are required to have a compliant mindset and follow commonly agreed process and practice or take instructions in a crisis. However, when the leader is unavailable to exert control, they expect their managers and teams to have an independent thinking mindset, to problem solve, and to take self-induced action to deal with situations and implement improvements.

Acting interchangeably between these two mindsets is problematic because—and I know I'm generalising here, but I do think this is a widely applicable generalisation—leaders who like to control like to admonish employees for failure or are overly critical of attempts at initiative. One admonishment is often all it takes for a manager to stop acting and think ing independently, not necessarily through conscious abdication but because they don't want another reprimand. I had a manager tell me that formal disciplinary proceedings had been started against him for repeatedly miss-ing a reporting deadline, and the next day he was on the third day of my empowering leadership programme! His point was that he really liked the training material but there was no way he was acting on it for the risk of further reprimand. If you want a motivated culture, it only works if you commit totally and it's accompanied by a no-blame learning environment.

As a consultant and trainer in this situation, I find it disappointing, as it becomes apparent that the organisation is not going to benefit as much as it might have. I have had discussions with leaders about the difficulties caused by operating in an uncertain cultural environment, and they have mostly been frank about having a degree of freedom they were prepared to give. In these situations, I have continued with the programme on the basis that building awareness and knowledge increases options and possibilities for change, albeit not now, but possibly in the future. It has made it very clear to me that change in the empowerment style that relies on motivation has to come with commit-ment from the top, because that's where control is taken or freedom is given.

In this chapter, I hope I have drawn attention to how employee perfor-mance during and after change is determined by the communication they receive and how this can be the difference between the success and failure of change implementation. By way of reminder, I offer a few key guidelines:

- Consider your own mindset; take your employees through a learning process
- Consider your own motives—employee involvement creates substan-tive successes
- Involve employees early in the process; give them the reasons for the change not the solution
- Give these reasons time to sink in, answer questions and explain as much background as you can. Take time to build their understanding—this is their motive to contribute
- Describe the situation as a problem requiring a solution and ask for suggestions and ideas
- If employee contributions are not part of the culture, run workshops to change the culture
- Don't focus on the few negative individuals, address the positive majority
- Implement simple suggestions quickly and publicise these with praise and recognition

Once you have your employees on board, you stand a much greater chance of achieving a successful outcome.

REFERENCES

Argyris, C., Schon, D. (1978). *Organisational Learning: A Theory of Action Per-spective*, Addison-Wesley, New York, NY.

Argyris, C., Schon, D. (1996). *Organisational Learning II: Theory, Method and Practice*, Addison-Wesley, Reading, MA.
Burnes, B. (2014). *Managing Change*, 6th edn, Pearson, London.
Gallwey, W.T. (2000). *The Inner Game of Work*, Paperback reprint, Knutsford, Cheshire: Texere Publishing.
Greenleaf, R.K. (1977). *Servant Leadership: A Journey into the Nature of Legitimate Power and Greatness*, Paulist Press, Mahwah, NJ.
Greenleaf, R.K. (2003). *The Servant-Leader Within: A Transformative Path,* Paulist Press, Mahwah, NJ.
McKinsey & Company. (2008). Creating organizational transformations, *The McKinsey Quarterly*, July, 1–7. Available at http://www.mckinseyquarterly.com.

9 Dilemmas, Doubts, and Decisions
Change Management—
A Personal Journey

Elaine Mottram

Having dabbled in writing for some time, albeit writing poetry rather than professional writing, one of the most important lessons I learned early on was a very basic one—be sure I have something to say and second, be clear about what it is I want to say. When I was asked to contribute to this book, my reaction was the same as always—say yes and think later! So of course when I thought later I asked myself the two aforementioned questions and concluded that I probably didn't have anything to say, leading to a redundant second question. Nevertheless, the prospect of a coffee with one of the editors sounded like an attractive and stimulating way to spend an afternoon, even if it were to result in an amicable parting of the ways in relation to a book chapter.

However, things didn't go according to plan and here is a contribution to a book. You as the reader will make your own assessment of whether or not there was anything that this change practitioner had to say, but through an evolving process, it became clear to me that I did have something I wanted to say which I thought would be worth sharing. And this is the first message in my chapter. Process is key to change and allowing a process to emerge is a fundamental aspect of progress along a journey involving change.

Perhaps at this stage it will be helpful to share some of my reflections on my career path, which is in effect my own journey of change. My working life began as a physiotherapist with ambitions only to become a supervisor of a small group of staff. As a result, I might improve the service to a particular patient population and improve the lives of those for whom we provided treatment. After around ten years, I needed another challenge, and training to teach physiotherapy presented itself as an option thus beginning my real learning process, including, possibly most importantly, learning about myself. The capacity and the willingness to do this continuously are in my mind crucial aspects of working effectively in the field of change management and remaining emotionally healthy and resilient. What training to teach physiotherapy taught me was that passing on information, the key component of my own professional training and all too frequently still a dominant building block in change processes, is a minute fraction of what is required to facilitate learning, development, and change. On many occasions, I have seen very engaging and even inspiring presentations and treatises on the importance of engagement, ownership, commitment, and involvement in change processes then seen on the ground the same practitioners neglecting the very pieces of the jigsaw which they themselves promoted.

However, returning to my personal journey, a period of being a physiotherapy manager followed until a point where my career path was "blocked" unless my own boss retired, and this coincided with the advent of general management in the National Health Service (NHS). This represented huge organisational change and was in fact probably the most significant change there has been since the founding of the NHS. No doubt there would be those who would argue that the development of NHS Trusts was bigger or that the purchaser/provider split was more significant—there is probably no right answer, because there are no reliable rulers with which to measure the size of a change.

This introduction of general management arrived at the same time as the birth of organisation development and my opportunity to become a "change agent". In those early days, there were multiple initiatives to be attended by every member of NHS staff, with the exception of doctors, and the whole process resembled a sheep dip or sausage machine approach. During the 1990s and early 2000s, opportunities to learn and develop change management skills came thick and fast with changes in structure, workforce changes, the need for multi-agency working, and the arrival of a target culture. In 2008, another opportunity presented itself. The decision to leave the NHS and to work independently was taken with a degree of trepidation; but the learning journey has continued, and this stage is proving to be perhaps the most rich in terms of learning and development.

As I write, I have current projects underway in the public sector, in higher education, in the private sector, and in both voluntary and charity organisations; and I hope you will agree that there is something to be said.

WORKING IN CHANGE MANAGEMENT—
A LEADERSHIP ROLE?

In common with many professionals, change practitioners invest significantly from their personal resources, because a large part of their role is negotiation, influencing, and persuasion. Indeed it became clear to me when I was working as an internal consultant, bombarded by external agencies offering their services, that when I bought services, I was in fact buying a specific person. On many occasions, I made it explicit that while I might enter into a contract with company X, the contract was entirely dependent on the delivery of work by practitioner Y. As I write, I am exploring my thoughts and asking myself what lies behind this view as well as why it is so important. The conclusion I am reaching, but like many aspects of this chapter and of my professional life this is "work in progress", is that being a change practitioner is to adopt a leadership role. Not all of us have the ability or the attributes or indeed the desire to be a charismatic, high-profile leader; but we do all have the opportunity to provide leadership in our lives. As change practitioners, we have a unique platform from which to provide leadership.

The concept of authentic leadership resonates strongly for me and confirms the importance of "the person" in relation to leadership capacity. The sense of purpose, the underpinning values and beliefs, the mindset are critical aspects of what we bring to a change role. In addition, a significant responsibility accompanies a change role—the responsibility to carry out duties with integrity, the responsibility to ensure that we protect those with whom we work from our subjective bias, and the responsibility to ensure that our personal ambitions do not dominate our decisions and actions illustrate the arena within which a change practitioner works. I do not ignore subjectivity and personal ambition, nor do I try to suggest that they should not exist; but self-awareness is the tool which helps to manage the risks that may exist if they dominate. Awareness of what judgements we make, what we like to pay attention to, what we ignore or distort to help us to remain personally and professionally secure is crucial. How we make sense of what is going on informs our proposals about a way forward both for an organisation but also for individuals, for example the chief executive with whom we are working.

ASSIGNMENTS—MAKING SENSE OF WHAT IS REQUIRED

Dilemmas appear at every turn, and a very common one is the dilemma which may appear when we have been contracted to "fix" a problem, whether that problem is a person or a situation. It can quickly become apparent that the solution lies somewhere that the client has not looked or is perhaps unwilling to look. The most severe example of this for me was a large piece of change management work which had been tackled by a number of different consultants with seemingly little or even no success. The stated aim was to improve the performance of the department in question through the development of new administrative processes. As a result of the multiple interventions, there was severe cynicism, demotivation, and lack of willingness to engage with the project among staff.

It became clear that a change in leadership style would bring enormous benefits and was indeed the key to delivering the required change. The reason for multiple attempts to "fix" the staff and their performance was that the practitioners previously engaged had either offered this solution and been rejected or had delivered new departmental processes which did not result in a high performing department. It seemed that the search for the perfect or at least most compliant practitioner or consultant was on! The dilemma to be managed was that simply discharging my responsibility to deliver new departmental processes would not result in improved performance. The realisation that the clients were unwilling to look at themselves led me to ensure that a second phase of this project would not take place, even though it would have been financially lucrative. My own professionalism and integrity would not allow me to work on something which I knew had so little chance of success. However, it is unrealistic to restrict work to only those projects where success is guaranteed. I would have worked on few if any projects!

Unfortunately, this issue is more complicated than a straightforward, inaccurate description of the assignment. The situation I have described illustrates another important factor, that is, the development of a sense of responsibility to others over and above the client. The process of gaining the support and trust of stakeholders frequently leads to a sense of responsibility towards them. In the situation mentioned earlier, the most significant group of stakeholders to whom a sense of responsibility developed was the staff. The process of re-engaging them in the project led to the development of relationships and a feeling of accountability to them. Not to put too fine a point on it, in order to gain their confidence, I promised I would do my very best to ensure that their views about how to "fix" the problem reached those who were in a position to respond—my client. The feeling I had of letting them down and even betraying them was overwhelming!

This area of assessing and understanding an assignment before embarking on it represents for me the most significant challenge associated with working independently. For most challenges connected to change activity, there is rarely a right answer. There are advantages and disadvantages and risks flowing from any decision and remembering who the client is and that the client has a right to be treated as the most important player has helped me to steer my way through many challenging situations.

While it may not be possible to "walk away" from work as an internal practitioner or as an external associated with a larger company or team, it is always possible to walk away when one is working solo as I am. In fact, I have walked away from only one piece of work in my six years working alone, but I have decided not to follow-up many possibilities because I have predicted the sort of challenges I have mentioned. It can be very difficult to create a clear and full picture at an early stage as an external person in contrast to the ease with which this can often be done internally. The fact of being around in an organisation allows exposure to organisational intelligence and the organisational memory which can help to build a picture which is useful.

ETHICAL CHALLENGES AND PERSONAL VALUES

A delicate balancing act must be performed by anyone working either internally or externally in the field of change. On the one hand, there are responsibilities which go inevitably with being contracted and paid to do a job, while on the other, there may be personal tensions related to ethical considerations. There may be no objective placing of an ethical boundary but there is no doubt for a change practitioner when his or her own ethical boundaries are being encroached on, leading to pressures to compromise his or her integrity. I well remember as a fairly inexperienced practitioner being instructed by my chief executive to present staff survey results in a way which was inconsistent with my own values and beliefs about what was right and acceptable. Colleagues had a range of views stretching from "Stop making a fuss" to "If it was me I would resign"! Faced with such a dilemma, one has to find one's own way through the maze in a way which balances responsibility to do the job with the need (if one has that need) to behave in a way which is true to oneself and authentic.

This can in some situations feel like a high-wire walk and is a critical aspect of ensuring that work is not adversely affecting health and well-being. Anecdotally, I have encountered a number of change professionals who have suffered from "stress" and many of these have described the core of their difficulty as being a divergence between the values of their organisation and its demands, and their own values and beliefs about what is the right way to live and carry out one's role. This does not mean that there is an inevitability around this issue. Rather it means that the tool of self-awareness is the one that allows us to recognise what is happening and find ways to manage the resulting tension.

ROLE, CREDIBILITY, AND WORKING TO STRENGTHS

Another important aspect of the change role relates to knowing where your skills and energy lie on the spectrum running from being an expert and providing advice at one end to being a facilitator at the other. I have often described myself jokingly as "content free", which I admit is an exaggeration, but I use it to make it clear that the change role I adopt is generally one of being a facilitator and coach rather than an expert or adviser. This clarity about my preferred way of working allows me to pursue work with clients which will match my skill set. The risk of unrealistic expectations by a client is much minimised as a result and the likelihood of doing good work enhanced. While I recognise that this may be a luxury for me due to the nature of my work arrangements, it is nevertheless important to anyone as part of their portfolio of self-awareness tools.

Whether we are working internally or externally, an understanding of personal needs, strengths, and motivators is crucial. For some of us, playing the "long game" is satisfying and motivating. For others, it is frustrating, and the buzz comes from well-defined and concluded pieces of work. As an external practitioner, it is inevitable that I will have less long-term involvement in pieces of change activity, although long-term relationships with clients are possible and can be very satisfying.

As an internal practitioner, I often engaged an external resource and asked myself three questions to help me to decide why I was planning to use external resources and to help me to make sure I engaged the best kind of resource for my purpose. The three questions were: Do I need more capacity/am I short of the amount of resources I need? Do I need different capability/am I short of the skills that I need? And lastly, will an external resource provide credibility that we don't have internally? As I have grown in experience, these questions have been fleshed out and the third is the one that deserves significant reflection. Credibility is about perception—the perception that if the organisation places enough value on a resource to pay for it then it must be of value and therefore worth listening to. The ability of the internal resource to see things with the fresh eyes of someone unfamiliar with the organisation is limited and avoidance of the blind spots which can plague us when we are too close to a situation can be impossible. The external is likely to be free from or perceived to be free from allegiances which could "get in the way". An external resource is unencumbered in this regard and can ask what may be considered daft laddy (*stupid* is the translation from the Scots term!) questions in a sincere way that the internal cannot. The perception around this can inspire confidence in a way that has been lost over time by the internal person.

It occurs to me that the term *change practitioner* is appearing frequently in this chapter and it prompts some curiosity about the term and what other labels might be available. We see the terms *change manager*—indeed it was one of my many job titles—*change facilitator, change agent, change consultant*, and even *change leader*. For me the term *change practitioner* reflects my belief that any change initiative needs a resource which, in the words of an ex-boss of mine, "gets its sleeves rolled up and works in the guts of the project". Over the years, I have worked on every element of change initiatives—from photocopying to strategy development, from coping with tears at workshops to speaking at national events! Versatility and a willingness to turn my hand to anything which will facilitate progress were attitudes that I learned the value of at an early stage. In more professional language, a change practitioner role may focus on crafting the change agenda, guiding it or managing the "fallout" and unintended consequences. The most effective and probably satisfying role is the one which allows involvement in all three aspects; and if this is not possible, at least being connected across all three is important. So much of facilitating change depends on continuous data gathering and analysis to inform the process, connections being made, and opportunities taken that without involvement across the whole process there are risks to success. Indeed the process is never linear; it is always iterative to some degree.

WHO IS THE CLIENT?

One of the features of the training I was exposed to at the start of my change role was a consideration of the "client", indeed many hours it seemed on working out "Who is the client"? At the time, and for several subsequent years, I didn't fully appreciate the importance of this; but I now believe it to be possibly the single most important question on which to gain clarity for anyone working as a change practitioner. As previously mentioned, with that clarity comes the answer to many subsequent questions, making life a whole lot easier.

On several occasions, I have been engaged by a client who then wished to leave all the work in the hands of one of their managers. It has taken discipline and assertiveness on my part to ensure continued contact with the clients themselves. Day-to-day working may well have been easier, but I have learned to my cost that however much the "clients" say they are happy leaving the work in the hands of another, it is wise to challenge that view. The client may well "not know what they don't know" at the outset and indeed the practitioner is likely also to be in a similar position. Again, when I recall projects carried out in my early days involved in change work, I realise that a lack of investment in relationships with clients on occasions made it difficult to re-engage with them when I needed to.

Securing the continued engagement of the client may be difficult but it is essential. An extremely difficult situation occurs when clients, in effect, abdicate their responsibility and the people to whom responsibility has been given are neither committed nor capable. One project I worked on as an external involved me being engaged by a director to work in a particular function with a specific manager who was ambivalent about the agenda on which we were to work. The "client" appeared not to want to become involved and certainly not to have to spend time on the project. The rigour of defining the work with the "client", exploring the risks, and agreeing on and defining the roles we each would undertake represent fundamental building blocks of a change project, whether working internally or externally. This process may also serve to gain the full engagement of the client. This is yet another example of the importance of continually reminding myself of who is the client and who is a stakeholder that has helped me to manage my way through many difficult situations.

As an internal resource we may remain on the journey with our clients over a long period, while as an external we may accompany our client on only a section of their journey. This distinction brings consequences which change practitioners may need to consider. Participating in the whole journey may lead to some personal recognition for the change practitioner although equally it may not. I am reminded of the maxim that we should strive to reach the point where our clients feel as though the achievement is theirs. Accompanying a client on part of their journey may well mean there is no recognition. I recall working on several projects with clients whose staff told me that "this work had been done many times before and nothing ever changes!" A familiar message I imagine to both internal and external practitioners! But in the same way that we encourage staff to see end-to-end processes and not focus on their section of a process to the exclusion of other components, we must try to see the entire journey a client is taking, perhaps over several years, not just the section of the journey, a few months, that we are part of. We may help to shift them to a place where the next intervention can have more impact.

Returning to the issue of long-term relationships with clients, even as an external resource, we may find ourselves in the midst of some of the risk areas that an internal practitioner faces, for example blind spots, reduced credibility, and "going native". There is a constant need for external practitioners to reflect on whether or not they are developing the characteristics of an internal practitioner. It is necessary to consider whether what the client needs is the benefit of knowing the situation over a period and all the risks that may entail or the fresh eyes and lack of bias that come with an independent resource.

INTERNAL OR EXTERNAL AND WHAT
SHALL I HAVE IN MY TOOLBOX?

To what extent the challenges of a change role described are common to both internal and external practitioners is an obvious next question for me. Having worked for many years as an internal resource and more recently, in the last six years, as an external resource, it occurs to me that the split, internal or external, may be oversimplifying a topic which has many more relevant variables. So working alone or as part of a team may present an interesting variable, working alongside a chief executive or working within an HR function will also present differences; working externally as part of a large consultancy will be very different to working as a sole trader like myself. Some internal conflict may arise as one manages the transition from internal to external, which may incorporate a shift from having some degree of corporate accountability and responsibility as an internal and less complicated accountability as an external.

While there are major differences between internal and external work, there are many areas which are similar and many tools which are equally applicable. The choice of tool is more related to the situation and the challenge itself than to the role of the practitioner. Many of the tools I used during my time within the NHS remain valuable today. Similarly, my development over the last six years has equipped me with tools valuable in any setting. This chapter would be excessively long and probably boring if I were to list all the tools and techniques I have used and found useful. I will, therefore, only mention the ones that have stood out and been the most enduring.

Beckhard and Harris's change equation was one of the first tools I learned, and it has stood me in good stead in many situations—it continues to do so to this very day. I find myself repeatedly in situations where those who need to change in order for something to be "fixed" are not the ones with the most or indeed any perception that there is something to be "fixed". All of those leading change need to remind themselves of this and consider the best way through. In my early days, I played around with trying to find ways to ensure that those who were considered as needing to change, e.g. the frontline staff, perceived a problem and believed that there would be benefits for them as a result of changing. On most occasions this proved impossible and resulted in a frustrated decision to "press on" in spite of lack of commitment and engagement. However, analysis using this framework has frequently provided me with valuable insight.

Another approach that I have found very successful is Appreciative Inquiry. Almost without exception, staff groups in all sectors are energised by dreaming about and imagining the future and the kind of service/product they would like to deliver. Interestingly, there is often very little difference between what staff want to deliver and what managers in an organisation would like them to deliver. The differences surface when the detail of "how" delivery will take place is under discussion. By that time, the shared view of the future can provide common ground from which to resolve differences.

Early in my career, I was also introduced to the phrase "form follows function" and was curious about this because it seemed obvious to me. However, as time went on and my exposure to different situations and clients increased, I discovered what an important foundation stone this phrase could be. The imperative to move quickly, to demonstrate visible action, sometimes even to cut corners often created pressure from clients to forget function completely. Whether it was an organisational structure, a management process, a workshop or a training event, or even a building there were frequent occasions when I acted as the guardian of this tool which contributes enormously to both achievement of the desired outcome and sustainability. I recall many conversations with both clients and colleagues where my rigour around identifying function (of a structure, of a process, for a workshop, etc.) before considering form was challenged. "You must have done a workshop like this tons of times, can you not take a programme off the shelf?" Of course there has to be a balance and time spent on design may have to be restricted. But there are so many times when it may seem easier just to transplant a solution—if the change practitioner is not the guardian of good practice then the risk of failure is significant. Yet again self-awareness and reflection are the practices which will stand us in very good stead.

Self-awareness serves another significant purpose in addition to what was outlined earlier. It allows us to make choices about how we interact with others whether they be staff who are subject to change, our CEO for whom we are the agent of change, or even, as is the case with the NHS and other service sector organisations, the public for whom services are provided. As a change practitioner, there is likely to be and should be direct contact with many different stakeholder groups and as a result an exposure to many conflicting views, all of them often legitimate and understandable. The job of the change practitioner is multifaceted in that it must try to make sense of the messages conveyed and find a path which will achieve the desired outcome in a timely and sustainable way. And herein lies a significant challenge. There may be those of you reading who at this stage are saying this is an excessively soft approach, change needs to be much more assertively led and delivered. There are no doubt times when that is the best approach; but there are also times, many I would argue, when change is not sustained and does not deliver what it set out to achieve for the very reason that insufficient attention has been paid to a wide enough group of stakeholders. This is not advocating an approach which is tantamount to seeking permission from stakeholders, but it is saying that unless multiple perspectives are heard and considered there is frequently a high risk that sustainability will be compromised. Snowden's Cynefin model provides a framework which illustrates this perfectly in that where there is complexity, and organisational change is always complex, there must be an iterative or action learning type approach. This means taking a step, reflecting on the impact/consequences of that step and then as a result determining the next step and so on. Often there is no or little change to what is being done in the name of change but how the implementation is managed may well be influenced by the reflective process. This leads to another critical message or aspect of my learning and that is that it is never enough to consider only what should be done, but it is crucial to pay equal attention to how a change project should be progressed. Unfortunately, the latter can be neglected; but that neglect is at our peril because it can be the "make or break" factor.

BOUNDARIES AND SUSTAINABILITY

The opportunity to remain on a change journey or initiative over a long period is one of the characteristics of working on an internal basis and along with that is the opportunity to see and follow-up on situations which may help or hinder the process and in effect to have a very "loose", or perhaps a better word is "permeable", boundary around the work. For many years I convinced myself that this was inherently a good thing if I wanted to be involved in work that would be sustainable. I began to learn, however, that there are two sides to every coin and in this case the other side of the coin was the risk of "going native". This accusation was often made, and I have reflected on it a great deal. What I have seen, including on occasions in myself, was a drift towards becoming the advocate of those affected by change.

Placing clear boundaries around work and then sticking to them can be another enormous challenge. The systems nature of organisations means that it is very difficult to contain a change project, and working within an organisation often entails working on multiple small projects which coalesce to move the whole organisation in a particular direction. So the temptation always exists to add just one more piece of activity and to move towards that critical mass or tipping point. At an early stage in this chapter, I mentioned how much a change role uses up personal resources, often mental and emotional, but this tendency to see opportunities to have more impact and just follow them through can lead to exhaustion and burnout if care is not taken. Keeping some distance, maintaining a sense of perspective are phrases that can be very poignant.

Working on an external basis is not easier than working internally, it simply has different challenges. However, placing boundaries round pieces of work can be easier as an external resource, especially if there is clarity at the start of a project. With increased experience comes the ability to predict areas to be defined as either inside or outside the boundary and, very importantly, to predict approximate time commitment which in itself may act as a boundary.

The lack of clarity about the boundaries which define organisation development work, leadership development, strategy development, and management development can also on occasions be very challenging as an external practitioner. For the practitioner, these different topics may easily blend into what could be viewed as a single organisational challenge with multiple facets. In contrast, the client may see these as very distinct and separate pieces of work which need to be contracted for separately. The challenge arises when it is difficult to see at the outset that the different facets exist. A project that I am currently working on is a well-defined piece of leadership development work; but it has become apparent, now that the work is underway, that there are organisation development and strategy development components to the challenges faced by the client. The old adage of requiring permission in order to become involved in an additional component has presented a challenge. Practitioners must be personally clear about their motivators if they pursue these additional components. Is it genuinely necessary to expand the initial contract or is it about business generation? As an internal practitioner, this may be easier to manage because of the absence of a contractual relationship. However, it can be very helpful to create some of the disciplines that accompany contracting.

SOME THINGS TO DO AND THINGS TO AVOID

DO try to lead by example and behave in a way which is consistent with what you advocate! Your client and stakeholders will notice if you don't, and you risk your credibility plummeting!

DO make sure you know what you want and need when you engage an external resource and similarly be clear what kind of practitioner you are and want to be.

DO work on developing and sustaining your credibility—it will stand you in good stead.

DO be clear about boundaries and if you can't identify boundaries then create and agree on some.

AVOID losing contact with your client; keep working on the relationship throughout the assignment.

AVOID embarking on something you are not prepared to see through.

AVOID growing assignments for your own purpose; if necessary, ask a friend/colleague to challenge you to make sure you are behaving with integrity and don't have a blind spot.

LAST BUT NOT LEAST!

Remember to take good care of your physical, mental, and emotional health. It is only by doing this that you will have the resources to keep going in what can be a very demanding role.

CONCLUSIONS

The process of writing this chapter has led me to the point where I realise that the lot of a change practitioner, whether internal or external, is very different now than when my change agent days began more than 20 years ago. I wonder if the continual succession of change initiatives leading to complaints of "insufficient time for them to bed down" has been replaced by an environment of constant change. The current volatile, uncertain, complex, and ambiguous context within which most organisations now have to function, represented by the acronym VUCA, means that the management and leadership of change is now the province of all those in leadership roles. This contrasts with the early days of my own change career where many managers facing change called in the "change expert". This was of course always an unrealistic and ineffective way to ensure that an organisation can be responsive and flexible enough to survive and be successful in the VUCA environment. As a result, the role of a change practitioner is now, I think, very different in that the skills of managing and leading change have to be at the core of managerial skills at all levels. The change practitioner is therefore no longer the "expert" but is perhaps the only person whose entire raison d'être relates to change activity. When others are challenged by the need to avoid being consumed by operational activity, the change agent can support and again be the guardian and facilitator of best practice.

Many important aspects of change have not been covered—the word culture has not even been mentioned. I set out to provide a personal perspective and have selected areas that have been important aspects of my experience and learning and hope they may have engaged and interested you the reader.

WRITERS AND BOOK THAT HAVE INFLUENCED ME

Bridges, William (1980) *Transitions: Making Sense of Life's Changes*. Cambridge MA: Perseus Books.

10 Embedding a Talent Management Strategy in the Middle East
Cultural and Consultant Obstacles and Levers

Norrie Silvestro

BIOGRAPHY

I am an independent Chartered Occupational Psychologist. I have also worked as an internal consultant in the National Health Service (NHS) as the Head of Organisation Development, (Grubb, Silvestro and Ward, 1994a, 1994b). In the last decade, I have had the opportunity to work on Associate contracting assignments in the Middle East. This gave me some insight into aspects of living and working in a new and different business and social culture. Prior to that, I had also had extensive experience of consulting with family businesses in the UK to support them to be more innovative (Reid and Silvestro, 2006, 2008). I continue to work as an independent Chartered Occupational Psychology consultant for leadership assessment, coaching, and Talent Management related projects in the Middle East and across the UK and Europe.

PURPOSE

My objective is to describe my immersion of working on a new start Talent Management project in the Middle East. It will not be a clean, organised, and sanitised account of a rational and logical project design and delivery success. It will be a realistic account of the technical highs and lows relating to the Talent Management interventions in this 'foreign' context. It will also describe and share aspects of my emotional journey as an Occupational Psychology internal consultant operating as a 'stranger in a strange land'. I am hoping that this case study will also illustrate and reinforce that as consultants in these 'alien' contexts, we need more that technical expertise to be useful to the host organisation. It takes expertise, emotional resilience, determination, and high-quality leadership support.

BACKGROUND CONTEXT

My new employers, the Saudi Family Business Group (SFBG) conglomerate (anonymised) was founded on printing and packaging and educational support services and products. It expanded through takeovers and new business creation into a wider range of business with over five thousand staff in total within a period of 25 years. It also operated a number of joint ventures and it exported to over 70 countries.

The Group had an organisational structure of a board and a Chairman, a Chief Executive, and a senior management team. It also had a new corporate HQ with a number of groups of businesses, with each group designed to be led by a Vice President.

The organisation was led by a Chief Executive family member who had a modern, ambitious, and international sales focus as a core thrust to his leadership and business style. They were a successful family business in Saudi Arabia, and they were also devout and conservative Muslims.

The Saudi government also enforces a social and economic policy which is designed to employ specific proportions of Saudi staff as part of their 'Saudization' requirements. The staff in this business were predominantly ex-pat recruits from the Philippines, India, and Pakistan, and to a lesser extent, from Europe (as senior professionals). The Saudis were in the minority of the workforce, but they often held senior and significant roles.

The organisation decision-making chain was strongly centralised and hierarchical in its business structure and in its orientation to engagement and control. This was associated with a very traditional management style that is control and status orientated (Hofstede, Hofstede and Minkov, 2010). This also mirrored the cultural power distance between the citizens and the Saudi king. The senior staff also seemed to work and get involved much more in operational decisions and issues than compared with UK or Western senior leaders.

KOTTER 8 STEP CHANGE MODEL

The Kotter change model (Kotter, 1995) provides a useful 'post hoc' framework to describe this project. However, I will supplement its core structure with my own observations about the Talent Management context and interventions and the changes in my emotional and confidence levels as I worked on this project.

Kotter (1995) identified an eight-step framework for successful change transformations from his own consultancy experience and additional observations of major change projects across a wide range of organisations.

Initially, he described these stages as 'errors', but he later came to represent them as vital stages or steps that were evident in successful organisational change programmes.

I did not explicitly use this model at the time of my new work role, mainly because I was feeling too overwhelmed by the transition into the new work and social culture in the Middle East. I was well outside of my 'comfort zone'. My first priority was to survive the transition and to seek to understand what was required. I also had to focus on identifying the levels

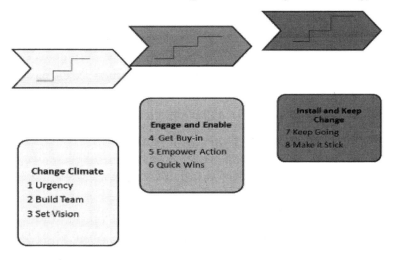

Figure 10.1   Kotter 8 Step Change Model
Source: Created by author

of support and resources that actually existed in the business context that I had committed myself to in my 24-month work contract. In this chapter, I have drawn on the illustrations from the actual PowerPoint presentations that I used during this project.

STEP 1: CREATE URGENCY

Kotter (1995) recognises that successful change needs to be built on either a frustration with the status quo or a need to seek better opportunities in the future market place. The family business that I was employed by had already conducted its own internal strategic review prior to my arrival.

It was a successful international family business (Saudi Family Business Group, SFBG). It had set a new and demanding strategic goal of raising its turnover from 1 billion US dollars to 2.5 billion US dollars within five years. The vision behind this growth challenge was shared in my recruitment interviews as an exciting, compelling, and challenging place to work.

The assessment and development of the existing leaders was seen as a critical and urgent step in this business transformation. This goal represents the 'Vision' for the business at the broader corporate level. At best, each operational project needs also to be aligned and organised so that its 'vision' (lower case) is also structured and planned as a change management plan in its own right. This case study will describe both vision levels associated with the corporate 'direction and speed' elements and of using operational talent management level visions as interventions to provide energy and momentum for transformational and local change.

The organisation also was committed to building its own Knowledge Academy to design, deliver, and buy-in technical and non-technical training services. This was created to support the business growth requirements and to manage and reduce the costs of these training services by minimising the need to travel outside the Kingdom.

I was hired and encouraged to get into the business 'as soon as possible' to get the core leadership assessment phase of the project designed and started. I arrived just as the region was celebrating an annual religious holiday break (Eid). This meant that I was stuck in a hotel with no access to work. I largely was on my own for a week as soon as I arrived. I was dislocated and lonely. This vacuum gave me plenty of time to doubt the wisdom of my decision to move to live and work in the Middle East!

All parts of the business were under pressure to improve through an extensive set of change projects about ERP, lean manufacturing, performance management, job evaluation, and the Talent Management changes. Nothing operates or exists in a vacuum. However, they all required time and attention from the businesses, sometimes competing time without coordination.

TRANSITION

The initial weeks were emotionally and professionally challenging on a cultural, business, and personal and domestic levels. There were lots of discussions with key stakeholders about their needs and expectations for the role and the services that I represented. I really did feel like a 'stranger in a strange land'. I initially came to doubt if my expertise was relevant to this social, religious, and management culture. My prior experience was based on the existence and operation of other human resource systems and skills being in place, such as competency-based frameworks, performance appraisal and job evaluation, and in devolved HR partnership practices too. Virtually none of these systems and practices existed in my new organisation.

The need for speed was a high priority from the CEO. One of my first meetings was to sit in on a vendor's presentation for a new SAP database. This was being sold on the basis that it could provide instant reports across the business about the competency levels of the staff. This prospect of a competency dashboard across the businesses was attractive to the CEO, as he wanted to have this knowledge, and he also wanted to be like other modern businesses that he admired that had these systems. His enthusiasm was pushing him to go from no formal competency assessment system to a highly technology-driven system in one step. He did not recognise or appreciate that this type of technology had to be based on the underlying skills and experience of performance management skills and practices. It also required the training, use, and ownership over a number of years of a robust and relevant competency-based framework. However, the SFBG competency 'system' was only two months old!

I was able to persuade the CEO and the VP to defer this piece of technology until after we had established the necessary building blocks for a period of at least two years. I was beginning to feel that I could add some immediate value given that my advice and challenge had been accepted!

STEP 2: FORM A POWERFUL COALITION TEAM

Prior to my arrival, the CEO took the advice of his trusted Senior VP and appointed him to lead the strategic HR projects over and beyond his normal business responsibilities. This involved creating the new Knowledge Academy, and a new performance management system, a new job evaluation system, and a new leadership assessment system. He had relevant exposure of working with these types of systems from his international work experience in large multinational businesses in the USA. The Human Resources Director continued to direct and run the operational services delivered via his HR team of recruitment and hiring from international locations and handling the payroll and benefits and the visa services.

Some good engagement work had already been establish for this emerging talent project. Some senior managers and staff in the business were involved in working in focus groups prior to my arrival. Their goal was to design and validate the vision and mission, the core values, and a set of behavioural competencies for all staff across all the businesses. This work was commissioned just prior to my arrival and facilitated by an external occupational psychology business based in the Middle East.

This process led to the development of the first corporate competency framework (see Table 10.1).

Each competency had a sample of expected behavioural indicators. Each competency was subsequently developed to show each competency indicator set across the four levels of management and leadership that was the foundation of the emerging Talent Management strategy focus on—supervisors, middle managers, senior leaders, and executive leaders. This served as a common framework of the behavioural standards that was expected to drive business success in the next five years.

Table 10.1 SFBG Corporate Competencies

• Team Working	• Communication
• Customer Focus	• Innovation
• Leadership	• Drive for Results
• Continuous Learning & Development	

Work Levels – Skills Performance Overlap

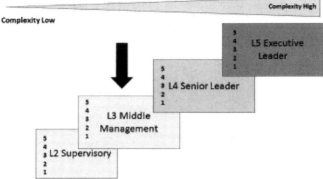

Communication, Customer Focus, Innovation, Teamwork, Learning, Drive, Leadership

Figure 10.2   Leadership Levels
Source: Created by author

This was an important and significant commitment by the organisation. However, Silzer and Davis (2010) make the general observation that it is a challenging task for any senior management team to predict the future business needs or the corresponding future skill priorities for their staff, as the future is inherently unstable and volatile.

I was hired as a Chartered Occupational Psychologist to lead a small internal team to create and run a new leadership assessment service. This project was led by a Senior Vice President to develop the strategic human resource services across the businesses. The existing human resources department tended to take a traditional and transactional approach to its services.

A small internal team consisted of the Director of the Knowledge Academy, the Senior VP, and me as the Assessment and Development Manager. We met regularly to develop the thinking and the scope of the leadership audit and assessment programme. We also met regularly with the CEO to inform him about our plans and to seek his support and feedback. We also met occasionally with the Human Resources Director to engage him and seek his support. This early thinking led to the need to develop a full Talent Management or Human Capital Strategy that was linked to core Development Centre process.

This close alignment of key stakeholders is regarded as fundamental to the success of any Talent Management programme by Thornton, Rupp and Hoffman (2015).

From this core team we extended the education, engagement, and debate about the shape of the emerging Talent Management strategy within the larger senior management and the general management team via specially designed workshops that were led and supported by the CEO. These workshops were convened every quarter. The CEO was a strong and active leader who made it very clear of his expectation for the businesses to participate and support the new talent strategy.

I also considered our external occupational psychology consultants as key partners in our specialist Talent Management team. Their involvement was also central to us, enabling us to meet the 'need for speed' and to partially satisfy our key senior internal stakeholders. Additionally, our psychometric test suppliers were also a key part of this team of advisers. Close collaboration with these external stakeholders was a vital part of my resource support plan. It was vital that we build close professional relationships with these stakeholders, as they could offer us an external insight into best practice.

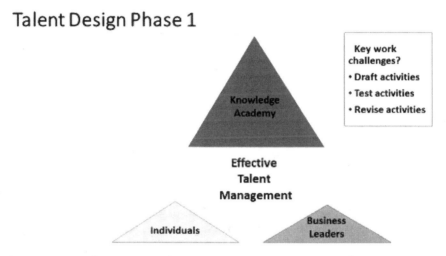

Figure 10.3 Talent Design—Phase 1
Source: Created by author

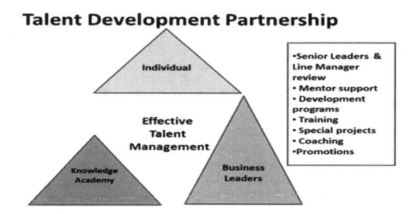

Figure 10.4 Talent Development—Phase 4
Source: Created by author

The relative responsibilities of this internal stakeholder team changed according to the stage in the Talent Management strategy. This is represented visually in the diagrams by the relative size of the stakeholder triangle (see figure 4).

The overall composition and work of this coalition satisfied Kotter's observation that successful transformations need to be owned and led by the business leaders (rather than by technical or HR specialists). Ours was led by the VP and the CEO.

STEP 3: CREATE A VISION FOR CHANGE

The corporate vision to grow the business turnover from 1 billion US dollars to 2.5 billion US dollars within five years had just been set and agreed upon prior to my arrival. As part of this future focus, the CEO wanted his business to become the 'business of choice for customers, suppliers and for employees'. For him it was all about the need to boost the brand and the experience of the stakeholders working with his business in new and more dynamic and professional ways.

It became clear to me within a short period of time of arriving that the business needed a Talent Management or Human Capital Management strategy rather than relying on a series of leadership assessments to deliver this ambitious business strategy. I took the lead to design and deliver this Talent Management strategy over the initial six months of my appointment. The extract shown in Figure 10.5 was from a senior management workshop used to engage and seek their support for the development of the Talent Strategy.

I created a proposal for a Corporate Human Capital Committee and for links into new group business Human Capital Committees to provide a forum for the periodic review of high-potential staff and their development. The Corporate Human Capital Committee had the Chief Executive, the VP of Human Capital, the HR Director, the Learning Academy Director, and the Head of Talent Management as its core members. The Business Group Human Capital Committees had a VP and the relevant general managers and the Head of Talent Management and an HR Manager as its core membership. These proposals were accepted and endorsed by the CEO and his general managers. I felt that it was necessary to create new structures and process to support the development of Talent Management talking, thinking, and action. It was both a practical and a symbolic plan.

I also set up these groups as I anticipated that they would become the central bodies to provide the assessment of performance and potential. It was not viable to use Development Centres continually in the future as this approach was too resource intensive. It also was an exclusive process in terms of the risk that the organisation became too dependent on internal experts to make these high-potential assessments.

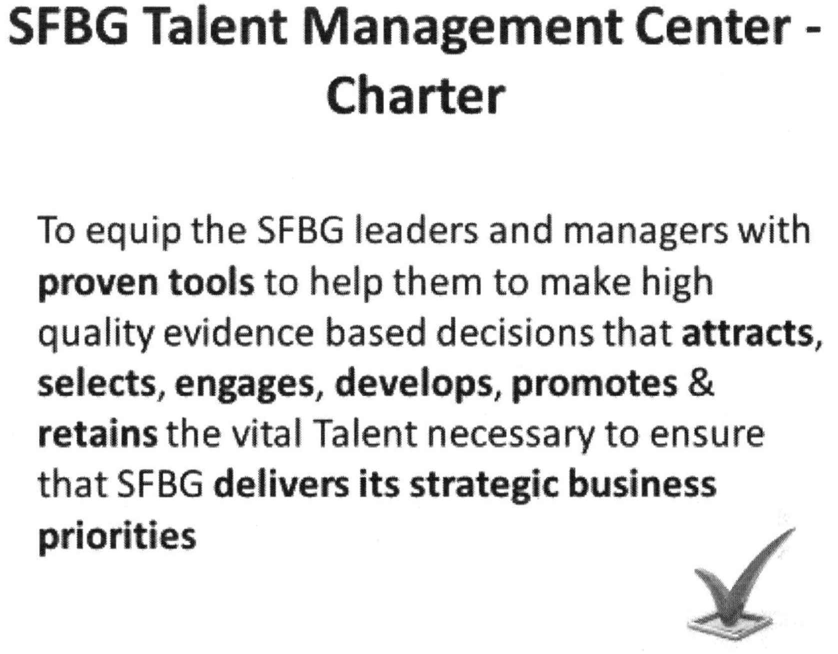

SFBG Talent Management Center - Charter

To equip the SFBG leaders and managers with proven tools to help them to make high quality evidence based decisions that attracts, selects, engages, develops, promotes & retains the vital Talent necessary to ensure that SFBG delivers its strategic business priorities

Figure 10.5   Talent Management Charter
Source: Created by author

This proposal also set the scene for high-potential staff to become recognised and developed as key assets from a corporate business level. This had previously not been done at the operational business levels. I anticipated that this might create some tension over 'who owns' the high-potential staff and who decides when that person should be assigned to a corporate project or moved to a new role in another part of the business to boost his or her experience and to stretch his or her development. Conaty and Charan (2011) were very clear that the high-potential staff were corporate assets when they commented, 'Leadership talent must be cultivated and protected as a corporate resource' (p. 267).

This potential development expectation was a radical and challenging perspective, as staff were generally seen in the Middle East as a commodity who were hired on a standard two-year employment contract. Trying to change this mindset to regard these key staff as assets to be invested in over a longer time frame was a very big step in our Talent Management vision.

STEP 4: COMMUNICATE THE VISION

In the broader context of the corporate vision, the CEO boosted his focus on internal and external communication by appointing a new Director of Marketing to deal with all aspects of branding and corporate communication. The Marketing Director worked closely with external consultants to review and develop new multimedia channels to communicate the business and the employer brand offerings. He also brought in a new Chief Financial Officer from a large and well-known international business to reform the financial planning and management of all the businesses.

In terms of the project vision associated with the Talent Management benefits, we advocated in management workshop meetings, and in internal emails and reports, that we should anticipate a better quality of candidate applications, improved staff performance, and a reduction in unwanted turnover levels. We also discussed and endorsed the potential benefits of hiring fewer supervisory and managerial staff in the future who were of a higher skill quality. We also advocated the use of our competency framework as a skills profile to improve the recruitment process and to link into the new performance management system that was planned.

The style and structure of communication in this Middle East business context was substantially different than that with which I was familiar. It was more oral and more visual and less about the written word. I quickly learned that I needed to become more aligned and more effective at influencing and persuading in this Middle East business culture. It also became clear to me that the levels of English language competence would also have a significant impact on the participants and managers within the planned Development Centre projects. However, the CEO was committed to the assessment being conducted in business English, as this was the preferred standard for his international businesses.

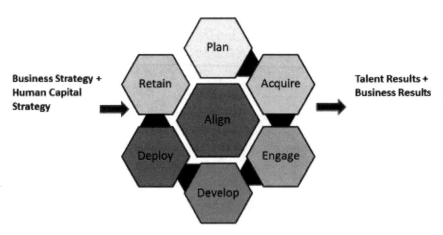

Figure 10.6 Talent Management Cycle
Source: Created by author

This was a tough and brave decision by the CEO, as it meant that those staff who could not speak, read, or write English to a good enough standard could not participate in the Development Centre diagnostic process. Later in the project, we explored the possibility of creating Arabic language versions of the bespoke leadership scenarios that we were creating. But this option was never developed during my time on the project.

I also had to learn to adjust my typical way of communicating with the senior stakeholder group to make it easier for them to engage, understand and participate in the Talent Management workshops.

I had to change from my typically conceptual and textual approach to structuring my briefing workshop presentations so that they became more visual and less textual. I also integrated more questions and feedback into the sessions to make the sessions more interactive and more engaging.

Historically, the centralised HR function was responsible for most of the support and development 'training' provided to staff in this organisation. We were aware of these working practices. We created the expectation of a more involved and active business manager role in providing support and development through stretch conversations with their own staff. We gave them some examples of the types of questions that they should be asking their key staff regularly through their ongoing work conversations.

It took me longer than normal to prepare these modified and much more visual styles of communication sessions. I had to simplify and check the accessibility of what I was trying to communicate. Initially, I was uncomfortable with this adjustment as it felt as if I was 'dumbing down' my presentations. However, the feedback that I obtained was positive.

What help do you need personally to support and challenge your key people even more effectively?

Figure 10.7   Manager Development Questions
Source: Created by author

This communication adjustment paid dividends in terms of better involvement and better questions and better support from the senior management stakeholder group. These briefing workshops were held every three months with the CEO and his senior team to educate and develop their understanding about the technology and the tools of Development Centres and to clarify our expectations about the different roles that existed between the assessors, the participants, and the line managers before, during, and after the Development Centres.

Within each Development Centre, we also had a short induction overview just to make sure that the participants knew why they were attending and what they could get out of the new Talent Management process. This was also followed up when we ran Personal Development Planning (PDP) workshops to help the participants to develop their own learning plans.

We were also very concerned about the challenges associated with keeping the Talent Management data confidential. In this Middle East culture, there was much more openness with friends and work colleagues readily sharing what would normally be regarded as confidential personal and corporate data. We explicitly tried to deal with this practice by contracting with the stakeholders about who should have access to what levels of data. Because the senior leaders were also scheduled to be part of the leadership assessment audit, it was also in their own interests to actively manage the confidentiality of the Talent Management data and its investment implications.

Talent Development Centre -Communication Plan

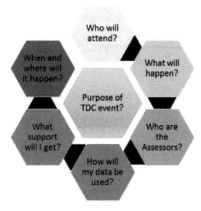

Figure 10.8   Communication Plan
Source: Created by author

TM Data & Confidentiality – Need to Know Basis

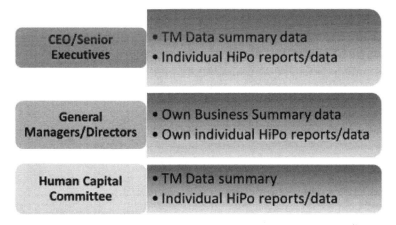

CEO/Senior Executives
- TM Data summary data
- Individual HiPo reports/data

General Managers/Directors
- Own Business Summary data
- Own individual HiPo reports/data

Human Capital Committee
- TM Data summary
- Individual HiPo reports/data

Figure 10.9   Data Confidentiality Contracting
Source: Created by author

STEP 5: EMPOWER ACTION AND REMOVE OBSTACLES

Overcoming Obstacles

Kotter (1995) talks about the critical need to overcome cultural, systems, or behavioural obstacles to taking forward the vision.

Even ordinary operational transactions required an extraordinary amount of time and effort to ensure that they happened as required and each and every time that they were required! In learning about this operational inertia, I often resorted to 'jumping out of the process' by bypassing it and obtaining materials and resources such as paper, pens, folders, and printer toner directly for myself or through my network rather than going through a tortuous and unpredictable procurement process.

Even the forecasting of how many eligible staff we had in each of the managerial categories had no easily accessible organisational data from the HR department. We had to define operationally what we meant by middle manager. This had to be translated into a number of criteria, such as being the head of a department that also included supervisors who reported to this role. However, it also needed to be flexible enough to include functional professionals who had no line management responsibilities. Each business had its own job titles and job grading process, and this had to be redesigned and resolved before we could get reasonably accurate numbers for how many staff we employed and how they fit into our managerial level descriptions. This process took over four months to resolve.

We also needed accommodation to run the Development Centres. The Knowledge Academy was being refurbished, but the completion of this 12-month plan eventually took more than 24 months to be completed. My project could not wait. I had to explore and cost a range of local business-based events and hotel- and business-based events. When these options were identified and costed, the Chief Executive pushed for us to find space within the headquarters building instead as the most cost effective option. This new option had to be negotiated delicately, as it involved persuading other departments to give up their office space so that we could design and build bespoke offices to run out Development Centre meetings. This process took over six months to complete.

Initially, I only had a small team: another business Psychologist, an Administrator who became the Centre Manager, and me. Given the strong expectations for the key stakeholders, we needed to make quick progress through the Development Centre phase of the project. I advocated the need to partner with external consultants to support some of the key bespoke development work. This proposal was accepted.

I set up a flexible modular invitation to tender design that mapped out the range of services that we potentially had a need for. Initially, this was set up for four managerial cohorts. The lowest level was supervisors, the next level was for middle managers, and then we had the general managers and then finally the executive-level leaders.

I had made some networking visits locally, and through my own professional network, to speak with five occupational psychologist businesses in the Middle East and in the UK to explore their interest and capacity to support out program requirements. We designed the initial Development Centre to run with six participants, three assessors, and one centre manager. The events would be designed to run for two days. Day one would be assessment and day two would be integration and feedback to the participants. Five external vendor businesses were invited to tender the services set out in the following sections.

The original plan was to begin the process by designing a bespoke Development Centre 'day-in-the-life' set of scenarios for the middle manager participants. They were identified as key players in the businesses, and we wanted to influence and develop them first as a critical asset. We also planned to follow this phase up with the second phase for supervisory staff. This would also be a new bespoke set of scenarios.

This modular design of the Development Centre allowed the organisation to 'pick and mix' how it assembled their service supply offers. We could create a design that was based on internal consultants and a combination of external consultant collaboration. This design was used to create a four-segment design with different number of staff predicted for each cohort. It was also designed this way to make it quick and easy for the vendors to complete too.

The initial plan was to buy-in or create a set of 'day-in-the-life' Development Centre scenarios for our middle management cohort of about 80 nominated staff. I reviewed samples of off the shelf exercises, and I rejected them all on the basis that they were either too complex linguistically and conceptually or else the scenarios were too alien from the Middle East work context. I decided that we had to create our own bespoke exercises.

The team of internal psychologists worked closely with the external psychologists to research and create a set of realistic work simulations that could be closely aligned with our corporate competencies.

This was not a quick process. It probably took about three months of elapsed time for the draft to be finalised. The major challenge was getting the scenarios written in a way that was easy to understand across a range of nationalities who did not have English as their first language. I also pushed the external vendors to create materials that were short and as visual as possible.

After much editing and re-editing to simplify the texts, I remembered that Microsoft Word had a readability statistical measure built into it. This was called the Flesch-Kincaid measure. Essentially, it calculates the relationship between the word syllables and the sentence lengths to produce a 'readability score'. I decided to experiment with this as a way of

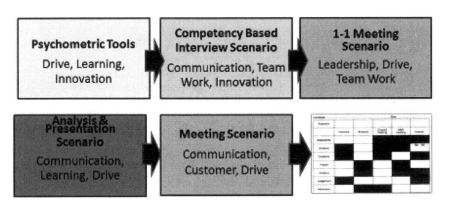

Figure 10.10 Business Simulation x Competencies
Source: Created by author

measuring the progress that we were making with simplifying the draft materials. By applying this tool and editing the drafts, we reduced the complexity of the text from an average graduate reading level to first-year secondary school level. We then tested these revised materials with focus groups to confirm their improved readability. We subsequently applied the same readability tool to the feedback and learning guidance reports that we produced.

This allowed us to move towards our vision of creating a set of bespoke materials that would be easy to read and absorb for non-native English speakers. We also wanted the materials to be quite short in length so that they could be covered in the time set aside for preparation. The materials also had to be designed so that they created no advantage and no disadvantage across the different organisational functions such engineering, finance, sales, HR or marketing for example.

The feedback that we received in the pilot and implementation phase confirmed that these design standard goals had been met. Out of the 85 participants nominated for the Middle Manager Talent Development Centres, we only had to send two participants back to their jobs because their command of English was not adequate for them to cope with the demands of the briefing materials and the scenarios.

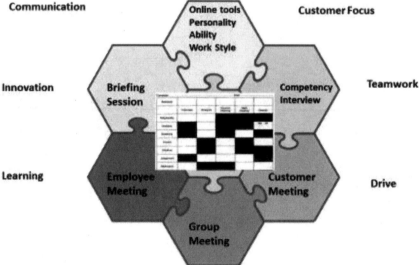

Figure 10.11 Middle Manager Development Centre Performance
Source: Created by author

PHASE 1—MIDDLE MANAGEMENT TALENT DEVELOPMENT CENTRES

In consultation with the CEO, it was decided to start the assessment process with the middle management cohort. They were seen as a key level in the organisation that had a pivotal role in developing the staff and the businesses. It was estimated that there might be over 80 odd eligible staff members who could be nominated for our two-day Talent Development Centre workshops.

Part of our plan was to embed the assessment skills in a broader group of line managers across the businesses. This would allow them to be trained to operate as assessors. It would also allow them a clear insight into the assessment and development approaches and skills used. It was also hoped that they would absorb these key assessment skills and begin to apply them into their recruitment practices and with their performance management meetings too. This was a sensible plan to grow the internal managerial capability and capacity. The CEO was very supportive of this goal, and he actively sought nominations from his business managers. A pool of ten managers and technical professionals were identified to be trained.

Initially, it was planned to offer a two-day training workshop for these assessors. It would also allow us to get further feedback about the suitability and the readability of the scenario materials, and it would allow them to be prepared and observed as assessors and as role players before subjecting them to these fuller responsibilities.

Unfortunately, it soon became clear that the skill set of these high-performing managers was not broad or deep enough for them to move directly into a full assessor or role player roles.

We added an additional day of assessor training to try to help build up their experience and confidence in the new roles that we expected them to play. We also modified the timetable and reduced the expectation so that they did not need to operate as fully independent assessors and role players. Instead, we designed opportunities for them to shadow the experienced assessors.

However, they were typically self-aware enough to be uncomfortable with the responsibilities associated with these new roles. They were also concerned about the time (and effort) that they would need to expend to gain the confidence in the new skills and to work as an assessor and role player, as they had busy and demanding full-time day jobs.

Even with this 'gentler' introduction to their new responsibilities, we noted a significant drop off in their availability and an increase in their reluctance to be available for the full day of each of the Development Centre events. This meant that we could not rely on them to support the roll-out of the Development Centre programme. HR was also seen by some practitioners as the most relevant role models to occupy this assessor role (Sharkey and Eccher, 2011).

This was the first major setback in the Talent Management programme. We had to break this bad news carefully to the CEO. We also had to break the news about his high-performance nominations in a diplomatic and supportive way, as we did not want to over criticise these participants. He accepted the need to drive the programme with experienced internal and external professional assessors.

However, we still concluded that there were benefits in that these key managers had a very direct insight into the Development Centre methodology and its robustness. They also had a better insight into the use of a range of behavioural and psychometric data when making important staffing decisions. There was also a new sense of respect from these managers for what it takes to operate as a 'professional' assessor.

Thornton, Rupp and Hoffman (2015) are clear about the benefits that trained internal assessors can bring to reinforce the corporate Talent Management strategy through their active and practical involvement.

Our managers were also able to support the implementation and use of the Talent Management data within the senior management briefing workshops because they had been exposed to the detailed working of the Development Centres.

Additionally, some real and symbolic staff blockages were removed by the CEO. The Director of IT and an internal HR Consultant, who was in charge of the Performance Management project, were invited to leave the business. There were strong general concerns with their performance and leadership. Remarkably, they were both Saudi nationals!

STEP 6: CREATE SHORT-TERM WINS

We had made good progress in terms of designing and running a series of bespoke Development Centres for 80-plus nominated middle managers from across all of the businesses. These bespoke business simulations allowed us to measure the *performance* of the participants against the key corporate behavioural competencies in a standardised and systematic way.

We also created an operational definition of potential after reviewing the literature and after exploring a number of internally generated models of potential. Eventually, our forecast of potential was based on a combination of each participant's score on the ability tests (a non-verbal test of general mental ability), the 'motivational' mapping of key dimensions from the personality tool, and how well each individual performed in the Development Centre. Each source of potential was weighted equally in our model. Silzer and Church (2010) advocated that this approach was a systematic and reliable way to measure potential beyond the conventional overdependence on past performance.

Potential

- "**Future potential is typically better measured by tests, inventories and individual *assessment* than by past performance.**"

Silzer & Davis (2010) Handbook of Workplace Assessment

- **Potential - the readiness and motivation to take on more responsibility at higher levels in the business and succeed**

Figure 10.12 Potential Definition and Measurement
Source: Created by author

TDC Potential Measurement

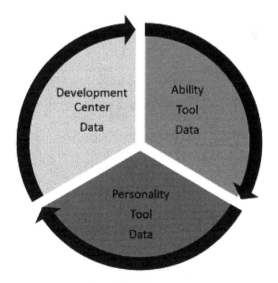

Figure 10.13 Potential Measurement
Source: Created by author

This allowed us to plot each participant on a nine-box grid comparing potential with performance. This was the first time in the history of these businesses that a cohort of its managers had been formally assessed with professional assessors to measure their managerial performance and their managerial potential.

The participants and their line managers also received short and clear feedback reports that included a separate developmental guidance framework. We also designed a development process and clarified the roles and expectations for the participants, their line managers, and the senior leaders before, during, and after the Development Centres. These reports incorporated the participants' own self-assessments on how well they thought they had demonstrated the key behaviours in the corporate competencies during the exercises. This was included to check their self-awareness and also to get an early insight into their expectations for feedback. We also revealed the key competencies that we were focusing on in the participant briefing prior to each exercise. This was designed to engage them and to help them to be more comfortable with the assessment process. This was the first time for the vast majority of the staff that they had ever participated in such a formal and professional development assessment process.

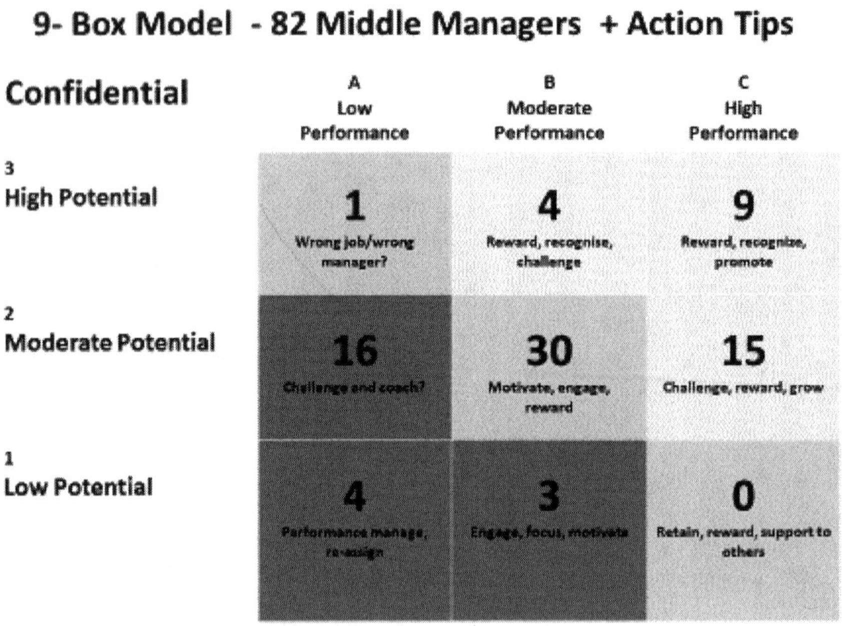

Figure 10.14   9-Box Model—Middle Managers
Source: Created by author

STEP 7: BUILD ON THE CHANGE

General Manager Validation

Although the senior stakeholders had been actively involved in several workshops to explain the concepts and practices associated with strategic Talent Management, we still needed to get further practical engagement with them with real data about their staff.

As soon as we had completed the first round of assessment for the middle managers and a nine-box grid had been produced, I set up confidential meetings with the Chief Executive and separately with each of the general managers to review our data and our predictions related to their staff. This also allowed them to check if it was similar or different to their knowledge and assessment of these individuals in their teams.

In general, this process was productive and collaborative, and the general managers found the data to be useful and relevant. However, one meeting stands out as someone who we had assessed as a strong performer with high potential was earmarked by the General Manager to be immediately dismissed, as his work style was unproductive and 'high maintenance', and he was not fulfilling his current role.

During these meetings, I agreed with the general managers that if they had good reasons and clear examples and evidence that specific individuals should be in a different box, then we would explore some transfers within the nine-box grid. In some cases, the general managers accepted that they had not been managing and stimulating some of their staff closely or well enough in the past and that they wanted to give them another chance through better coaching and supervision. This was a major breakthrough in ownership and accountability. However, it took quite a long time into the Talent Management project before we had this real data to have these powerful review conversations.

The next phase of the Development Centre focused on creating a new bespoke set of business simulations for the 120-nominated supervisory level staff. We improved the process considerably by getting the staff to complete the online psychometric tools under supervision. We also designed the bespoke tasks without the external consultants. We also created the feedback reports internally in a much shorter time period than the initial reports.

We also created another cohort of internal assessors and role players for this second phase. And, just like the initial phase, they could not acquire the skills and the confidence quickly enough to play a full part in the roll-out of the Supervisory Development Centres. This time I was ready for this, and I dropped them from the programme as they represented a big risk to the quality and the credibility of the assessments. This decision was endorsed by the senior leaders.

This phase of the project was delivered with 120 participants, and we were able to provide them with action-orientated feedback reports and to plot their location on the Talent Management nine-box grids.

This Talent Management tool is strongly supported by Charan, Drotter and Noel, 2011 and by Caplan, 2013, as it allows strategic calibration across the business and this also raises the visibility of the staff in the grid. It also enhances the focus and the accountability of the senior leaders to support the development of these key business assets. However, Clutterbuck (2012) is much more critical of this tool as he sees it as too elitist, too reductionist, and too restrictive.

STEP 8: ANCHOR THE CHANGES IN CORPORATE CULTURE

Development Action Planning

In anticipation of the emerging talent pool of people being identified, I explored through my professional network the educational institutions that might be suitable to provide our advanced development training and qualifications. This review of potential providers took me to MBA fairs in Riyadh with over 100 international educational providers.

I also conducted Internet searches of the top 100 educational providers for leadership development programmes in institutions such as Harvard, London Business School, and INSEAD to look at advanced leadership programmes and post-graduate qualifications. The financial and organisational implications of selecting and sending key staff onto these types of elite events were not fully understood or originally budgeted for. The business would need to prioritise who they could invest in and support for these development opportunities.

The new roles and responsibilities for this development and support were explored and debated during a series of internal leadership workshops.

As this assessment work was going on, we were also building up training and development resources so that they could be aligned with the corporate competencies at the different levels of expertise. Additionally, these programs were being shared on the company's new Learning Management System. Most of these were planned to be hosted in the new Knowledge Academy.

We also made attempts to offer a roadmap for the managers to clarify the different roles and responsibilities at every formal workshop opportunity. It is my belief that this 'conversational control' by managers is mostly informally exercised through the content and style of their everyday work talk. With this in mind, we were always careful about the words we chose to represent new concepts and new work role responsibilities.

At the senior leadership workshops, we explored the business need and fairness of investing differentially in staff across the different cells in the nine-box grid. We had productive conversations and consensus about the

Talent Development Actions

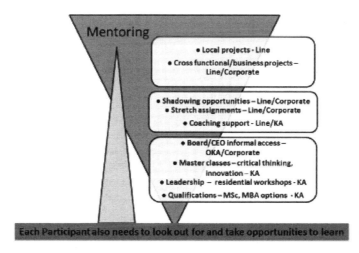

Figure 10.15   Talent Development
Source: Created by author

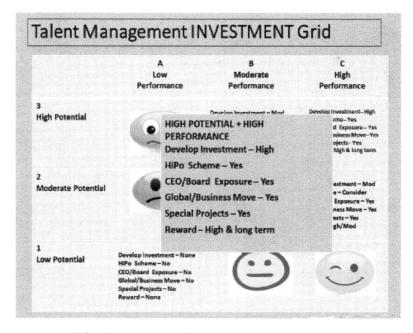

Figure 10.16   Talent Investment Grid
Source: Effron, M. and Ort, M. (2010). One Page Talent Management. Boston: Harvard Business School Publishing Press, p. 88.

need to prioritise this leadership reward and development according to the forecasted business returns.

Some practitioners, (Silzer and Church, 2010), are very clear at the need to treat the nine-box model as an ongoing and dynamic judgement that can change where people are positioned based on new data. Effron and Ort (2010) also believe that these systematic reviews allow a better and deeper insight into the talent needs in the business and where to invest it. Even Clutterbuck (2012) concedes that this tool still has value as a workforce planning tool and as an enabler for the managers involved to think more systematically and more objectively about talent in their business.

In these regular workshops, we also mapped out our expectations about how we needed the different stakeholders to behave in order to keep a momentum that flowed from the leadership assessments towards ongoing development actions.

We also provided the senior leaders with an outline 'script' for what they were expected to use in the future in their business with their general managers and within their Human Capital Committee meetings. This approach to link business reviews with people reviews is well represented in the work

Talent Management INVESTMENT Grid

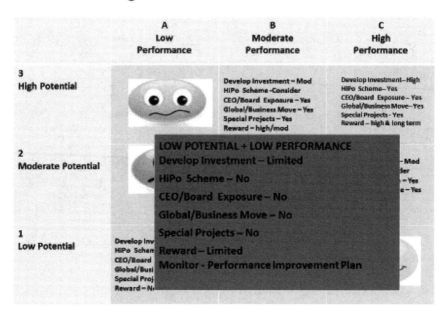

Figure 10.17   Talent Investment 2

Source: Effron, M. and Ort, M (2010). One Page Talent Management. Boston: Harvard Business School Publishing Press, p. 88.

Next Steps & Responsibilities?

What?
- Review Feedback Data

- Draft Action Plan PDP

- Use Action Plan

- Monitor and Recognize Progress

Who?
- Participants, Line Managers & Senior Leaders
- Participants & Line Managers

- Participants

- Participants, Line Managers & Senior Leaders

When?
- Within 3 weeks of report & Quarterly

- Within a month of report

- Ongoing

- Quarterly

Figure 10.18   New Responsibilities
Source: Created by author

Chief Exec/VP's – Support & Challenge Conversations

1. What are your key business challenges? (Do you have the skills in your teams to meet these challenges?)
2. What are you doing to support your key people? (What support do you need from me/others?)
3. Who are the successors for your key roles?
4. What will progress look like? (Let's review progress quarterly)

Figure 10.19   Support and Challenge Conversations
Source: Created by author

of Conaty and Charan (2011) as a key way to reinforce the strategic significance of this type of integrated review.

Overall, our key focus was on creating experiential work-based development opportunities (rather than formal classroom training), as this was endorsed in the research as the best way to acquire new skills and experience

(Byham, Smith and Paese, 2002; McCall, 1998) alongside deliberate practice and reflection (McCrae and Furnham, 2014) and as action learning methods (Charan, Drotter and Noel, 2011; Colvin, 2014).

REFLECTIONS AND SUMMARY

Strengths—What Went Well?

This Talent Management strategy project was a professionally demanding and stretching assignment. We were able to create a Talent Management strategy that had the support and involvement of the key managerial and staff stakeholders. It was a business-driven initiative.

It was also important to focus on the potential of the personal, operational, as well as the corporate business benefits to motivate the stakeholders. It was also critical to recognise that the Development Centre process was demanding and potentially scary for the participants.

The project that I led delivered a positive experience for the participants, and it produced high-quality assessment and clear and action-orientated feedback and reports. It also put in place a development framework to help guide the various stakeholders on how to invest in key talent conversations and practices in the business. Their experience with thinking and talking in this more practical and focused way was emerging during the project.

Talent Tool Model Benefits

Figure 10.20   Talent Benefits
Source: Created by author

Another key breakthrough in the project was the recognition that formal and informal communication had to be more personal, simpler, and more engaging to work effectively in this Middle East business context. The need to focus on language and supplement this with clear and reinforcing visuals was also vital to the successes achieved.

We put in place design improvements in the Development Centres between the first and the second phase. This allowed us to do most of the design, delilvery, and reporting internally. Additionally, the bespoke exercises and competency measurements were technically a better balanced and more robust assessment design when compared with the initial phase. Learning from reflection is still a practical and powerful resource.

While it was useful for me to to draw on the literature to guide these types of interventions, there was also the need to recognise that the achievements in Talent Management practices delivered elsewhere take time, resources, and considerable leadership support. To emulate these best practices is not easy or quick. Indeed, Hunt (2014) suggests that it takes about three years for users to get comfortable and experienced at using new HR processes.

I am proud that I helped to guide the business to move more towards a staff investment mindset depite working under extremely stressful conditions within an unusual cultural context. I left a professional and practical legacy for my successors and for the business.

I was also satisfied that I was able to negotiate extra trips home to support my wife and family. However, with each extra trip home, it became harder to leave again and return to work. The lesson here is that it is possible to renegotiate stakeholder expectations and assumptions about the need to work on-site all the time. Technology makes it possible to be productive on-site and off-site too.

We also made a reasonable attempt to engage and build up practical conversations with the general managers and the Executive about the talent pools model of Talent Management that we were proposing (Byham, Smith and Paese, 2002) rather than a more elaborate talent pipeline model (Charan, Drotter and Noel, 2011).

I did not want to risk creating doubt or confusuion amongst the stakeholders about our Talent Management model if we explored and debated the strengths and weaknesses of more than one model. Indeed, Clutterbuck (2012) is very critical of the limited and static assumptions built into both these models and with the general overdependency on competency models within Talent Management.

LIMITATIONS AND LESSONS LEARNED?

The plan to include internal managers as assessors was right, but it was also naive. This approach absorbed too many resources. But they did not reach the required skill levels to operate effectively within the Development

Centre. We did not even expect them to provide feedback sessions or write the feedback reports. In the future, it might be more realistic just to invite senior managers to shadow the professional assessors at the Development Centre to let them observe and experience what goes into collecting, integrating, and reporting on the performance and potential of their staff.

However, I was still frustrated and disappointed that I was unable to see the whole 24 months of my contract through. My wife became ill, and I had to leave the project permanently and return home to look after and support her. Consequently, I was not able to add as much value to the business in my time as I had hoped to do. But, as I anticipated this risk, I set up a contingency plan with my Line Manager to create a pool of travelling associates to replace me. They eventually appointed a new set of occupational psychologists to continue the next phase of the programme.

I needed to be more aware of my stress limits and triggers and manage these better to reduce my levels of anxiety and frustration. It was clear on reflection that the intense levels of stress that I was experiencing were predictable. (ACAS; HSE, 2008). I also needed to find ways to manage my own stress levels more productively. In the final phases of my work, I started going to the gym virtually every day and this helped me to cope more effectively.

I also could have read the signs better about what I perceived as the narrow focus on assessment productivity and made a better case for what I was offering. I needed to set the Development Centre phase of the work in a better learning context to show the senior stakeholders that a 'slower' approach would be more beneficial in the medium term.

Alternatively, it might have been useful for me to have negotiated to have more assessment resources so that more assessment phases could have been achieved in a shorter period of time. I should have also insisted on appointing my own team members rather than accepting my Line Manager's judgement of the need to push ahead quickly with this key appointment.

The stakeholders needed time to elapse so that they could 'play' with the Development Centre Talent Management data and then experience the next stages of having more developmental and feedback and coaching conversations. This opportunity to learn from the different phases of the Talent Management programme was not understood or appreciated enough in the general push to just complete the assessment phase.

It also might have been useful to invite successful Talent Management leaders from successful international businesses to share aspects of their journey with our senior stakeholders to give them a better insight into the time and effort required to do these things well.

It would also have been more of an achievement if I had managed to spend more time making better connections with the HR managers. They were still running the corporate recruitment processes in a traditional interview- and CV-based way. They resisted our repeated suggestions to try out competency-based application forms and to use psychometric tools and competency-based interviews to boost the reliability of their recruitment practices. They were also more comfortable focusing on assessing technical and functional skills, whereas we were more interested in these and broader managerial and leadership skills and potential.

At that stage, we were not able to offer them our definition of potential as this emerged from our gathering and interpreting of the assessment and the psychometric data. Some practitioners regard it as fundamental to create this working definition of potential from the start (Thornton, Rupp and Hoffman, 2015).

However, there was downsides from them taking our advice. They might have lost their autonomy, and they would have needed to learn and apply new skills and to become more accountable for the standard of the staff that they appointed from international locations.

We also probably did not provide enough attention to supporting the line managers to run their own Talent Management reviews. These practical steps at data collection and calibration are seen as essential to good Talent Management decisions (Charan, Drotter and Noel, 2011).

We also did not allocate enough time and attention to define and map the critical roles across the businesses for Talent Management appointments. We did not have enough resources to do this, and the organisation did not have an established job evaluation system to help to do this work.

We also should have spent more time and energy focusing on creating experiential development opportunities for the key individuals emerging from the Talent Management diagnostic phase. We did not move quick enough to recognise and reward and stretch those who had come through as high-potential staff. There were plenty of business challenges and issues relating to marketing, business development, and cost reductions that would have made excellent developmental projects.

FINAL OBSERVATIONS

I was not prepared emotionally or professionally for how stressful this project would be. It brought together a number of factors that I had never experienced before. I did not have the luxury of working in an organisation that had a full repertoire of HR systems and tools.

I was typically working with inexperienced managers and very operational senior leaders. I was not successful enough at building flexible and trusting relationships with my own line managers or with some of my own team members.

I also did not realise how difficult it would be to live full time in a Middle East cultural environment. However, one unexpected paradox was that I felt physically safer in this community than I did in my home town!

I did not anticipate the emotional drain extended domestic separation would bring. Having access to daily Skype sessions home only made the loneliness more intense.

Operating as an internal consultant was much more difficult than being an external consultant back home. I could not just 'walk away' when I had a major disagreement with my line managers about their excessive workload expectations or the narrowness of their work agenda. I felt like leaving many times, but my passport was held by the HR department.

Some of my general manager colleagues had refused to surrender their passports. However, others could not tolerate the alien work environment and they just chose to 'walk away' after only a few months in their roles. I could have been more assertive in holding onto my own passport and this might have restored my sense of personal control.

Finally, this Talent Management strategy was also demanding on the managers and leaders. They were more comfortable getting HR to deal with all staffing issues. Development was typically seen as a training course. They were also used to hiring in consultants to make recommendations about how they could improve their business processes.

In this Talent Management strategy, I worked hard to promote and to reinforce a number of key messages:

1. We need to be better at defining and assessing performance and potential
2. Most useful learning comes from work-based projects and experience
3. Nothing changes unless behaviour changes

Kotter and Cohen (2012) are much more explicit that effective change needs to focus on behavioural change and also from a perspective that shows insight and understanding that speaks powerfully to the stakeholders' feelings and their emotional needs.

It is also true for me that the emotional needs and well-being of the consultant also need to be recognised and nurtured in a foreign culture like the Middle East to maintain motivation and to mitigate against burnout.

It is my hope that as time has passed since I was actively leading this project that these key themes and insights might be getting gradually absorbed and acted on by the managers and leaders that I worked with. I would be very satisfied if this was my legacy.

REFERENCES

Byham, W. C., Smith, A. B. and Paese, M. J. (2002). *Grow Your Own Leaders*. New York: Financial Times Prentice Hall.
Caplan, J. (2013). *Strategic Talent Development*. London: KoganPage.
Charan, R., Drotter, S. and Noel, J. (2011). *The Leadership Pipeline*, 2nd ed. San Francisco: Jossey-Bass.
Conaty, B. and Charan, R. (2011). *The Talent Masters*. London: Random House Business Books.

Colvin, G. (2014). *Talent Is Overrated*. London: Nicholas Brealey Publishing.

Clutterbuck, D. (2012). *The Talent Wave*. London: KoganPage.

Effron, M. and Ort, M. (2010). *One Page Talent Management*. Boston: Harvard Business School Press.

Grubb, I. M., Silvestro, N. W., and Ward, D. F. (1994a). Stop the world I want to change it! Part 1. *Industrial and Commercial Training*, 26, 1, 23–27.

Grubb, I. M., Silvestro, N. W., and Ward, D. F. (1994b). Stop the world I want to change it! Part 2. *Industrial and Commercial Training*, 26, 4, 15–21.

Hofstede, G., Hofstede, G. J. and Minkov, M. (2010). *Cultures and Organizations: Software of the Mind*, 3rd ed. New York: McGraw-Hill.

HSE (2008). *Working Together to Reduce Stress: A Guide for Employees*. London: Crown.

Hunt, S. T. (2014). *Commonsense Talent Management*. New York: Wiley.

Kotter, J. P. (1995). Leading change: why transformation efforts fail. *Harvard Business Review*, March–April, 59–67.

Kotter, J. P. and Cohen, D. S. (2012). *The Heart of Change*. Boston: Harvard Business School Press.

Macrae, I. and Furnham, A. (2014). *High Potential*. London: Bloomsbury.

McCall, M. W. (1998). *High Flyers*. Boston: Harvard Business School Press.

Reid, R. S. and Silvestro, N. W. (2006). *Celebrating Innovation and Creativity in the Family Business*. Glasgow: Caledonian Family Business Centre.

Reid, R. S. and Silvestro, N. W. (2008). *Positive Solutions for Female Leaders: An Innovation Qualification*. Glasgow: Caledonian Family Business Centre.

Silzer, R. F. and Church, A. H. (2010). The perils and pearls of identifying potential. *Industrial and Organizational Psychology: Perspectives on Science and Practice*, 2, 4, 377–412.

Silzer, R. F. and Davis, S. L. (2010). Assessing the potential of individuals: the prediction of future behaviour. In Scott, J. C. and Reynolds, D. H. (Eds). *Handbook of Workplace Assessment*, pp. 495–532. San Francisco: Jossey-Bass.

Sharkey, L. D. and Eccher, P. H. (2011). *Optimizing Talent*. Charlotte: Information Age Publishing.

Thornton, G. C., Rupp, D. E., and Hoffman, B. J. (2015). *Assessment Center Perspectives for Talent Management Strategies*, 2nd ed. New York: Routledge.

11 Change Practice
What Works?

Tricia Boyle

I have been consulting on change in organisations for 25 years. It is my occupation and my obsession. My current context is as the head of a small organisational development team in the National Health Service (NHS) in Fife in Scotland. We work as an internal consultancy service for our Chair, CEO, and the Director of Organisational Development. We work by invitation, across the NHS system, as a corporate service, assisting leaders with changes they wish to achieve. I have been in post for seven years.

NHS Fife is a medium-sized territorial health board and includes both community services and acute hospital services. The overall headcount at the moment is 8,896. Nursing and midwifery make up nearly half of the staff at 4,086, doctors and dentists are 631. The others include administrative, allied health professionals, health-care scientists, support staff, other therapeutic staff, and managers. General practitioners (GPs), although largely funded by the Health Service, are almost exclusively independent contractors and are not counted as staff.

The most significant of many current national change initiatives is the integration of health and social care services. This involves bringing together around five thousand staff from Fife Council Social Services departments and NHS Fife Community Services under an additional structural arrangement. A new Director of Health and Social Care has been appointed and reports to the two Chief Executives of the NHS and the Local Authority. Staff will remain employed as they are now in an effort to minimise disruption and allow everyone to focus on accelerating the creation of better and more appropriate service delivery for more people at reduced costs.

This change is bigger than the changes I have been involved with in the NHS so far. People tell me that this change is bigger than all previous changes, as all the others just remodelled the NHS. This change will take us beyond the worst of our competition, the best of our cooperation, and invite collaboration. I have been anticipating this direction and our Fife Partnership won a COSLA award last year for our post-graduate certificate in Collaborative Leadership accredited by St Andrews University. In Huxham and Vangen (2005), the authors explain the difference between Collaborative Advantage and Collaborative Inertia. We all know what the Inertia feels like, and we are trying to help staff develop the skill set and conceptual understanding to get to Advantage.

In this complex context, there is never a shortage of work for us, and prioritising it is the issue, making sure we are working on the long term and not just reactive short-term fixes. During my time so far, we have been commissioned by the leadership to help with decision making for changes, the preparation of staff for restructures, closure of buildings and services, the building and opening of a new hospital wing and other specialist facilities, the relocation of services geographically, and the remodelling of services where they are. We also help teams whose performance or relations have deteriorated, and they need to resolve differences and return to effectiveness. We help with the diagnosis of issues, design interventions, coach leaders, and facilitate tricky conversations. The Integration work at the moment requires us to help with decisions about processes to involve staff and stakeholders and designing and facilitating events, analysing data, and using it to help inform next steps.

The way we measure the success of interventions varies. It includes quantifiable measures, such as better attendance/reduced absence, reduced complaints, better approaches to services identified and established. It also includes qualitative measures, such as colleagues feeling more positive about each other, misunderstandings cleared up, different perspectives explored and resolved, increased self-awareness and organisational dynamic awareness, increased leadership capacities within and across teams, increased capacity to stay in and resolve conflicted conversations, increased resilience, increased empathy and understanding, more compassion, more collaborative enquiry and generative dialogue, less professional defensiveness, more open appreciation and the trust to explore difficult issues with others, forward thinking and less just 'doing the do', more calm and less anxiety, and better delivery of services. We also hope to increase the capacity of leaders and managers to identify and commission Organization Development interventions where needed, to grow their appreciation of conversational design and its contribution to leadership of complex issues.

The NHS aims to use best-evidenced clinical practices and scrutiny is part of the way things are done. I am torn at times between evidencing the value of the work we do and getting the next job commissioned and completed. We are practitioners not researchers, and we would offer significantly less help if we were to aim to do everything as a research project. I have decided, however, to commission some action research activity as part of the Integration work, to support our practice and to write it up, as it is a significant long-term endeavour with multiple stakeholders' involvement and stretching and articulated outcomes that we want to be able to track progress against.

The question 'what works?' is something I regularly find I have been musing on when I return to conscious thought. 'What's not working and what can I do to help change these circumstances?' is probably a more frequent visitor and gnaws away at any sense of complacency I might permit myself. I visit and revisit issues, searching for new insights, new angles, something I might have overlooked. Sometimes I flatter myself that I might have made a half-decent detective if I'd made different career choices and the height restrictions had been kinder to short women when I was in my youth. I was too short then and too old now. I think it will be best if I just stick to reading Ian Rankin!

Accepting the invite to write a chapter for this book has just deepened the neural pathway that I've been creating all this time. What's working, what's not working, what can I do next? The noise in my head has been amplified and everything has got louder. I hate to fail, and it drives this way of thinking and being. I have been in post long enough to see many successes and also to be challenged by the lack of progress on many others. I have eighteen years external consultancy experience in addition to seven years in the NHS. There isn't a sector I have not worked in, including: multinationals, government departments, local authorities, charities, theatres, small start-ups, large media organisations, police, military, and so on. Before external consulting, I was a manager in local government in the Careers Service in London. I went independent and started out doing assertiveness and personal development training before management and then leadership development. I have an MSc in consulting, and a coaching accreditation from Ashridge Management College. I might be expected to feel confidant, yet committing my ideas to paper seems like a risk, a presumption even. Success is often short-lived and in the eye of the beholder. I wonder how explaining my practice model will be of any help to anyone else. Even although I have had feedback from others that this is the case, and I have learned from others too. I decide this is just a defence against the difficulty of attempting the task and resolve to get on with it. I have been given a time frame, made a window of space, and am taking an optimistic stance that, in spite of misgivings and fear, this will be a useful exercise, for me at least, if not others.

Many academic studies conclude that most change initiatives fail. (Beer & Nohria 2000, Hammer & Champy 1993, Hughes 2010, Kotter 2008, Senturia et al 2008). My practical experience tells me that even the best of my work with leaders can wither quickly if circumstances change or if there is insufficient attention and maintenance of new practices. There are many theories to explain this phenomenon. We all know that change can be short-lived. We only need to look at our own New Year's resolutions if we attempt to make them. Taking more exercise, losing weight, stopping smoking, and so on are not easy. We all know how quickly old habits re-establish themselves. I have been resolving to be more cheerful for years. The old adage 'at least no one died' does not apply in the NHS. It's not the cheeriest place to work, I am not the cheeriest character I know, but my work is a privilege and is very satisfying.

At a larger systemic level, there are different organisational theories that offer different explanatory lenses for the tendency to not change. For example psychodynamic theory suggests current practices are there for a reason, often unconscious, providing some protection to those in the system (Obholzer et al 1994).

There are 'unwritten rules' around all systems (Scott-Morgan 1994) that people can no longer see. If they can see them, they are often so embedded that no one wants to attempt to deal with them. They bring positives as well as negatives, so best we leave them until a later date.

Others suggest we can settle for the 'low hanging fruit', which offer some short-term satisfaction for those who want some quick wins. Difficulties arise when there are no more of these to be had, or they start creating different issues through unintended consequences (Watzlawick et al. 1974). It is also easy to create the perfect fix to the wrong issue (Mitroff & Silvers 2010).

Sometimes it seems that no one really wants any change anyway and having an activity is enough, a 'tick box' exercise is sufficient in those circumstances.

At other times the political environment changes and what was wanted shifts halfway through a change. Decisions are made to stop and revert back to what was there before.

Sometimes I also wonder if the execution of a change intervention was not skilful enough; it does happen. On a bad day I realise I can get in the way of something going well, I don't always get it right.

In the life of this job, I have reached my 'seven-year itch'. Am I still offering what is needed? There has been a great deal of change in my wider environment over this time, including government policy and direction, preferred processes for change, new local leadership with different styles and priorities. Some of my relationships are in good shape and some have deteriorated, others have gone due to retirement or new jobs. I am at the point where I am thinking about what I need to do next and differently. This includes the team, the system, its customers and myself. I want to stay well and stay committed and vibrant. This writing challenge is timely for me.

I have decided to offer observations on two levels.

(1) 'What works' in terms of what has helped us help our clients progress their issues and make changes, fixes, improvements, or transformations. This encompasses how we are positioned, how we do our work, how we are supported by and support the leadership in return.

(2) 'What works' when I think nothing is working. This is particularly important to me as a practitioner and team leader. What do I do when I might want to give up and walk away? What holds me and helps me grow resilience when facing 24/7 ongoing, intractable issues and slow progress or worse than that, when things seem to be going backwards? When the stakes increase and the 'ask' makes no sense to me? When there is no obvious solution to conflicting demands, for example national uniformity and local autonomy, strong top-down

leadership and citizen-led initiative. When people attack me rather than the issue?

(1) What helps us help our clients?

(A) Positioning of the department

There are all sorts of ways to do OD. It is a broad term encompassing many disciplines. It is both a process and a function. Each workplace has its own version which is subject to its changing environment and the choices of the people who put the team together.

The department in Fife is set up as a corporate function reporting to the Chief Executive. This model confirmed me as an applicant for the post. We perform our internal consultancy role anywhere across the system, at any level in the hierarchy. We aim to stay on the borderline, the edge, just inside but not fully incorporated into daily business. We work for others who have issues to address. We don't own these issues. If we owned them there would be too much work for such a small team to do, and at the same time, it would make us too powerful. For both reasons this needs to be avoided. Our positioning and freedom to act is an advantage and has to be executed with care, integrity, and with senior support. We gather a broad understanding of the people and the issues and develop a unique lens on what is going on, translating between perspectives and fostering constructive responses to difficulties. I am summarising our offer in my PhD work with lots of Cs. 'We aim to contribute to the creation of constructive conversation in circumstances of change, complexity and conflict.'

An organisation needs to be large to require an internal OD department and scale normally creates hierarchy. The more senior a person becomes, the more people are likely to tell them what they think they want to hear. Part of the permissions granted to OD in NHS Fife has been to speak of what is more often left unsaid. This takes courage as an internal consultant; it is akin to the role of the court jester and can only work with the protection of the senior staff involved. The OD staff in turn must be saying what needs to be said for the protection of the senior staff. We are part of the checks and balances that create good governance.

This has worked in Fife, as the CEO has delegated a clear mandate and invited it in and has been appreciative rather than punishing for providing the service. I have survived seven years where I might not have elsewhere. In the worst of systems, this is not permitted, and the OD function doesn't last very long. Senior OD roles can be very precarious. They can raise the issues that need to be attended to and, sometimes, instead of the issues being attended to, they are not, and the OD team become the issue, one that needs to be erased. I have been around this type of work long enough to see OD being abolished and reinstituted many times. Restructuring into training, HR partners, re-engineering or privatisation are classic ways of internalising and neutralising the 'edgy' OD team with privileged access and knowledge. This is less likely to be the case when the leaders know that systems are bound to be fragile at times and that s/he needs feedback and help to find a way through. Real strength permits uncertainty and vulnerability in my view, like the concept of yin and yang, one is enveloped in the other (Brown 2013).

(B) Remember who owns the issue

My second 'what works' is to remember that I am in service of my client. The issue is theirs and it's my job to help them resolve it, if I can. This is particularly relevant to the Relational Consulting model we offer, which I will explain later in section E. It is always important to avoid the seduction of taking on the responsibility that belongs to the client. We have to remember that we are working for others who are responsible for the outcomes. We find it helps to identify as quickly as possible our primary 'client' for a change project and a more senior sponsor who can help if things get stuck. We in OD assist, come alongside, think and design, coach and facilitate, but we do not own the issue. When issues are tricky, difficult and complex, it is natural for people to want to resolve them and even more attractive sometimes to get rid of them. If OD consultants are too keen, they can find themselves going beyond their relational role and taking on the leadership that more correctly sits with their clients. It can be tempting. Power is seductive. The OD practitioner is there to help the leader lead and help with additional insight and conversational design. If you find you need to take ownership and prove something, then best you do a different kind of consulting or take a line management and leadership role. Some people are just not temperamentally suited to OD work. The lack of visibility and kudos can make life intolerable for some. A good practitioner needs to be able to hold confidences all around the system and be valued for behind the scenes, informal, constructive work. As a result, good OD practice can go unnoticed or be misunderstood until it's not there.

(C) Levels/orders of change

OD work often needs to start with help for the client to identify and decide what level/order of change they want to achieve. Fix/improve/transform? Is it critical, tame, or wicked? (Grint 2008) The initial requests we have to the team are often for a fix. After deeper data gathering, this is not always what we agree to support.

A fix does not require a change of core function; it is enough to return it to good service delivery. There are all sorts of reasons why services might deteriorate, and the job of the OD consultant, in support of the local leadership, is to help diagnose what has been going on and design and often facilitate conversations between the parties to support a resolution and a type of rebirth. To achieve this, we usually contract and work in pairs; and if it becomes a large team conversation, we coach and support the leadership and help hold the teams' anxiety while the work to change their circumstances happens. We might work alone as OD or bring in other support services, such as HR or quality improvement, information services, etc. Sometimes they invite us in.

There are many approaches to diagnosing what has been happening and what might need to be explored and how to get to resolution. It has been a long time since the Hawthorne Effect showed how team performance improved when people's working conditions were given attention (Taylor 1911). My experience leads me to agree with this, and yet I notice that some fixes/improvements/transformations are more sustainable than others. In my experience, this can be influenced by the maintenance work done and other factors, such as the quality of initial engagement, the individual and group insights gained, the process of healing the disagreements, the honesty of the renewed relationships, and the complexity of the system and the issues. A particularly helpful skill set to develop in teams and senior individuals is the capacity for skilful conversation and dialogue. This skill set can help people deal with whatever the system throws at them. David Kantor in *Reading the Room* (2012) explores dialogue in depth.

We have been using Kantor theory and practices in a great variety of settings in the system for seven years. Dialogue and Structural dynamics are particularly useful in situations where a transformation is sought and there are many players involved. Bringing a cross section of the system together to talk and understand the big picture and create a way forward is not a simple task but very rewarding when it creates a generative solution based on the best of a groups' collective thinking. It is demanding of all concerned to attempt to talk and really listen to each other. Few people enjoy the process of giving up their cherished negative assumptions but the end results are often convincing, even if difficult to get to. Having the recipients of the service as part of the conversation is usually very helpful, as their presence stops professional viewpoints and rivalries from limiting the creation of solutions.

Kantor's early research was with conflicted families, and he concluded that it was not enough to help them resolve their immediate conflict. He found that to thrive, they needed to learn how to have disagreement constructively. I think this skill is as useful at work as it is at home.

Big organisations like the one I currently work for are bureaucratic by nature and encourage people to follow established routines, focus on the known approach to the task, getting it done rather than thinking about how it could be done more effectively. This is an excellent approach for routine, best practice, which is already known and agreed. It is less useful where situations are more uncertain and there are many conflicting views on the way ahead. A good dialogic conversation is more likely to generate new solutions that more people will enact with commitment than one imposed through the hierarchy without enough appreciation of the task or the people process involved.

(D) Unconscious metaphor

My fourth 'what works' is to remember there is no such thing as a successful formula or recipe for resolving issues. People often want a simple recipe, a quick way forward and one that can be universally applied everywhere for positive outcomes. It is tempting to suggest there might be such a thing when your clients are anxious and they want quick reassurance.

To find different ways through situations I turn to metaphor to understand the dominant mindset in the situation and for ways to unlock and shift the situation. Morgan (2006) provides a good introduction to organisational metaphor and its impact on how we think and act. There are no right or wrong metaphors, and the task is often to identify those unconscious metaphors already dominating the way people are thinking and acting then help them see and use other more appropriate metaphors to deal with the issue. The next steps can then be more thought through and conscious. It may or may not create instant changes, but the new way of understanding a situation offers new ways to understand feedback and the creation of new actions. Often people are using inadequate, mechanistic, linear thinking in situations of complexity. Every assignment is unique and requires fresh thinking. Our job is to help resolve issues and the capacity of the leadership at the same time. This requires space for reflective conversations before, during, and after interventions so that feedback can be given and received and self-awareness grown.

(E) Role clarity

My fifth 'what works' is to be clear with my client about what kind of internal/external consultant I am. The type that we offer in our OD team is variously called Relational/Process /Collaborative consulting. In Block (2011), he includes a description of this and others, including 'Expert', 'Delegated', and 'A Pair of Hands'. They are all legitimate and relevant in particular settings. It is frustrating, however, when you are attempting to deliver one and the client wants another. Agreeing to a clear contract with your client as soon as you can is your best strategy, even if it changes as the work progresses and it becomes necessary to update and renew.

The relational model of consulting that we use requires us to get alongside our clients and help them to help themselves. We focus is on the leadership challenges they have and what the particular leaders or groups need to do in their situation to unstick the situation or themselves. We pay attention to their personal leadership development needs and the organisational issue, often helping them work out who needs to talk to whom about what to move an issue on. Sometimes we also design and facilitate the necessary conversation, sometimes we don't, depending on the situation. If the client wants to be in a conversation and not have to hold the space and lead it also, then we are usually well placed to facilitate it and are seen as 'neutral'. It is not true that any of us are entirely neutral, however. We in OD are paid to pay attention to the whole system, not the parts alone; and we aim to create constructive conversation, even if that includes facing cross system paradoxes and dilemmas.

We also attempt to uncover and explore any skill deficiencies or knowledge or insight gaps that might have been unseen and caused the original impasse. If the unsticking is not within the grasp of the individuals concerned, then at minimum, they will be clearer about the impact this is having on them and whether they will be able to live with it and how or whether they will need to find another place to put their energies.

(F) Appropriate form of intervention involving the customer

Taking an appreciative, asset-based, dialogic approach as part of the work can help everyone rebuild their confidence and strength to move towards each other and the issues that need to change. It also supports the personal, inner enquiry they will need to make to find a way through. In service of more sustainable solutions, my team and I have built our capacity to use dialogue approaches to service change. We use it when there is a need to develop a new joint approach to service delivery. A top-down approach does not always work. In the NHS there is a great dependence on relatively autonomous and powerful individual practitioners, and if they do not understand the direction of a service change, they can thwart it. The use of large-scale dialogic methodologies to involve many voices offers increased opportunities for people to create a new narrative together and to use it to guide their actions and deliver enhanced service models. These conversations are at their best when the client/customer is also part of the conversation, as he or she tends to offer both praise and a clear direction for improvements and transformations.

In consulting contracts with clients, the challenges faced can be acute or chronic or both. Building a client relationship robust enough to go into these uncharted territories happens over time. This work is anxiety provoking for all concerned. The client team benefits from having people to help contain their anxiety and to hold the space for new conversation that they would really rather not have, but need to. The most senior client needs to give the permission to take them and others to places they have consciously or unconsciously avoided and make it safe for them and for the consultant. If the hierarchy cannot permit this, then an internal OD person may be asked to commission an external consultant to help or sometimes work with an external; a successful blend can be one from inside and one outside the organisational boundary.

(2) What helps when nothing seems to be working?

(a) Personal work

My model for OD often involves helping senior players develop new insight. In my experience, organisations often get stuck when the senior leaders are personally stuck. The best way to develop the capacity to help people develop insight is to work on your own. Staying curious and open is fundamental. Fallibility and vulnerability are cornerstone attributes. High levels of optimism and trust are also useful. You never know where your next best piece of feedback is going to come from, so not closing down the shutters is vital. With high self-awareness, OD practitioners can bring their confidence about this to conversations. The more you understand your own perspective, the more you can be 'critically subjective' and offer your lens for what it is, without it being presented as the only way and the truth. Clients can learn to do the same. I work from the assumption that there is no such thing as objectivity. It is however a great advantage to know as much as possible about my subjectivity and help others see theirs so that a wider field of options might be uncovered without an inappropriate right or wrong developing. Over time I have found that I have built up a group of clients who are open to this approach and are able to do the same. Developing generative dialogues with them is easier than with others. Finding solutions is quicker. Creating more leaders with this capability is an aim.

(b) Taking support

In my experience, developing personal insight and self-awareness is a relational process. I am a strong extrovert and may need to be in conversation more than others. I learn from reading; but what works best for me, is taking my reading and my lived experience into conversation with knowledgeable others who will hear, witness, and understand as well as challenge. I take help of this sort regularly to understand what is going on for me so that I am supported enough to offer this service to others. It helps me enact what I espouse. It guarantees that I don't fall into the trap of always being the one with either the insightful clever questions and/or the answers. I explore my stuckness (Petriglieri 2007) as preparation for helping others to do the same with me. These opportunities help keep me topped up and positive.

The job is demanding and more time is spent with those in difficulty than those without. It can feel like the legend of Sisyphus. He displeased the gods and was doomed to an eternity of rolling a stone uphill for it just to roll down again and then start again. The work is never complete and it is easy to lose sight of the positive and focus on the negative.

The NHS deals with patients/customers who are anxious and in pain, and it rubs off on the staff. If the OD team is part of the 'health service' for the people who deliver the health services, we need to stay as well as we can so that we can be of use to the people who ask us for help. To stay able to do this, we face our own vulnerabilities. An easy trap for health practitioners is to deny their vulnerabilities and project them all onto their patients. They are fine and the patient is ill. They are strong and the patient is weak. My service model demands of me that I stay in touch with my weak and ill self so that I can work alongside my clients and empathise, while I help them find a way through to health.

The people I take support from are also practiced in organisational development theory of a variety of disciplines and have concepts and practices that help me separate out my own issues from the systemic ones. I particularly appreciate help to notice when I am acting out systemic issues unawarely and unhelpfully for myself and others. In addition, having help to work on my own worst emotional experiences and reducing the pain attached to them helps me be in the here and now more effectively and to avoid overreacting to small situations that restimulate my old hurts when I am leading my team or doing client work.

(c) Timing, patience, and the long view

Moving towards conversations rather than away is vital if progress is to be made. Getting stuck in avoidance or monologue or debate is not generally enough. More skilful conversation brings together different perspectives so that some new solution can be generated. Even though everyone wants a good solution, most want to avoid the pain and fear involved in taking the time to resolve the situation. Sometimes things need to get really bad before people are prepared to invest the time in a proper rethink of their situation. Patience is vital here with yourself and others, not giving up and waiting for the time to be right and acting as soon as it is.

(d) Time out, stray dogs, and other interests

I have discovered how important breaks away from work on annual leave are. I also now realise this is what I need to do when I think it is the last thing I can do. When I think like that, it is a sign that I am overtired and overinvested. The best thing I can do is get out and put my attention on something else. The NHS is a never-ending task. There is no destination I can get to; there is always more to be done.

'Stray dogs' is a term my supervisor used to describe the issues that I see in the system at any point in time that no one else seems to be owning and I am 'holding' meantime. I have not found a way as yet to have them all homed or to stop myself hearing their barking. I suspect I would just pick up some more as soon as I got my current ones homed. I am energetic and keen to see progress, and setting boundaries is a daily challenge for someone like me. Not everyone is like this, and it makes me more susceptible than others to introjecting the systems pattern of noticing what's wrong rather than what's good.

To help switch off this 24/7 NHS, I find doing some creative practical work a pleasure for me. I manage to do a weekly upholstery night class now that I don't travel all over the country for my work. It's amazing how refreshing some physical work can be. I can see and touch the product of my labours and doing it uses different parts of my brain and gives parts of my intellect a rest. Being at home enough to do this class is restorative in its own right also. The items I have worked on are symbolic of a much-needed restoration of my own domestic life.

I have also practiced meditation for many years, and it has helped me a great deal. I am currently experimenting with 'Timefulness' as part of a programme I am doing (Kantor 2012). I know I don't take enough exercise now as I drive to work. I can't do it all.

(e) Keep honing your skills and avoiding complacency and contempt

I choose personal development processes every year to keep stretching my skill set. We also do this as a team to help us work with our clients more effectively. We work on our difficulties between ourselves so that we can remember what it feels like when we encourage others to do this. We can find ourselves mirroring the system and introjecting the nature of our clients' issues between us. It is important that we work with these issues in team supervision and team development sessions. (Obholzer 1994).

I believe I can only take my clients as far as I have gone myself and it is important therefore to keep exploring and learning. We are currently on a programme designed to help us work with others in 'high stakes'. It is a further development in our dialogue training based on the work of David Kantor, through the Kantor Institute and Dialogix. We are being helped to look at what puts us into high stakes so that we can more effectively stay in low stakes when we might not otherwise be able to do this, especially if working with others in high stakes.

Another writer in the field of group conflict (Mindell 1995) suggests that the people drawn to work in the field of conflict normally have 'wood to burn'. Mindell argues that you are unlikely to be interested in this type of work if you have had a life of blissful harmony. If you don't do any work to identify your own old issues and hurts and angers, then you are more likely to bring it into your client work unawarely. The more aware you are of what you bring to a conversation, good or bad patterns, the more able you will be to be present and to stay in 'humble enquiry'(Schein 2013) rather than the unconscious advocacy of inappropriate solutions.

(f) Reading and education

My job and my family take up most of my time, and reading has got harder since I now drive to work and have not got the trains and planes and hotel rooms I used to read in when I did external consulting. The NHS has fantastic library services. I can order any book, and they also proactively produce lists of the latest research articles in topics such as leadership, change, culture, etc. I am well supported. There is a Knowledge Network, virtual and actual networks. I am in a group of OD Leads who learn and work together. There are journals and periodicals available to me. My team members are also readers, and they bring books to my attention. My individual supervisor and our team supervisor also recommend books or I hear of them from my action learning set, the radio. I am an associate with Ashridge, and they also provide me with extensive leadership and management resources and colleagues who are exceptional learners and teachers. The web allows me to browse and to receive information from writers, researchers, talks, conferences, and more.

Narrowing it all down is the big issue for me. There are mountains of theories and researched evidence, more than I have time to read. I prioritise my reading by subject, recommendations of trusted mavens, and by the hours left in the day!

REFERENCES

Beer, M. and Nohria, N. (2000) Cracking the code of change. *Harvard Business Review,* 78(3), 133–141.

Block, P. (2011) *Flawless Consulting: A Guide to Getting Your Expertise Used,* 3rd Edition. Hoboken: Wiley.

Brown, B. (2013) *Daring Greatly: How the Courage to Be Vulnerable Transforms the Way We Live, Love, Parent, and Lead.* Harmondsworth: Portfolio Penguin.

Grint, K. (2008) Wicked problems and clumsy solutions: The role of leadership. *Clinical Leader,* 1(2), 54–68.

Hammer, M. and Champy, J. (1993) *Reengineering the Corporation: A Manifesto for Business Revolution.* London: Nicholas Brearly.

Hughes, M. (2010) *Managing Change: A Critical Perspective.* Wimbledon: CIPD Publishing.

Huxham, C. and Vangen, S. (2005) *Managing to Collaborate.* London: Routledge.

Kantor, D. (2012) *Reading the Room: Group Dynamics for Coaches and Leaders.* San Francisco: Jossey Bass.

Kotter, J.P. (2008) *A Sense of Urgency.* Boston: Harvard Business School Press.

Mindell, A. (1995) *Sitting in the Fire: Large Group Transformation Using Conflict and Diversity.* Chicago: The Independent Publishers Group.

Mitroff, I.I. and Silvers, A. (2010). *Dirty Rotten Strategies, How We Trick Ourselves and Others into Solving the Wrong Problems Precisely.* Palo Alto: Stanford Business Books.

Morgan. G. (2006). *Images of Organisation.* Thousand Oaks: SAGE.

Petriglieri, G. (2007). Stuck in a moment: A developmental perspective on impasses. *Transactional Analysis Journal,* 37(3), 185–194.

Obholzer, A. et al (Eds) (1994) *The Unconscious at Work: Individual and Organizational Stress in the Human Services.* London: Routledge.

Scott-Morgan, P. (1994). *Unwritten Rules of the Game: Master Them, Shatter Them and Break Through the Barriers to Organizational Change* New York: McGraw-Hill.

Schein, E.H. (2013). *Humble Inquiry: The Gentle Art of Asking Instead of Telling.* San Francisco: Berrett-Koehler.

Senturia, T. et al (2008) *Leading change management requires sticking to the plot.* [Online]. Available from www.bain.com [Accessed: 2/9/14]

Taylor, F.W. (1911). *The Principles of Scientific Management.* New York: Harper and Brothers.

Watzlawick, P. et al (1974) *Change; Principles of Problem Formation and Problem Resolution.* New York: Norton.

Part III

Managers as Consultants

Julian Randall and Bernard Burnes

There are as many definitions of management as there are management practitioners (Stewart, 1991). Every job description contains that final clause that you will do anything reasonably requested by management. So responding willingly to a variety of demands is a characteristic of the role. Mary Parker Follet's (1942) definition of 'Getting things done through other people' suggests a general definition, if largely of a supervisory role. In contrast, Fayol's five categories of planning, organizing, motivating, controlling, and coordinating, is another which suggests that there is a mental process that underwrites what managers do (Fayol, 1949). This may have been the case when workplaces provided rungs on a promotional ladder which proficient managers used as they climbed their way up to the top of the organization. But how valid is that model now? The Shamrock Organisation suggested 25 years ago that core staff would serve up to the age of 47 (later the author reduced this to 35) and that workers would then have a choice between the consultancy route or contracting out low-tech, no-tech services (Handy, 1989, 1992). This trend has been compounded by an increasing cohort of workers on zero-hours contracts. So how does the manager motivate such a diverse group of workers, especially during change?

During the upbeat period of Business Process Reengineering, workers were encouraged to think of themselves differently. Senior managers were now rebranded 'enterprise managers', middle managers rebranded 'expertise managers' (IT, HR specialists, etc.), first line managers were rebranded system and people managers, and ordinary workers as 'self-managers' (Champy, 1995; Hamel & Prahaled, 1994). It seemed that everybody had become a manager now. The only certainty is that there is no necessary promotion path, no assurance of job security, the likelihood of a short-term tenancy in the organization, and the need to manage your career portfolio as you go from job to job. For many managers in HR there is now only an interim contract. For example, a recent job with a large bank, which required training and negotiational skills and was based between business teams in two locations only offered a salary of £14K and an 18-month contract. We are all entrepreneurs in our own right now and definitely bricoleurs—making our job up as we go along (Gabriel, 2000).

Apart from the fragmentation of the traditional organizational model, what else is there that affects those seeking to create order out of chaos in that process of becoming that which is management (Tsoukas and Chia, 2002)? Once again the spectre of change rears its head. This time it is not just incremental change, not even punctuated equilibrium, but continuous change. Now that might suggest that there will an increasing demand for external consultants. They could almost be forgiven for taking up permanent residence in the organization. But the fact is that another development seems to be emerging which sees the manager brokering change and exercising those facilitational skills which were once the preserve of an external consultant parachuted in to solve problems.

The manager is now a consultant. She comes in with experience of facilitating change; she has experienced this either as an external consultant herself, or she has acquired the skills from involvement as an internal change agent during her previous job roles elsewhere (Sturdy et al, 2014). Indeed, we might almost say that since workers are busy managing themselves, there is one significant role that a manager managing people has: brokering change for staff whose lives are bedevilled by constant change. Sturdy suggests that there are four important factors that need to be included here:

> *(1) adopting an external focus by drawing on the pro-change orientations and knowledge of outsiders, (2) a strategic 'value-added' approach, (3) use of 'non-hierarchical' styles of interaction and (4) deploying formal methods of change management and cross-functional project work.*
> (Sturdy et al, 2014: 2)

The authors see this in an increasing trend to recruit external consultants into management roles so that they are familiar with the techniques which support change initiatives at work. But increasingly, too, the managers involved with continuous change must necessarily find themselves embroiled with change on a daily basis and become adept at handling the challenges that change events always give rise to.

For our four chapter writers in this section, it would appear that this new world has already come to fruition. The first chapter is written by Dave Ennis who has been through the management journey of helping to site a foreign company in what was once regarded as a hostile environment of rigid unionism, convincing both workers and the new owners that a different approach to manufacturing was both possible and feasible. But nothing stays the same forever and for reasons that he explains, the company eventually sought to relocate its operations offshore, leaving him with the challenge of radical change or a management buy-out. More recently he has adapted to a consultancy role in his son's company and describes this transition in which he deploys similar skills and knowledge applied in a very different context.

Managers are sometimes involved in change early on in their careers and having found an aptitude for it enter into the role full time. Our second chapter is written by Stephen Banyard who did exactly that in the Civil Service, amalgamating two departments and coming to the conclusion that change is not just normal in a service that once considered itself impregnable to the business trends of the private sector but that change and learning are synonymous—and to be welcomed as such.

Keeping a business refreshed with new talent which fits into the ethos of the changing organization does not happen by chance. Our fourth chapter writer, Sarah Smith, describes her role as graduate recruitment manager for Aberdeen Asset Management in which there are two streams of entry, which include apprentices who have chosen not to go the a university but to go straight into the world of work. The initial experience for both entry streams involves an extended internship which allows all those involved to make choices about joining a changing and dynamic sector which encourages enjoying both work and social life together.

Our final chapter is written by Dave Sherrit who started in the NHS and moved on to the oil sector shortly after the Piper Alpha disaster when oil companies realized that they needed to take training a lot more seriously. Dave is an OD practitioner who has developed his own views of being an internal consultant and developer of people using activities that he has found help people to embrace change successfully. He demonstrates his belief that OD interventions should put philosophy into practice. He believes that return on investment needs to be balanced by humanistic values and that 'an ounce of action is worth a ton of theory'.

The overall advantages of this move to the manager as consultant can be summarized as follows:

> Whereas previous measures of managerial contribution might have been more easily quantified or, at least, were implied in the production process (e.g. cost-minimisation), neo-bureaucratic management relies upon perceptions of 'added-value' and market-based mechanisms. Hence, while the contradictory nature of management has been a recurring theme in critical studies, the application of neo-bureaucracy through practises, such as management as consultancy, suggests that it may serve to further de-value management in the long-term, as managers' work becomes more ambiguous and less tied to the relative certainties of traditional patterns of control, much like external consultancy.
>
> (Sturdy et al, 2014: 18)

We hope that our chapters illustrate the diversity of some of the work that has defined the work of these managers and accounts for their success in a world of continuous change.

REFERENCES

Champy, James (1995) *Reengineering Management*. London: Harper Business.

Fayol, Henri (1949) *General and Industrial Management*. London: Pitman.

Follett, Mary Parker. 1942. *Dynamic Administration: The Collected Papers of Mary Parker Follett*. Edited by Henry C. Metcalf and L. Urwick. New York and London: Harper & Brothers Publishing.

Gabriel, Yiannis (2000) *Storytelling in Organizations: Facts, Fictions, Fantasies*. Oxford: Oxford University Press.

Hamel, Gary and C.K. Prahaled (1994) *Competing for the Future*. Boston, MA: Harvard Business Press.

Handy, Charles (1989) *The Age of Unreason*. Boston, MA: Harvard Business School Press.

Sturdy, Andrew, Christopher Wright and Nick Wylie (2014) Managers as consultants: The hybridity and tensions of neo-bureaucratic management. Organization published online 15 July 2015 DOI: 10.1177/1350508414541580.

Tsoukas, Haridimos and Robert Chia (2002) On organizational becoming: Rethinking organizational change. *Organization Science* 13 (5), 567–582.

12 The Inevitability of Change

David Ennis

I'm David Ennis, and until 2006 I was the Managing Director of OKI (UK) Ltd based in Cumbernauld, Scotland. I moved to OKI—a Japanese-based company, as their Director of HR and Corporate Affairs, having previously worked for Philips Electronics and Plessey Telecommunications.

Currently, I'm associated with my son's company, NSDesign; an SME digital consultancy founded in 1999, providing web design, digital marketing, and social media training. I am still employed by OKI on a consultancy basis.

Mr Kibataro OKI founded OKI Electric in 1881 to supply equipment to the Ministry of Communications in Tokyo. With a reputation for innovation and quality, its main products are telecommunications, semiconductors, and computing and Internet products.

Many of OKI's traditional customers were large multinationals or government-backed organisations such as the Japanese post office. With a global network of sales companies in each of the continents, in line with many Japanese manufacturers, OKI decided to establish a base in Europe to supply an ever-increasing market and also to offset the rising yen.

To achieve this, OKI (UK) Ltd was setup in 1987 as a printer manufacturer. The first plant outside Japan, its purpose was essentially commercial rather than part of an overall strategy. A key reason for this plant was the recognition that the market responsiveness and flexibility that could be offered was going to be increasingly important. In addition, in the absence of a European plant, the tariffs levied on printers entering the EU would threaten the company's long-term competitiveness. Bottom line, our objective was to be at least as good as Japanese manufacturing in terms of efficiency and, more importantly, quality. To put this in perspective, we have to remember that in 1987 the economic and industrial relations conditions in the UK were far different from what they are today. Scotland, for example, had just lost out on attracting a major engine manufacturer simply because management and unions could not agree on the basic conditions of employment.

Our task, therefore, was to take the best of Japanese management practices and combine them with, what we believed to be, the best of UK practice. Having worked in European and British companies where industrial relations were a major issue, I was well aware of the challenges we faced.

At the time it felt as though we knew 'what not to do', rather than 'what to do'. There were many misconceptions on both the UK and the Japanese sides. UK managers were concerned about long-term commitment from the Japanese company, who in turn was concerned about the UK work ethic. These concerns ranged from day-to-day issues, such as tea breaks to the more complex issues of absenteeism and flexibility agreements. They were also understandable given that the plant had been previously operated by Burroughs, makers of business machines, who had experienced absenteeism averages of over 20 per cent.

A key decision, made in the early stages of the project, was that we would not formally recognise trade unions but instead set up a Japanese-style member's council drawn from all parts of the labour force.

I still have the slides which were prepared by our small management group to address the challenges associated with this very different approach. They summarised the discussions, arriving at a set of key issues, which were recruitment, flexibility, motivation, and communication.

A strategy was then developed for each element and a more extensive list of 'messages' was drawn up which sought to define the culture within the plant and how the company should try to present itself to the outside world.

The 'messages' were divided into internal and external.

INTERNAL TO OKI

- Is a successful company
- Cares about its workforce
- Involves workers
- Communicates well
- Will not accept poor performance
- Promotes from within where possible
- Is a single status company
- Believes

  - hard work = more jobs and more pay
  - poor work = termination of project

EXTERNAL TO OKI

- Is a professional company to deal with
- Is a successful company
- Is in Scotland to stay
- Is Japanese but understands UK
- Works with suppliers and customers
- Is tough but fair
- Has respect for people
- Has a name for high quality

The company adopted a culture of continuous improvement, one of 'kaizen'. However, due to the diverse background of its managers, early agreement on what kaizen meant, in the new company's context, was not achieved.

Some managers had experience with the Deming approach to Total Quality Control, some supported Crosby's more holistic philosophy, and for others Taguchi was *the* guru. Eventually the group recognised that an 'off the shelf system' could not be adopted. Instead, a customised system of supplier-customer relationships was developed.

What this meant, for example, was that line A was the *supplier* of line B, and line B in turn was not only a *customer* but also a *supplier* of line C.

This approach was also applied at the operator level where each operator was both a customer and a supplier.

Quality charts were set up at each stage of production to not only monitor and control quality levels but to act as feedback for the previous operation. These quality measuring points displayed hourly statistics. The targets were tightened as the product progressed through each operation until it approached zero defects for the final operation.

Defects were therefore identified at the earliest stage and the operator fed this back to the previous stage for instant action. If the number of defects exceeded the target, then the operator had the ability to stop the line until the issue was resolved. This meant that a 'no blame' culture had to be adopted, because any 'identification of blame' would put at risk the independent assessment of the individual employee. Management attempted to stand back and only manage the system, thus empowering the employees to manage their own jobs. Training was critical to the success of the operation. This change in attitude was not achieved without problems. Engineers, for instance, were used to having the final say in how an operation should be set up. When operators were given control, some saw this as a reduction in their authority and some saw it as 'madness' to allow semi-skilled operators to have the power to stop an operation. Supervisors sometimes found it difficult to stop being the 'overseers' rather than the providers of services. It was easy to say that mistakes were opportunities to learn but quite another to put it into practice.

Another outcome of this process was the collection of key data which was fed back to our suppliers in Europe in an attempt to improve the quality of incoming parts. We went to the extent of flying about 20 suppliers to Japan to show them what benefits could be achieved by this cooperation. This led to huge advances in quality that soon equalled and then surpassed the Japanese quality levels. Many awards were showered on the company from external organisations and, more importantly, from its customers, which included major companies such as ICL—a major computer company at the time.

In an effort then to do the 'right thing', we instituted a process of multitasking and moved employees regularly between jobs. Little did we understand that in doing so we would cause a reduction in quality levels. This reduction resulted (understandably) from employees who no sooner were trained in one role, were then moved to a new role. Clearly this multitasking approach required more thought!

THE EXTERNAL CHALLENGES

At the international level, we faced many choices and dilemmas. We had been operating effectively and successfully with our distributor, Technitron, for many years. However, it became obvious that as we became larger and increased the product range into Europe and the Middle East, we could not continue with the hands-off approach we had hitherto adopted.

After many discussions with the board of directors of Technitron and the board of OKI in Japan, it was agreed that the company would start negotiations with Technitron management to take over the eight countries that distributed our products. There were eight separate companies in Europe to negotiate with, all with different legal systems and employment practices: UK, Germany, Norway, Sweden, Denmark, Holland, Italy, and France. We also had to satisfy the monopoly commission in the UK that we were acting fairly from a corporate point of view and with due regard to the individual shareholders, many of whom were the managing directors of these companies.

I was involved in the decision process as the only non-Japanese Director of the company in the UK; and after more than a year of discussions and negotiation, we were successful, resulting in the establishment of the OKI Systems' group of companies in 1990. The Managing Director of Technitron then became the Assistant Managing Director of the new sales company, with engineering and support services being absorbed into the Cumbernauld facility.

The sales organisation and manufacturing organisation worked very closely together. There were inevitable disagreements on how the schedule of production was set. Sales forecasts were seldom accurate and production problems and material lead times occasionally resulted in a mismatch against the sales promises. Mistakes led to missed deliveries, high inventory, or shortage of product.

Teams were set up to try and solve the issues and gradually an understanding developed.

Customer visits were a regular occurrence and relationships were improved with customers.

By the end of the millennium we had opened new distributors in Eastern Europe and in the Middle East. Sales were booming, and we had the reputation for high quality from a responsive and friendly company.

But . . . Success Can Be a Fleeting Thing

By the year 2000, events were changing in manufacturing. Many manufacturing companies set up in Scotland were now loOKIng at China and the Far East to reduce their cost base. OKI was no different.

The wage rates in China were one-tenth of what was paid in Scotland, and this led to a review of the Scottish operation. Our initial reaction was 'How dare they'? But the brutal fact remained that no increase in efficiency, and no amount of cost reduction, could compensate for the difference in wage rates between the UK and the Far East.

At this point, together with the management team, I proposed a management buy-out, which recognised the need to manufacture in the East but also gave a real role for the Scottish operation.

The intention of this proposed solution was to approach other electronic companies and try and set up a cooperative venture where Cumbernauld would produce for a range of companies, such as Sun, Motorola, IBM, and others and also manage part of their supply chain. In doing this, we reckoned we could keep the cost base down but also provide local (European) support for products and processes.

The process of a MBO is fascinating, and this was one of the most challenging times of my career. The process started with me presenting our proposal to the board of OKI in Japan. Within a few days we had a team of eight Japanese senior executives and local advisers led by the Finance Director descend on us to negotiate the complex deal.

However, despite our efforts, in the end we saw many of the prospective target companies go elsewhere in the world, and the MBO became non-viable.

Some benefit can be found in most projects. An interesting development that came out of the process was that we understood our total assets better than we ever had. The land, for instance, was a valuable asset that we had previously ignored. After lots of negotiating with OKI headquarters and the local council, we managed to obtain permission to convert the existing factory space from industrial to commercial classification and used the increase in value to sell this to a retail developer.

OKI, in return for the capital infusion, promised to retain 500 employees as a minimum for at least five years. This is an example of how driving for change in one direction can lead to a change in a totally different area. By doing this, we gained a lot of respect from Japan.

Many companies see change as cost reduction, improvement in efficiencies, or the adoption of new equipment—but these are usually small incremental changes within an overall static framework. For change to be more than a one-off, it has to be focused on customers, driven by a never-ending process, and accompanied by a cultural shift.

Change is a search for a different approach and must result in something better. The process is as important as the decisions reached and within that process must be a robust communication system which concentrates on the truth of what is taking place.

Change is very difficult if the need for it is unclear. Some see change as a threat, and this needs to be recognised by management. Small changes in strategic direction require significant change in culture and often changes in people and systems.

Key Success Factors . . .

Communication is at the heart of almost everything. When I was asked by my Japanese boss to describe what type of communication system we should introduce, I responded by describing the Industrial Society model.

> He then asked what it really meant. I described a process that started with the Managing Director and the board preparing a brief each month that was cascaded down the organisation and everyone then should understand what was happening.

> He then asked me if I was married (a strange question at the time). I replied that I had been married for over 20 years.

> He then asked if my wife would be pleased if I only talked to her once a month.

I'm not sure of my reply, but it did bring home to me that communication is an endless process that cannot be switched on and off and should not be confined to a monthly meeting.

OKI now has *chokai*, which in Japanese means 'morning meeting'. Each team meets first thing in the morning and goes through what happened yesterday, what is happening today, and what problems need to be fixed. Other issues of a personal nature can be, and are, also raised. This is not regarded as downtime or waiting time or personal time. This is work time, doing the things that we should be doing.

The process of change can only work effectively if it is seen as an integral part of doing business.

AND NOW?

My current role at my son's company is dramatically different from my previous positions of management in what were considerably bigger organisations. At its peak, I looked after 1500 employees at OKI. At NSDesign, I'm one of nine employees where phrases such as management structure and employee review are alien concepts.

You probably haven't heard of NSDesign, but you may have heard of a slightly bigger Internet organisation called Google. In actual fact, it's easy for me to explain a little bit more about NSDesign by comparing the two companies—which are remarkably similar!

- Google was formed in late 1998, NSDesign just a few months later at the start of 1999.
- Google was started by a man named 'Larry' when he was working for Stanford University.
- NSDesign was started by a man named 'Gary' when he should have been working for Strathclyde University.
- Fifteen years later, Google is worth $300 billion.
- NSDesign is worth . . . a little visit. Always open for a chat and a coffee!

The point is—NSDesign is NOT Google.

NSDesign is the definition of a micro-business. That is, businesses of less than ten employees. The reality is that *in the UK, 95 per cent of all businesses are micro-businesses*. If every micro-business in the UK hired just *one* employee, there would be zero unemployment.

The concept of 'change' is very different in a small organisation compared to multinationals. Unlike the bigger organisations, where change is often difficult, unwanted, and avoided, in small businesses it's almost a part of the day-to-day process of business.

Small businesses don't have the luxury (some would say headache!) of taking time to pilot things, user test them, run a focus group, and have a committee spend three months deciding what changes to implement. The stages of this process are done 'on the fly', often on the hunch of the 'boss', or on the advice of one of the other members in the team.

Small businesses exist in a constant state of change and require the ability to adapt quickly and respond to external factors critical to small business success.

One of the more pertinent examples of change at NSDesign in recent years was the decision to sell off part of the company. Since its formation in 1999, NSDesign has provided domain name registration and web hosting services. At its peak, it provided such services to over ten thousand businesses, large and small.

While profitable, the 'high volume, low value' model meant that creativity and growth were being somewhat stifled, as members of the NSDesign team often found themselves bogged down in small trivial tasks around support and accounting. This would often limit the 'bigger ambitions' and more enjoyable work of creative design, consultancy, and training—requiring a higher commitment of people time.

After a team meeting in early 2012 to discuss the future direction of the company, it was unanimously agreed that if the resources required to run the hosting business were freed up, everyone would have more time to focus on other work deemed to be both more appealing and also more profitable. The decision to change and sell up was made; and within six months, NSDesign had sold that side of the business to Broadband Cloud Solutions (BCS)—a new, growing company loOKIng to expand its user base by acquiring hosting companies.

Whereas, to bigger businesses, the repeat revenue almost guaranteed by domain/hosting customers would be considered minute, to NSDesign, it represented close to 40 per cent of their total income; so the decision to give this up was a massive one and a big risk in terms of replacing it with other income from elsewhere. Such decisions of this scale at bigger organisations would have taken years to agree, plan, and execute. At NSDesign, it was more or less made over coffee!

Gary structured the sale in such a way as to minimise the risk, by agreeing to continue running the operations for BCS as a service. This, combined with the exclusive digital marketing agreement for BCS, meant that NSDesign continued to receive significant ongoing revenue after the sale, as well as a lump sum to immediately invest in extra staff and give some breathing space to pursue new income streams.

It was a bit of a gamble, but one that has paid off with the 2013–2014 accounts loOKIng the healthiest yet. The sale of one part of the company allowed a 140 per cent growth in the more lucrative consultancy and training services, now a key part of NSDesign's future.

NSDesign have agreed on three main values which are interesting:

- Be Nice
- Be Great
- Be Remembered

The company really does believe that it should be nice by not just saying the words that appear in any customer service manual. They genuinely want to help people. Once a year, NSDesign offers a free day of training to anyone who wants to come along.

Being 'great', in their eyes, means exceeding customer expectations. Perhaps not being the best all of the time, but giving more than expected. To be remembered, they try to create a lasting impression and strive to be novel in their approach.

Despite the many differences between OKI and NSDesign, one of the values both companies share is that of the importance of communication. OKI pushed for regular daily meetings to keep everyone in the loop. NSDesign also employs a process of continuous employee engagement. Indeed, customer engagement too; in their case, not through daily meetings but through the use of social media.

The rapid increase and growth of tools such as Twitter and Facebook has shaken up the business world. Many have been slow to adapt to embrace such tools, citing excuses such as 'We're not that type of organisation'. Worse still, some play the stereotypical 'It's just for the kids' card. The truth is social media is not a radical concept. Good businesses have always been doing it, having regular conversations with stakeholders. Tools like Facebook have just made it easier, more transparent, and turned it into a two-way dialogue—not just the broadcast afforded by a company newsletter or a typical CEO briefings.

Today, the most common demographic on Facebook are the 25–35 year olds; it's not 'the kids'. I know of no business that doesn't consider this market segment critical to ongoing success. Ignoring the communication tools that allow direct engagement with your audience is business suicide. Indeed, you might not be there, but they are. And they're talking *about* you rather than *with* you.

NSDesign utilises all the social media tools, enabling them to engage continuously with clients, seeking feedback and sharing advice on Twitter, building community on Facebook, and growing their supplier and partner relationships on LinkedIn. Customer surveys are now a rarity, as they have their finger on the pulse of customer satisfaction, because they never stop talking to them. If social media had been around in my days at OKI, I reckon the same attitudes would have been employed. It's all about communication—use whatever current tools are available to you.

This growth and change in attitude to social media as a business tool is actually one of the current growth markets for NSDesign. Approximately 40 per cent of our turnover now comes from business consultancy around the usage and implementation of tools such as Twitter within businesses big and small. From changing attitudes in the board room, to training the shop floor how to use the tools, NSDesign is an advocate on the correct business usage of social media to communicate with your customers.

Twenty years ago, email was 'new'. I remember it well. Many in our organisation resisted change: 'What's wrong with internal memos in my pigeon hole,' or 'I'm not good with computers'. I now know of few individuals (let alone businesses) who do not rely on email. Email quickly became mainstream communication and people had to change, embrace it, or miss out. Social media is no different. It's an evolution of the way people talk to one another. The way they engage, support, complain.

To quote Erik Qualman, 'The ROI of social media is that your business will still exist in 5 years'

WORDS OF WISDOM . . . FOOD FOR THOUGHT . . .

1. The quality of our products will never exceed the quality of our people. Hire people better than you.
2. Work on strategy—what not to do is important. It is easy to say yes to everything that looks profitable but this can utilise resources that could be better used to develop other aspects of the business. Short-term profits can be very seductive, but the organisation must constantly review the direction it is taking and for that you need resources.
3. Empower people. Employees can only be empowered if they have the skills and knowledge base to start with. Managers must instil a passion to make a difference to enact the necessary change.

4. Think global, act local—be glocal. To your customer you should be seen as a local resource for them to call upon quickly. At the same time, you must take advantage of global assets. The idea of 'not invented here' is present in some companies. This leads to narrow thinking about any issue. It is now quite common for products to be built and designed in several continents and assembled and packaged in the sales area.

5. Managers must get used to serving—If managers cannot embrace change, get new managers. The idea of a manager as the one who tells others what to do and when to do it is disappearing. It stifles innovation and treats employees as nothing short of robots. Managers are responsible for the 'system'; employees are responsible for their own jobs. One of the roles that managers have is to ensure that employees bring more than just their hands when they come to work.

6. Customers can be a pain—but they are always the customer. The relationship between the company and the customer is crucial for success. Many orders are lost because of a misunderstanding between each other. Let the customer feel a part of your business. Let him feel as though he can influence your actions. Customer visits, company presentations, shared knowledge, and complete trust can help.

7. Change is inevitable (except from university vending machines)—It is the search for a different approach and must result in something better. The process is as important as the decisions reached.

8. Communication is like dieting—If you do not make it a way of life, it is a waste of time. Change is very difficult if the need for it is unclear. It is the manager's role to communicate this need. You need to be brave enough to open a dialogue with employees on all issues—not just the pleasant ones. It is no sign of weakness to say, "I have cocked things up"

9. Change is not just a search for cost reduction, improvement in efficiencies, or the adoption of new equipment—It must be focused on customers, driven by a never-ending process, and accompanied by a cultural shift. Operational excellence is vital to establish credibility—use it as a base. Many companies concentrate only on operational excellence, devoting all of their efforts to improving the current operation. It is certainly true that this is important, but it should not be the sole objective of an organisation. True leadership demands that we look at and understand the key organisational challenges present and future. Products, technology, and markets are constantly changing and to equip your company to deal only with the present is to risk being excellent at something that is no longer required.

10. Have fun!

13 Making Change Work in a Large Public Sector Organisation

Stephen Banyard

1 INTRODUCTION

This chapter has a practical focus on making change work successfully in a large public sector organisation. It is based on changes I have experienced as a manager and leader. My key theme is the value of taking an inclusive approach for successful outcomes, which is described in part 3.

How did I get into change? I wasn't born a change manager nor trained as one. In two quite different careers, the professional training I received was aimed at carrying out an essentially expert role and leading small groups of professional people. But working in a large and varied organisation, I was given the opportunity to play an active part in large-scale change, and I quickly caught the change bug. Most of my subsequent career involved trying to make change work well in large organisations in a variety of roles: as strategist, as change leader, and as operational manager.

Change has many attractions for me: the opportunity to envisage something new and make it happen, the challenge of resolving the many issues which arise in a major change programme, the ability to see a result you delivered or contributed to, and the pleasure (and privilege) of working with people you meet on programmes with their remarkable commitment and can-do attitudes.

To start at the beginning, my first career was as a Post-Doctoral Research Scientist in the mid-1970s—working out the structure of large protein molecules using a method called protein crystallography. This was an exciting field; but in the late 1970s, there were far more post-docs than permanent research jobs, so I decided to look elsewhere. I wanted to be in the public sector and to have a professional training. Inland Revenue[1] offered that in tax law and accountancy—they also promised significant responsibility within five years—so I took a big leap and joined them. I later found many other PhDs had made the same jump around that time.

Working in a large government department (it varied between 65,000 and 100,000 people while I was there) was hugely interesting. The professional training was demanding, and from the word go there was also practical application in the many challenging situations I was thrown into.

My managers were encouraging and supportive. We were placed into responsible jobs early on, and the work was intellectually demanding and interesting. What more could you ask for?

Yet what really made it for me were the subsequent opportunities to move into a wide variety of change-related roles. *Some were as strategist.* I led the production of Inland Revenue's first strategic plan in 1993 and two subsequent strategic plans in 1996 and 2006. *Some were more policy focused*, for example trying to influence other areas of the department to reduce the burden of red tape on business. *Others were on large-scale change programmes*, first as team leader, later as Programme Director and finally as Senior Responsible Officer. Some of these changes majored on *reorganisation*. They included a programme to move a large amount of work (around 1200 jobs) away from London, where recruitment was difficult; and leading the merger of Contributions Agency (then an Agency of DSS with 8000 people) with Inland Revenue (with some 70,000) in 1999. *Some programmes involved* a *heavy IT component and process change*. Between 2006 and 2012, I lead several such large (£100m+) change programmes, most with a focus on developing online services for the public.

In between these change roles, I was a Leader and Manager of large service delivery units. My first management role was with a small team of 20; later I became a Regional Director, then Director of Operations (responsible for 47,000 people in 950 local tax offices across the UK), and finally Director General of Personal Tax, a member of the department's executive board. In all the senior management roles, a core requirement was to lead the introduction of large-scale change while maintaining day-to-day service levels—so change has been my career anchor.

Moving fairly regularly between quite different types of roles meant I became an expert in my organisation (Inland Revenue and then HM Revenue and Customs) rather than in a specific professional specialism. My employer benefited in that, having experienced a range of different roles at one level, I was better equipped to carry out a broader role at the next. I found it hugely motivating to regularly face the new opportunities and the challenges this career pattern brought, if at times it took me beyond my comfort zone—and I still felt motivated when I retired at 64.

2   APPROACH TO CHANGE

i   The Public Sector Dimension

Managing change in the public sector has similar pressures to those in the private sector with one key addition: everything you do is in the public eye, problems can be very visible, and you are publicly held to account. The National Audit Office reviewed our work, and two Parliamentary Select Committees regularly examined our senior officials in public hearings on the department's work. I attended 14 as a witness over 12 years. These hearings usually last two to three hours, are often televised, and make the word accountability very real.

Another difference in the public sector is over *what* we change in our change programmes. Our market is public policy and this is determined by ministers and Parliament. The changes we implement give life to that policy. Often the issue is therefore not *whether* to do something but *how best* to do it.

I found ministers themselves (I worked with ministers from both major parties) are a real plus in the change process. Having signed up to a programme, they were accessible, helpful, and supportive in the change process, aware of the pressures faced by people on major programmes, ready to listen and understand problems and keen to help resolve them.

Making changes to processes used by the public also means there can be a lot of people affected (the Pay As You Earn tax process, for example, covers over 30 million taxpayers.) These users, unlike many normal customers, do not have the choice to go somewhere else and buy a competing product. This has implications for how to consult stakeholders and users of government systems in developing and implementing a change. Early on I concluded that an inclusive approach to them was the best way—sometimes the only way—to deliver change successfully (see section 3).

ii   Where Do You Start the Change?

Most of the change I have experienced had its genesis in a broad need to improve performance, usually doing more for less. With a general challenge like that, where do you start?

There are many ways to change an organisation—for example, redesign the processes, increase the levels of automation, change the culture, and reorganise the structure. Each has their merits. Sometimes it is obvious which aspect most needs improving—and there is a general appreciation that it needs to be tackled first. But often the business challenge is less specific and there is scope to consider where first to focus any change. In that situation, with the benefit of hindsight, I would start by looking at the processes (and products)—because they are the core of what the organisation is about and the easiest place to achieve real, lasting benefits.

Process Redesign

Process redesign can be large scale, big picture, top down; it can be small scale, limited impact, bottom up; and everything in between. Some organisations have been successful in inculcating a culture of continuous process improvement which has the added benefit of achieving greater staff engagement. I have seen this done very effectively in the 1990s under the TQM (Total Quality Management) banner (for example in Toyota and Nissan in Japan) and in recent years in the UK—under regimes which combine lean process improvement with a linked focus on culture change and leadership improvement. Unipart (in Oxford) has been a successful private sector proponent of this approach and HMRC's Pacesetter programme has been a good, externally recognised, public sector success. I have seen many examples where our HMRC front line teams working under Pacesetter have not only made significant improvements in performance but have also become much more engaged as a result. It was always inspiring to meet the people involved and hear them describe what they had achieved. For this approach to be successful though, we found there has to be real, visible senior buy-in, and it has to be sustained over many years to get the best out of the initial investment. The results we achieved in HMRC were impressive both in terms of business improvement and staff engagement.

I have also experienced very useful benefits from shorter-term process improvement exercises, perhaps lasting between six months and two years. We found the best formula for doing this was a mixed team made up of three groups of people: national experts in the specific process (for example Pay As You Earn tax), specialists in process redesign (people skilled in how to tackle process redesign, perhaps external consultants), and front line staff (who, of course, have the knowledge of how things really happen, what works, and what doesn't). Each group was essential to the success of the exercise, and we achieved significant improvements in the performance of PAYE in this way.

Once you can see the way forward in redesigning a process, you can consider changing other dimensions—adapting the IT support, looking at the culture and reorganising the structure—and probably in that order. Sometimes though, there are greater imperatives which override this approach. Taking paper processes online (for example tax returns) is an example I have experienced. In this case, the main driver for change was the need to remove vast amounts of paper processing, storage, and retrieval by moving the process online. But we sought to maximise the benefits by doing this in tandem with a thorough review of the process and customer experience to best exploit the new opportunities presented. An example is in section 3.

Structural Reorganisations and Mergers

Reorganising the structure is often the first response to a perceived problem, and at times I have witnessed somewhat greater enthusiasm for structural reorganisation than for reforming the underlying processes or working culture. This may be because a structural reorganisation is easier to envisage—the change and the outcome can be illustrated in a simple diagram, and it all seems pretty clear and straightforward. So people are drawn to it as a first option. By contrast, process redesign can be less easy to envisage and the outcomes less easy to describe—so it is more difficult to get excited about at the outset.

In some cases, structural reorganisation is the right answer. But alternatives should be considered first, because, in addition to the easily quantified costs (of moving around people, equipment, and IT), there are considerable costs which may not be so apparent on the surface. *One* of these is the time taken for people to become effective in their new roles, learn the work, learn to work with new colleagues, and build relationships with them. *Another* is the breaking of links between different parts of the organisation. Large complex organisations sometimes struggle with internal signposting and people develop, over time, a personal knowledge of who they need to contact in their everyday work. Reorganisations struggle to capture these essential links, and the new people often have to rediscover them from scratch—which is doubly difficult if the roles themselves have also been changed. This is all human capital and rebuilding it takes time; in the interim, performance can fall.

Merger is a more radical form of reorganisation which can also be the right solution and produce long-term advantages. The two mergers I have experienced certainly were and gave benefits for both the government and its customers. But before setting out on this route, it is worth considering alternative ways of achieving the same goal. Merging two organisations probably means tackling, at some point, the integration of IT systems, processes, staff groups, HR terms and conditions, accounting processes and systems, brand and culture on top of the costs of any equivalent internal structural reorganisation. It is difficult stuff and requires the best people in the organisation to make it happen. As a result, there is a large opportunity cost. Many government mergers have a further degree of challenge in that their underlying processes are set in law. The different legal systems being brought together may have different foundations and a different definitional structure. So patience is required, as there may be limits on what can be achieved in the short term.

iii   The People Involved in Change

The Value of Good Management

One of the welcome trends I have witnessed over my career has been a greater appreciation of the need for good leadership and a professional approach to management (including the management of change).

Management was not a career specialism when I joined the Civil Service in the late 1970s. Management roles were often combined with professional roles in a single job. For example the senior person (called the District Inspector) who led a local Tax Office (which was then responsible for all the taxation in a particular geographic area) would combine their management (of some 75 to 150 staff) with personal casework on the tax affairs of the largest, most complex taxpayers. The two areas required different skill sets and could compete unhelpfully for priority.

Over time the balance of importance between professional and management roles shifted significantly—and much greater emphasis was placed on management at all levels. Management became a specialism in its own right.

People were selected for their management potential, trained and developed in some considerable depth, and placed in specific key management roles. For some specialist management roles, for example managing contact centres, specialist managers were recruited from the industry. Today, the management role is much more highly valued; the people holding these roles are judged on their management and leadership ability, helping their team get the best out of their work rather than focusing on their own individual casework. At the same time, people in professional roles can better focus on developing and practicing their specialism. The resulting performance of our organisation[2]—its responsiveness to change and its professionalism—strengthened significantly over the years as a result.

Care is needed though in the transition, and this example illustrates that. I mentioned earlier that the leaders (District Inspectors) of Inland Revenue's local offices held a combined management and specialist role. Under the Area Management change programme in 1999, several tax offices were grouped together under a single Area Director (who focused mainly on leadership and management) and the District Inspector role was abolished. The former District Inspectors who did not become Area Directors in the new structure were redeployed to a pure tax specialist role, giving a welcome boost to the senior resource we deployed to counter tax evasion and avoidance. They were the people most personally affected by the change. Their roles changed significantly as did their status. Conscious of this, we tried to be careful in helping them through the change and in valuing them in their new specialist roles. Most of them had been in the organisation many years, so the change was a particular wrench and that was undoubtedly a difficult period for them personally. And yet, with support, most of them set about tackling their new roles very positively and made the transition well.

Leadership

The value of good leadership has also become better recognised in the public sector. All management roles require an element of leadership but the balance varies. Recognition of the importance of the leadership component has grown significantly over my career in government and much greater emphasis is placed on this now.

Books have been written on what constitutes good leadership. There is no single definition. Setting direction, setting the tone, and setting an example are important components—and there are many more. The many successful leaders I have seen (inside and beyond government) have shown a huge variety of personal qualities—there was no single blueprint for success; and in fact there were only two qualities I could see that they all held in common: *first* was the ability to look forward and envisage the future, even when current pressures crowded in, and the *second* was having more energy than anyone around them.

Managing and Leading Change

The government-preferred model for managing change developed, over time, a number of senior roles which require leadership and management skills—but in different proportions. Large programmes now have a Senior Responsible Officer (essentially the sponsor or owner), who is accountable for the success of the programme and a Programme Director, whose role is to ensure delivery. Both roles require people who can both lead and manage. The balance is different though, with the SRO concentrating more on looking forward and outwards and the Programme Director focusing more on the specific management of delivery. I found this division worked very well for the larger programmes I led. The appreciation in government of the demanding nature of these roles on major programmes has also grown in recent years and, as a result, the people going into them are much better prepared and supported.

The place in the organisational structure where change is managed from has also varied. Inland Revenue's model in the early 1990s was to manage it from separate teams, for example a Change Management Division, where the line of command was outside that of the day-to-day business, even at executive board level. But I have also experienced change managed from roles with combined responsibility for both today's business and change, at all levels. Both models can be made to work. Using a separate external team gives an undivided focus on change but runs the risk of winning little buy-in to the change programme from the team running the current business—because they don't experience much sense of ownership, and it feels as though change is being done to them. Using the alternative model of combined current business/change roles gives a much better chance of acceptance of the change but runs the risk of less change being achieved—because when there is a clash of priorities (for management attention or resources), the immediate day-to-day problem usually wins out. The most successful model I have seen is one where major change is carried through by a dedicated leader and team—but where the links with the team running the current business are positive and strong, with a common line manager who sets an inclusive approach as a priority for their two teams, and the current business feels a real engagement and say in developing the change.

Senior Teams

That of course requires senior teams to work well together. How do you achieve that? The starting point is not always promising, as many people in senior teams will have got to their present position through some degree of single-minded pursuit of their or their own team's goals.

Sometimes you have the opportunity to pick a senior team from scratch. But those situations are rare. Usually the leader's role is to get the best out of the people already there—and this is a good test of leadership ability.

How easy is it to build a strong senior team? One key factor is the degree of common purpose. If there is little or no common purpose or goal for the team—which is a collection of people of similar but independent inter-ests grouped together—then team behaviour may be less needed and it is certainly more difficult to achieve. These situations do exist—I have been a member of some—and it is worthwhile recognising the reality and not spending too much time trying to produce something that is not really needed. Focus instead on finding elements that benefit from a common, cor-porate approach and work on them to build the team.

A good example of this was when I was one of a team of senior direc-tors whose work responsibilities were close but had little or no day-to-day interdependence. The need to play as a team was more important for the long term and as a signal of the desired behaviour to the rest of the organisa-tion than in achieving immediate business outcomes. Although this was not fertile ground to produce a high-performance team, our senior manager did achieve this—through a range of methods. *One* was setting a clear expec-tation that we would behave as a team—and support and encourage each other. That was written into our performance agreements. *Another* was looking for a common purpose which we would work together on—in our case, this included the need to develop our top-150 people. Instead of doing this separately in our individual directorates, we worked on this together, running joint workshops, action learning groups, and so on—developing our top-150 people as a single group in a single coordinated exercise. A *third* was carrying out our own personal development together, as a senior team, including our team leader herself (which was brave). This was sustained over several years and so progressively became the norm.

Senior Change Teams

On a major change programme, the common purpose and interdependency within a senior team should be much more evident as should the benefits of working closely together. So the starting point for the senior team play-ing together is that much stronger. But there will always be the need for the leader to encourage collaborative and supportive behaviour.

If you do have the luxury of recruiting a change team, there are several factors I would look for in addition to the necessary skills and experience.

The *first* is to look for people who can be relied upon to deliver, however big the challenge. Programmes usually require an outcome in a given time and are an unforgiving environment in that respect. So your key team needs to be people you know can deliver—people who are driven, as you probably are, and who do not entertain failure as an option.

Attitude to slippage is a good test. Small slippages quickly grow into big delays, and the culture of accepting them can quickly become the norm—so your approach to them is important. We once had a Programme Director on an outsourced programme whose "back to green" approach (how they got back on track when slippage had occurred) was to re-baseline the programme timetable with the slippage consolidated. It took a little while to convert him to the practice that "back to green" meant recovering the original timetable.

The *second*, linked to achieving the first, is to recruit people who are resourceful, innovative, and creative in solving problems. This was an important element in the successful delivery of Self Assessment online and Real Time Information for PAYE. My Programme Director there (and the team we recruited round him), apart from never entertaining the idea of failure, was incredibly resourceful in finding ways round apparently intractable problems—both from his own knowledge of our business and his ability to find and involve others with an innovative and creative contribution.

The *third* is about your own personal attributes and self-awareness. As I progressed through my career, I better understood my real strengths and the areas I was less strong in. It's useful to recognise these when selecting people to work with you; and I tried to complement areas where I am less strong with the people I recruited to my team.

Having chosen your team, I think it is very important to take a real supportive interest in the careers of each of them, making time at the outset to understand their aspirations and concerns, reviewing their progress and development periodically—and not letting it get crowded out by day-to-day pressures. They will undoubtedly be giving you 150 per cent commitment and they deserve your interest, encouragement, and support.

Involving Key People at the Beginning of a Change

Current models of the early growth of our universe envisage a period of very rapid expansion in the first few billionths of a second. The early stages of a change programme feel very similar. Once the business case is agreed and the preparation for the programme is complete, it moves off and expands at the outset very quickly. Two areas in particular can create long-term problems if not addressed effectively for this period. The first concerns *what* is to be done, the second *who* is to do it.

The what. When a new programme is envisaged, an organisation may need to commit to it (or not) fairly quickly. And while a thorough review will normally be conducted, it is not always practicable to go into every last detail at that point. A decision to commit has to be taken relatively quickly. But new programmes are often conceived in a strategy (or in government, sometimes a policy) environment rather than a practical delivery environment. It is important then to involve in the initial decision-making process the (experienced) person who will lead the programme as Programme Director if it does go ahead. His or her practical delivery experience brings three particular strengths—knowledge of aspects that might be difficult or costly to deliver, the ability to spot opportunities that may otherwise be missed, and knowing who to involve to resolve these issues. Knowing that you yourself will be leading the programme also brings a particular focus to this task. Experienced Programme Directors are usually in short supply and difficult to free up from the programmes they are already delivering. They may seem an expensive luxury at this early point. But their contribution at the earliest stages can be crucial.

The who. Once a programme is given the go-ahead, it will often start with a very small team—aiming to grow as the work increases. The work actually increases very quickly indeed in the early stages and programme teams can rapidly become stretched. Yet in many organisations, staff with the experience and the aptitudes needed on large change programmes are in short supply, and HR processes can seem very slow in finding and releasing them—against the accelerated timescales experienced by people working on programmes. Having learned this lesson early, I have subsequently tried a number of remedies. The best is to try and envisage at the outset the team you think you will need at points in the future, have a recruitment plan to match, and make sure you start the process for each role in good time—which is often well before the need for that particular role is apparent on the ground and so can be difficult to sell to colleagues as a priority against other more immediate pressures. Change is much more a way of life in large government organisations now, and this challenge is much more widely appreciated so help is often available, but it can still be a significant issue.

3   AN INCLUSIVE STYLE OF IMPLEMENTING CHANGE

I learned the value of an inclusive approach early on in my career, seeing both the difficulties that can arise if change is planned by a small group behind closed doors and the advantages of working beforehand with groups of people that might initially feel threatened by the change.

An inclusive approach to managing change therefore became a personal priority. It offers many advantages: wider involvement in the development phase can produce a better design by surfacing earlier potential problems and opportunities; inclusion can win the support of various groups affected by the change process that is going to impact on them; and when you get to implementation, it can provide valuable allies who may make the difference between success and failure.

But the inclusive approach requires effort, and it has to be sincere. Effort because it is time consuming and sincerity because you can't just go through the motions of listening to stakeholders: you have to be prepared to respond to them and that means at times adopting their suggestions—which may not be what you originally had in mind.

If an inclusive approach is followed, who should be "included"? In many of the changes I was involved in, there were usually three broad groups of people to be considered: the customers (in our case, taxpayers) who use that particular system, the relevant staff in the organisation (who also use it), and the people (some on outsourced teams) who contribute to delivering the change.

It is easy to say you want to be inclusive. How do you achieve that among customer groups, who are affected by the change, spread across the UK? How do you achieve that in a large, multilayered, geographically dispersed organisation? What is the best approach with outsourced contracts?

An Inclusive Approach with Customers

Thinking first of customers, here is an example which illustrates the approach I adopted. It was clear to me that an inclusive style was essential when I was asked to lead a major upgrade of the process of submitting Self Assessment tax returns online. This was to be a £100 million plus change programme involving a substantial investment in infrastructure with the aim of transforming a complex paper-based process to one that is online. Every year, about ten million people have to complete a Self Assessment tax return, accompanied in the case of self-employed people by their accounts for that year. In 2006, most people still submitted their returns and accounts on paper and HMRC wanted to significantly increase the proportion who submitted online. Over half of these returns are completed for taxpayers by an accountant or tax agent, so this was a key group to win support from. Unfortunately, that group had only recently very publicly fallen out with HMRC over other plans to change the Self Assessment process and although these plans had been withdrawn, the relationship with tax agents remained pretty strained. I couldn't see us succeeding with the new programme unless we got them onside at the outset.

This is how we went about it. Tax agents mainly belong to one of six different professional associations, and we approached their leaders to ask whether they would work with us on the programme. The response was positive (because they wanted to be involved in something that affected them all), but they felt we needed to rebuild trust and demonstrate to their profession at large that we were genuine in wanting to work with them and listen to their needs and concerns.

The opportunity soon arose. Our framework for the new service involved building a more robust and easier to use online tax return. The tax return is a long and complicated document. Every tax agent submits large numbers of these in the peak filing season, so the new service had to work well for them from the outset. We therefore had an enhancement budget to make improvements to help achieve this. To find out agents' priorities for improvements, the agents' leaders on the Joint Working Party (that we had established with them) wanted to canvass and poll all the UK's 50,000 plus tax agents through their weekly journal, read by almost all in the tax profession. But they didn't want us to run the survey. They felt there would be a better response if they led it themselves. We could see obvious risks in agreeing to this but also some real advantages in terms of buy-in to the process. So we went ahead. After the survey poll, the agents' leaders met us and presented a large resulting list of desired improvements. Somewhat troubled, we said we could probably only afford to build about five or six of them. Their response couldn't have been better. "We know you can only afford a few improvements but we want to be involved in choosing the 5 or 6 you can afford."

This was the start of what became a very productive relationship, and the key for their part had been our agreeing to their canvassing their profession (rather than doing it ourselves). In addition to the Joint Working Party (which I chaired myself, because of the importance of the relationship to us), we involved agents in other ways: I invited two of them to join the programme board on a personal basis. They were able to take a full part and saw all internal programme papers. Their judgement and contributions in this environment were seminal in helping us work through the many challenges. We also built a number of personal links and all of the contact enabled us to build up two-way trust.

Conversations weren't always comfortable, but over the following three years we built a strong relationship with them; and the high involvement of the tax agents was a key part of our success. On many occasions they took the lead in suggesting workarounds to potential problems. They also acted as an essential two-way channel between the 50,000 plus tax agents around the country and our programme team—surfacing and helping resolve potential issues and more generally reassuring the agent community that they were being listened to. Together we ran workshops to optimise the design and (as implementation approached) roadshows in most parts of the country to introduce local tax agents to the online process and listen to their concerns and issues. The involvement of agents' leaders in fronting these events themselves was a key factor in their success.

The new Self Assessment online programme was delivered on time and worked well from the outset. The numbers submitting online increased significantly year on year and currently over 95 per cent of tax agents' Self Assessment returns (and over 80 per cent of all Self Assessment returns) are submitted online—which is remarkable given the complexity of the tax return. The active positive involvement of the tax agent community was a key element in that.

An Inclusive Approach with Outsource Suppliers

The inclusive approach also needs to be practiced *internally* within the organisation both with those leading the change and with the staff and managers affected.

Thinking first of the change team itself, a large programme will often involve components to be built by other organisations (outsourced in some way). That applies for example to IT where government had outsourced most of its IT provision to the private sector. And they in turn further sub-contract specialist elements. I have experienced two broad approaches to managing these relationships in large change programmes. One is a contractually based, arm's length approach; the other is full involvement in the programme team and board. (The inclusive approach needs to be accompanied by an open-book relationship so that the supplier is not able to exploit the partnership.) The inclusive approach seemed to build much greater commitment to the change from the supplier. It also clearly provided a much better framework for dealing with the issues that can often arise on a large complex programme.

I had watched, in other organisations, situations where problems in the development of large outsourced programmes organised on an arm's length basis led to disputes and the inevitable souring of relationships—which in turn became major occupations in their own right, sapping energy and morale—all resulting in late delivery and the associated problems for the business.

By contrast, the inclusive approach has driven the teams involved to work together to resolve issues and problems. A good example from programmes I led was in building a major new IT system for a modernised tax process. The IT supplier had initially quoted a price which had formed the basis of the programme case and approved budget. Once underway, their detailed design work revealed issues not previously apparent (and which could not reasonably have been foreseen) with a cost some 20 per cent higher. We simply could not afford that. Nor could we de-scope to any significant extent. One approach we could have taken was to insist on the original price. But that was unrealistic for the supplier and meant we would have entered a complex contractual dispute; and as a result we would probably not have delivered the IT we needed in the time available. Instead, we approached the problem using a partnership approach with an agreed formula for sharing any eventual cost overrun. A joint team was constructed to review the business and IT designs and to look for ways to reduce cost in a collaborative manner. By working together to a common purpose, they were able to identify elements in the business design which involved very high IT cost but relatively lower business value—redesigning these had little impact on the business outcome but considerable impact on cost. The process proved very productive and gradually, over several months, the cost was brought down, eventually dropping slightly below the original quote—a real win-win.

An Inclusive Approach to a Merger and for the Staff Involved

Another aspect of inclusion is the need for stakeholder groups outside an organisation to have a champion within. Large organisations have a lot going on within them at any time, and it is very easy for their focus to become inward rather than outward. For the voice of the external customer or stakeholder to be heard, someone senior inside the organisation needs to act as their informal champion. On major change programmes, if the primary impact is on the external customer, the need for them to have an internal champion is all the greater. That might well be the person in the most senior role in the programme or someone who has their ear directly.

A similar situation can exist in mergers. When two organisations are being brought together, it can be very helpful for each to have a senior champion in the other organisation to give them a voice that is more likely to be listened to during the discussions on how the merger should be effected.

This example of a merger I led illustrates these ideas. In 1998, I was asked to lead a review of whether the Contributions Agency, the body that administered National Insurance Contributions, should transfer from the

Department of Social Security (its then home) to Inland Revenue. The reason for looking at this was that an employee's National Insurance Contributions are collected directly from their employers alongside their Pay As You Earn tax—and there could be benefit for all involved from having it all administered by a single organisation.

I recommended that there was, and it was decided to go ahead and merge the Contributions Agency with Inland Revenue. Personal accountability was always important in our culture, and once the recommendation was accepted, I was asked to back my recommendation and lead the resulting merger programme.

The Contributions Agency had some 8000 staff and the Inland Revenue had over 70,000. We believed the Contributions Agency had much to bring to the combined organisation from its different culture and approach, but there was risk of that being lost in the larger organisation. We therefore set out to run the merger programme in as an inclusive way as possible in order to maximise the benefits as well as to reassure the staff of both organisations—who were inevitably worried about how they would be affected.

This involved us in two broad strands of activity. The first was about involving people in decisions about their future. It comprised a large programme of joint workshops—each of which involved the relevant people from both organisations working together through one of our many processes and deciding whether or not it should be merged, and if so, when and how best to do it. It was a large undertaking involving over the many workshops several hundred managers and key staff. We sought to run this activity on the basis of an equal partnership so that the voice of the smaller organisation was not drowned out. To achieve this, we needed to build trust between the two groups of people involved at all levels.

To help accomplish this, I as the Inland Revenue Programme Director and my opposite number in the Contributions Agency acted in effect as internal champions for each other's organisations. With the uncertainties people feel during a merger, misunderstandings can easily arise within one or the other organisation and assume undue importance. Our aim was to avoid this by ensuring that each organisation got a fair and sympathetic hearing in the internal discussions of the other, and we worked closely together to achieve this. Key to our success was building an open relationship and a willingness to understand the other's point of view.

We also worked hard at building trust between our immediate programme teams so that we could model the behaviours we wanted others to follow in the workshops and other merger activities. We achieved some considerable success in this and were able to move the merger process forward in a collaborative manner and yet to a tight timetable.

The second strand was a large-scale exercise to communicate both ways with the 70,000 staff involved, spread over hundreds of different sites nationwide. The aim was both to enable everyone to know what was going on and to give them the opportunity to have their views heard and responded to. This involved a variety of media and approaches, as well as a normal Q&A process, a rumour line where people could phone in to ask about rumours they had heard and which we undertook to answer in 24 hours. We held a large number of face-to-face sessions with groups small and large—these were always lively and gave first-hand experience of what people were thinking that day.

Our news bulletins were avidly read by the teams in both organisations. But there were times when we had little of substance to report—reviews were taking place but weren't yet due to report. I learned there that there was still a need to communicate. Silence would easily be misinterpreted by staff who were about to join a new organisation and rumours would be quickly generated. Yet all we were able to tell them at that point was that a particular review was taking place, various workshops were taking place over the next week (say) and would report at a particular time. But front line staff told us that was sufficient: when there was little of substance to report, simply telling them about the process reassured them that they knew what was going on and when they would learn about changes.

Inclusion Takes Senior Time but is Crucial to Success

It is worth saying that an inclusive approach requires considerable investment of time to be successful, and it only really works if the change leaders are committed to the process and involved in it actively. If they are not, it takes too long for important messages to get through to them from outside and the people you are aiming to include quickly become frustrated. In my experience, the investment is hugely worthwhile, opens up new opportunities, helps solve problems, and can be the crucial factor in achieving success.

Change, at the end of the day, is about people and can affect their lives profoundly. Apart from the business benefits, it has to be right to involve those affected in working through how best to make the improvement needed.

4   DOS AND DON'TS

Here are a few short dos and don'ts that I have found useful and tried to follow.

Do at the outset **define the change** you are seeking **in terms of improved performance** and how that is best delivered. Start with the assumption that process improvement is the first place to look and structural reorganisation the last.

Do focus on and **agree what success will look like before signing off** the business case for the change. And keep your focus on that throughout.

Do **involve the person who is to lead the change programme in the initial decision to go ahead.** Aside from the focus that comes from future accountability, that person will bring a wealth of implementation experience to a concept that probably started off in a policy or strategy team.

Do **choose your top team at the outset and get them and other key people in place early.** Projects expand very quickly in the early phases, often outstripping the pace of supporting HR processes.

Do **take a real interest in the careers of your individual team members.** Take time at the outset to understand their aspirations and concerns; make time to review with them their progress and development and *don't* let this get crowded out. This is the least you can do for people who give you 150 per cent.

Do **adopt an inclusive approach** and lead it yourself from the front. Listen to the people who are affected by your change—inside and outside your organisation—and respond to their input. When internal change issues are competing for your time, an inclusive approach may not always seem a priority—but the payback can be considerable and the risks of not doing it are very high. An effective inclusive approach requires empathy on your part.

Do **manage risks and issues.** At the leadership level they often blow up faster than the formal programme process provides for—so you need, in addition, your own informal list, which you work through frequently.

Don't **accept even small delays.** Small delays quickly grow into big ones and their acceptance quickly becomes the norm.

Do **have open and transparent relationships along the supplier chain** both to best engage everyone in the process and gain their commitment, as well as to ensure no part of the chain is hidden from your view.

Do get out and **visit frequently your front line staff and external customers.** This is an important role for leaders. It keeps you in touch with people at the front line, short circuits communication chains, avoids messages getting shaded on the way to you, and lets people see who you really are. It is also useful to get feedback about how your visits were received and learn from that.

Don't **rubbish your predecessor.** Staff will often have a longer tenure than their leaders. Undermining *what* has gone before can say to them that their previous work is not valued or wasn't worthwhile. Undermining *who* has gone before can cut across personal loyalties that have been built up. Better for the incoming leader to say they are building on what has gone before and focus on the future.

Do make time frequently to **think about the future,** however much current issues crowd in on you. If you are the leader, that's a core role. I used to do this thinking at home on a Sunday morning looking out on the countryside over the road to have a different environment and a clear period of uninterrupted time to reflect.

Do **use your time carefully and deliberately.** I once heard Andy Grove, then CEO of Intel, speak about how he had learned to distribute his time according to Intel's strategic priorities rather than in response to day-to-day issues and meetings. Decide for example how much time a month you want to spend with customers, with front line staff, and thinking about the future and timetable all that in upfront.

NOTES

1. Inland Revenue merged with HM Customs and Excise in 2005 to become HM Revenue and Customs (HMRC).
2. Inland Revenue, later HM Revenue and Customs.

14 Developing a Culture
The Balance between Change and Consistency

Sarah Smith

About Aberdeen

Aberdeen Asset Management PLC is a global investment management group, managing assets for both institutional and retail clients from offices around the world.

Our mission is to deliver strong fund performance across diverse asset classes in which we believe we have a sustainable competitive edge.

We've been growing steadily, both through acquisitions and by expanding our own business, since we started out in 1983. We're based in Aberdeen, Scotland, and have been since the day we began.

BIOGRAPHY

Sarah Smith graduated from Aberdeen University in 1999 with a MA in management studies. She has worked with Aberdeen for the last 14 years, beginning her career in the finance sector as a customer services assistant and has held numerous roles across operations from junior to middle manager. Her current role with human resources as graduate recruitment and programme manager has provided a platform for her to build and strengthen the graduate programme but also create an apprenticeship programme along with other talent initiatives. She manages the graduate programme globally, overseeing them in Europe, Asia, and the United States. Sarah holds a certificate in professional coaching practice and is an accredited Insights and NLP practitioner.

Organizations develop around the founding fathers, according to Edgar Schein. The way we do things round here governs whether newcomers feel at home and want to stay and develop. Increasingly, knowledge workers have a personal agenda based on developing a portfolio career, being able to showcase their experience in a variety of roles and relevant experiences. Staying around has ceased to be a desired outcome in their employment aspirations unlike "generation x". So why does Aberdeen have such a high retention rate? Aberdeen and its employees have witnessed many changes throughout the finance sector from advancing regulatory requirements to becoming a FTSE 100 company.

Aberdeen has grown and developed through its people. But it has been careful to ensure that aspiring employees are aware of the Aberdeen culture and are exposed to it in an extended experience over an eight-week period prior to making a commitment.

Aberdeen boasts a unique culture; from its creation, Aberdeen has maintained a flat structure where people and teams are at its core, no individuals are singled out for performance. Aberdeen has a strong entrepreneurial spirit, and employees are encouraged to seek out and improve processes and apply their own ideas. The culture has not been orchestrated or carefully planned; it has grown organically with the company, with the CEO and senior managers leading by example, and is maintained and nurtured by its employees. Having been employed by Aberdeen since 2000, the culture was not part of the induction, no teachings or examples given, it just exists. The culture has grown from employees being a part of a team and able to work with senior leaders on a daily basis. No individual offices are allocated, which results in an open plan office with no segregation of management facilitating the sharing of ideas and problem solving.

Aberdeen's aim is to recruit and promote from within the business before going to market, encouraging employees to move across departments and a divisions, enriching their knowledge and experience in turn. This is reflected in the graduate and apprenticeship models as rotational programmes.

The continually high retention rate demonstrates the passion and loyalty employees have for Aberdeen.

In this chapter, we will examine the way in which this unique culture has been developed and the ways in which Human Resource Development interventions are managed. I will also focus on the graduate and apprenticeship programmes as prospective employees will primarily be employed via this route.

This will cover:

- Recruitment and selection
- The programme
- Introducing a new recruitment pipeline
- Changes in expectations
- Feedback and appraisal
- Change and a growing business

This chapter will also explore a changing workforce whose members increasingly look for a more proactive management style and ongoing feedback about their working lives and their career prospects. In a changing world, some things will change around the company, regulation, client needs, and the employment market for example. By keeping the founders values alive in a global market that means there is a balance to be struck between change and consistency.

Changing expectations in the workforce with regard to reward, work-life balance, and progression opportunity has become a focus of human resources and learning and development departments. Performance appraisal and regular feedback is fundamental to the graduate and apprenticeship programmes as well as for all employees.

With a changing landscape and workforce, how can a culture be sustained and be consistent?

RECRUITMENT AND SELECTION

Since inception, Aberdeen have nurtured young talent and valued graduates. The early 1990s saw the beginning of the graduate programme, a training programme primarily designed for the investment side of the business. Graduates were (and still are) encouraged to explore different areas of the business in order to build knowledge as well as relationships. The UK programme structure has now broadened out across all areas of Aberdeen globally to include the US, Asia, and Europe and covering operations, risk, and distribution divisions also. The purpose is still firmly fixed on learning about the business, local markets, and building relationships within Aberdeen as well as understanding client demand.

The selection process is kept simple, keeping the company culture and values at the forefront. Like our approach to investing, we like to keep things simple and straightforward. No test centres or psychometric testing are used, as graduates have become adept at performing a certain way with the help of guides and tips online, common interview questions and suggested answers and how to act are readily available. A straightforward online application form for the graduate programme is opened once a year, the second and final stage of the application process is an interview.

Aberdeen doesn't favour any one university over another, but we do attend several recruitment fairs in Scotland. Relationships between Aberdeen and Aberdeen University, Robert Gordon University, and Edinburgh University are strong. In addition to attending graduate fairs, we are invited as guest speakers at a number of society events. Aberdeen also has links with universities in England but does not favour one over another. It is important to attract applicants from various backgrounds. Linking with one university restricts the application pool.

As the apprenticeship programme grows, more pupils from additional schools are invited to apply. Like most new initiatives at Aberdeen, a pilot scheme is created where lessons can be learned early without creating a negative impact.

The compulsory eight-week internship for graduates and two-week internship for apprentices allows performance to be measured and the real person to be revealed while the individual explores his or her skill set. We consider this to be a part of the application process.

There is a reliance on existing employees along with human resources to select the best people; we don't use external agencies to employ our graduates or apprentices. Along with the CEO, Martin Gilbert, being involved in the selection process, senior managers as well as past graduates are included in the recruiting. Graduates and apprentices are recruited with the broader business in mind rather than recruiting for specific areas, so it is important to include a variety of interviewers. Human resources personnel conduct the traditional competency-based interview at the same time. Employees included in the selection process are aware of what to look for and will have a breadth of experience within Aberdeen and an awareness of the qualities sought after.

Applicants for the graduate programme are expected to complete an internship before being selected for the graduate programme as a part of the recruitment process. The recruitment and selection process is non-prescriptive, Aberdeen is agnostic in terms of degree disciplines and providers, helping to attract and capture a diverse group of talent. The internship allows candidates to demonstrate how they use their initiative and interact with others. The internship includes all areas of the business from operations, marketing, front office, to risk. Human resources is then able to assess the area that would perhaps suit candidates' the best longer term, utilising their skills as well as suiting their personalities and personal objectives.

Spending time with the interns allows HR and department heads to test ability but also allow the interns to "try before they buy"; the culture does not suit everyone. The stereotypical city image of working twenty-hour days while wearing a pinstripe suit does not match the reality of working for Aberdeen. The flat structure, open plan offices, and good work-life balance (and rarely a pinstripe in sight) is often not what is expected of a FTSE 100 global asset manager.

Interns attend an induction day before joining their teams; the day consists of a welcome from our CEO, guest speakers from the heads of departments, and a variety of icebreakers. The day allows interns to get to know each other also. Although spaces on the graduate programme are limited and the interns are competing with each other, we encourage camaraderie and teamwork from the interns. The interns are introduced to their supervisors and a social event is organised for employees, graduates, and apprentices to meet the new interns. The development of the intern day has been a result of feedback from the interns; we depend on them to tell us what works well and less well.

Following a one-day induction, the intern is seen as part of the team they have been allocated to. They perform daily tasks and are given real work to do; no projects are created specifically for the internship. Being integrated into the team means that the intern has the opportunity to add value and experience what it means to work at Aberdeen; they are then able to make an informed decision before putting themselves forward for final interview.

(turn

The continuous moving trends in recruitment techniques and increased sophistication have not escaped Aberdeen's attention. Simulated work situations and avatar's have become on-trend as well as longer and weightier first-stage, online questionnaire's. Assessment centres remain firm as a tool for recruitment, but the reliance on the recruiter to single out key performers from a short period of performance is not in keeping with Aberdeen's culture. The assessments tend to be driven by highlighting key players, those who take charge and stand out from those around them. Those who prefer not to be the centre of attention but perform well can be overlooked. There is also a danger of those successful candidates being similar in personality and lacking a variety of skills. The unconscious bias of the assessor is also important to consider; involving a spread of interviewers provides a spectrum of interns and, in turn, graduates and apprentices.

Keeping up to date with developments is key, but only those that are relevant and match the values of Aberdeen are adopted. Aberdeen still, however, depends on face-to-face interviews first and foremost, keeping it simple. As interviews are conducted by HR as well as the business, we are able to recruit a variety of personalities, skills, and academic disciplines. The CEO interviews all candidates as a second tier of the interview process at the end of the internship, which adds to Aberdeen's unique style.

The successful interns return the following year for the graduate programme with a group they are already familiar with, having spent the eight-week internship together. The peer support has already been established.

Aberdeen has grown substantially over the past 30 years, but the principles in recruiting young talent remains the same: keep it simple and find people who suit the culture and remain within the business for many years. The number of interns, graduates, and apprentices being recruited has seen a steady increase; and as a young FTSE 100 company, it may be expected for Aberdeen to adopt less traditional recruitment processes and look to outsourcing or buy on-trend tools, but this is not the case. The graduates and apprentices become mainstream employees and recruiters themselves, the buy-in on the process and procedure for recruiting has already been established.

Once selected, our graduates embark on a two-year rotational programme, crossing divisions as well as countries and asset classes to build knowledge and relationships. During this time, they find their skill set and settle into a permanent team. Having a retention rate over 80 per cent gives reassurance that allowing individuals to explore the business and be challenged in different role capacities has proven successful.

THE PROGRAMME

The graduate and apprenticeship programmes are training programmes rather than fast track. As full-time, permanent employees from day one, the graduates and apprentices are classed in the same way as all other employees and receive the same benefits.

All graduates have been interns and received the one-day induction; during the first week as a graduate, they become a part of a further tailored one-week induction. Feedback from past graduates has helped create the most effective induction possible, being refreshed yearly. The induction week prepares both graduates and apprentices and manages for their expectations for the following two years. Not all new graduates will have a financial background, so an introduction to investment is provided along with systems training, guest speakers from within the business, as well as presentations on training and development opportunities for them. The groups are expected to work together and help one another throughout their programme.

In addition to on-the-job training through their department rotations, they are expected to complete industry exams which comply with the regulators requirements but also equip them for future roles as well as career development. Graduates and apprentices, like all employees, are given a great deal of support to aid success. Continuous learning has been highlighted by the graduates and apprentices as being important to them personally. They value the opportunity given to continue learning.

The learning and development team (as part of human resources), is responsible for the programme and the development of the individual, providing soft skills training as well as personal, support such as coaching and mentoring.

Rotation supervisors also provide feedback on the development needs of the individuals, and this will be covered later in the chapter.

INTRODUCING A NEW RECRUITMENT PIPELINE

Most recently, Aberdeen identified an alternative pipeline while performing employability skills workshops in schools and launched a modern apprenticeship programme which provides the same opportunities as graduates but for school leavers.

More commonly, pupils are looking for employment straight from school in order to avoid student debts or believe that further education is not for them.

School leavers are being offered an alternative route to higher education by a variety of business sectors called a "Modern Apprenticeship". Apprenticeships, traditionally associated with trades such as joinery, plumbing, and mechanical work have crossed over to the business world. The modern apprenticeship came under fire as they were being viewed as cheap labour by some organisations, offering minimum wage (and often unpaid) with no vocational qualifications offered, often with no employment offered at the end of the programme. Although I am sure that these issues still exists in some organisations, more guidance and benchmarks are offered to help businesses set up a successful apprenticeship. Support and funding is offered by local authorities and organisations, such as Skills Development Scotland for vocational qualifications. Providing high-quality training that benefits both apprentices and employers is key to an apprenticeship. This is an opportunity for businesses to grow their own talent, so it pays to invest heavily and early.

With youth unemployment at an all-time high, Aberdeen was able to provide opportunities as well as grow new talent.

The Commission for Developing Scotland's Young Workforce was established by the Scottish government in January 2013. The commission was chaired by Sir Ian Wood and the purpose was to make recommendations on how young people can make the transition into employment. Aberdeen provided information on our apprenticeship programme and remains committed to not only continue providing employment opportunities to young people but to maintain strong relationships with schools in order to educate on employability skills as well as opportunities available.

The Aberdeen apprenticeship programme is designed to be an alternative to university, open to those with university grades, and provides opportunities to learn with on-the-job training as well as study for professional qualifications. Pupils are offered a two-week internship where they follow the same recruitment process as the graduate programme interns.

The apprenticeship programme began as a pilot, like so many of Aberdeen's new initiatives, and has become a mainstream offering; it follows the rotational programme model and is at present based in the UK only. We opened the opportunity to seventeen and eighteen year olds (in their penultimate and final year of school) but only recruit pupils who have finished their last year. By encouraging penultimate year pupils to apply, they have the opportunity to spend a second period in the summer to try a different department and apply to be interviewed for the programme. An understanding of the working world often comes from parents and family members, and they will rarely have first-hand experience of what an office looks like. It is important that the pupils experience what working life will be like for them and meet the people they will be working with. In our experience, the individuals feel much more comfortable with what they are applying for, and it helps to alleviate any worries they have about fitting in.

Now in its third year, the programme has proven to be a success, with all apprentices to date securing permanent roles within Aberdeen. An increase in demand for apprentices has created job opportunities and increased interest within local schools.

Having a recruitment pool at hand, Aberdeen very rarely recruits outside of the graduate and apprenticeship programmes and has always encouraged internal movement first and foremost. Our young talent learns from those around them and carry the culture with them. They grow and develop and pass their knowledge to the next generation.

CHANGES IN EXPECTATIONS

It feels as though the days of being enthused to spend an afternoon filing or reorganising the stationary cupboard for brownie points are long gone.

Being one of the MTV generation, I spent a good deal of my summers cleaning out cupboards and mass filing without any complaint in order to impress and get noticed. We now live in a much more efficient environment where files are electronic; we are working in paperless offices and stationary is ordered "just-in-time", consuming less space. This generation are problem solvers, and they want to help make practices faster and more efficient.

The stereotype of Generation Y and the Millennials not being loyal or willing to pay their dues is not one I agree with. It is how we adapt our own management style to get the most out of these generations that count. In my experience, any task with a clear purpose and feedback on performance will provide lessons to be learned and a sense of satisfaction.

Having graduated with a sense of purpose and a drive to make a difference in the business world, I was confused about why my SWOT analysis of reorganising the stationary cupboard or applying Porter's Five Forces to the file reconciliation were not more appreciated. The expectations I had graduated with were out of kilter with reality, and it took some time to realise that the business tools I had been armed with were not useful at this early stage in my career. I had to learn how to use systems I had never heard of and take minutes in meetings noting half the acronyms and abbreviations only to research their meanings afterwards with great discretion. I couldn't admit that I didn't know what they were talking about. I had a degree after all.

The first thing our interns, graduates, and apprentices are told is that there are no expectations for them to know anything, they are starting a new chapter in learning. Expectations are set early in terms of working hard, asking questions, and being sceptical. Aberdeen looks for sincerity, work ethic, and loyalty, none of which can be found on an academic transcript. Qualifications are not irrelevant but a base unit to be built upon. The qualities that we look for in an applicant have not changed over the past 30 years. In addition to those mentioned earlier, curiosity, cynicism, flexibility, and being a team player are ranked highly. These qualities are present in all of our employees and not reserved purely for our graduates and apprentices. Aberdeen views these individuals as the future of the company, and they are nurtured to become the leaders. All employees play vital roles on a day-to-day basis, as well as during acquisitions, for example, and graduates and apprentices are no different. Many of our past graduates are in senior positions heading up countries and departments, and we expect our apprentices to aim for the same degree of success. The experience, knowledge, and relationships built during their many years with Aberdeen equipped them with the vision to move the company forward. This extends to all staff where movement across divisions and internal promotion is encouraged and priority.

FEEDBACK AND APPRAISAL

Aberdeen has the same expectations of apprentices as they do graduates, having left school with little expectations of the world of work but with the same desire for purpose and an even bigger thirst for feedback, the more constructive the better.

Appraisals are seen as a chance to reflect on performance but to set objectives over the coming year, taking into account the company vision, values, and future objectives as well as individual. Core competencies are chosen by department heads for employees to be graded on, "change management" being a core competency. The culture at Aberdeen, as previously mentioned is entrepreneurial in nature, and managers adopt their own management style, therefore appraisals and feedback are adapted to fit the receiver. The standardised appraisal form provides consistency across the global business, while allowing employees and managers to set goals together. Competency, development needs, and objectives sit at the centre of the process.

Graduates and apprentices are part of the annual appraisal process but also receive monthly one-to-one meetings to assess performance. Feedback is vital for growth; constructive feedback is welcomed by graduates and apprentices, as they are keen to learn from experience and openly talk about what they can improve upon. We have seen that our apprentices and graduates seem more interested in what they do less well in order to improve than in praise for a job well done. Feedback from those they work with on a daily basis provides context when applying to competencies. As mentors and managers, we look for continuous development but also provide guidance and support. Expectations of our graduates and apprentices are high; we invest heavily in their development so concerns are addressed early.

Teams who host a graduate or apprentice are aware of the expectation and need for constructive feedback and provide it formally. Aberdeen also expects graduates and apprentices to offer feedback on their experience within the team and department which is fed back to them. This ensures that the graduates and apprentices are getting the most out of their experience and human resources is able to manage their expectations on workload and responsibility.

As well as on-the-job training, the learning and development department provide opportunities for continuous personal development (CPD). Training courses cover a variety of topics, including time management, project management, presentation skills, as well as providing mentors and delivering coaching. All employees, including graduates and apprentices, are expected to develop their soft skills throughout the year. The suite of training is provided throughout the year by internal and external providers.

CHANGE AND A GROWING BUSINESS

Through numerous acquisitions and organic growth, Aberdeen has experienced a number of transitions which have brought the challenge of integrating staff into a unique culture. With a high retention rate, legacy Aberdeen staff are experienced in coping with these changes and in turn able to help new staff integrate. Adapting to change is therefore a skill that most AAM employees are proficient in. Graduates and apprentices are exposed to the variety of tasks undertaken by each department during such a transition, and the knowledge travels with them during their programme and onto their permanent roles. They are then able to share and apply their learned knowledge. They are also able to assist those who are perhaps experiencing the changes for the first time.

Keeping up to date with the changing landscape of the finance industry and increased regulation demands immediate reaction and adaption from Aberdeen's workforce. HR is able to plan strategically around this, which is made easier by the view that change is part of everyday life for Aberdeen employees.

Because of the rotational structure of the programmes, the individuals are able to spend four months concentrating on one area of the business; for example, it is vital that our graduates learn the importance of having a risk division. Having an understanding and knowledge of regulations, how we comply with the regulator, and the risks to Aberdeen as well as our clients can only be advantageous.

During acquisitions, many changes can take place from systems and processes to department restructures. Employees of all levels are familiar with the lifecycle of the acquisition process and involved in the work undertaken; teams become equipped to plan and strategise for the process. Although each acquisition is unique, teams are already aware of the demands and expectations and can plan accordingly. The team culture assists in this preparation; the responsibility of the project is spread and graduates and apprentices included with a high level of support for learning.

We acquired Prolific Financial Management from Scottish Provident, which made us a UK top-10 unit trust manager.

In contrast, in 2003, Aberdeen saw the major sale of UK retail unit trusts to New Star, bringing the company £87.5 million but causing a number of redundancies, myself included. A high number of those who left Aberdeen have returned, which demonstrates how well the process was executed and how highly Aberdeen is thought of as an employer. For me personally, I was overjoyed to return to Aberdeen, and due to the high level of communication regarding the reasons for job losses, I understood why it had happened. This took place six years after the company became a UK top-10 unit trust manager and acquired an international equity and bond manager in 2000, creating a recruitment drive.

Employees remaining within the business saw friends leave and a new chapter of Aberdeen begin. Becoming a FTSE 100 for the first time in 2012 is testament to Aberdeen's resilience and, I believe, staying true to its values and its people.

SUMMARY

People are at the heart of Aberdeen's culture, but it does not suit all people or organisations and is not a prescription for success; it demonstrates how a culture can be sustained through change.

Keeping the recruitment process simple and straightforward matches the investment philosophy of Aberdeen, stating away from overly complicated processes and language.

Having an open and transparent way of working, Aberdeen employees are able to be led by example by senior management, the culture being fed from the top down. Using apprentices and graduates, Aberdeen has continued to grow their own talent from the company's creation in 1983. Learning about the business is key, training programmes are tailored for the graduates and apprentices, and they have the opportunity to find their skill set while rotating around areas of the business as well as international locations. Aberdeen has grown through many acquisitions as well as organic growth and managing changes depend on employees being adept at adapting to change. By employing young graduates and school leavers, they carry the culture of Aberdeen with them when they rotate around different teams. The feedback given by these individuals is vital to the continuous development of the programmes.

Aberdeen's graduates and apprentices are expected to contribute in the same way as regular employees do and take responsibility for adding value to teams. Constant feedback from both parties, team supervisors and individuals, ensured growth and development of the employee and the programmes.

The changing landscape of the finance sector means that change is regular and often challenging. Aberdeen depends on its people to move the business forward during these changes and successfully managed this for the last 30 years.

15 "Is OD Just a Big Bag of Interventions?"

David Sherrit

INTRODUCTION

The purpose of this chapter is to critically explore whether People and Organisation Development (P&OD) is more than just a "big bag" of interventions used by practitioners in the field. By doing so, I hope to explore several facets of OD from a practitioner's viewpoint.

I aim to do this by addressing the following questions:

- Who am I and my take on Organisational Development (OD)?
- What is Organisational Development and my own definition?
- Who does OD serve?
- How effectively does the field of OD meet the needs of organisations through OD interventions?

WHO AM I AND MY TAKE ON OD

In writing this chapter, I feel it's important that you get a sense of how my view of the field has evolved through my career and what I now do as a practitioner in the twenty-first century. I started working in the field of OD 28 years ago, not having a clue that what I was doing was defined in the field of work we now refer to as OD. I see my career in a couple of ways, defining it by both the industry sector I've worked in and by roles I've performed. In terms of industry sectors, I have worked in the retail sector, the NHS, and, for the last 22 years, the Oil and Gas industry in both service and oil companies. In terms of roles, I have worked as a trainer, internal consultant, team leader, and in manager roles, all in the field of learning and organisational development. The extent to which the journey through these roles has shaped my practice as a facilitator, leadership coach, trainer, team builder, internal consultant, and as a leader of change has been significant. I don't claim to be a jack of all trades but have found comfort in some interventions that have served me well over the years, underpinning my practice and allowing me not only to make a difference to the organisation and people I have supported but also pay my mortgage.

The bulk of my experience as a practitioner has been around the sharp end of people and organisation development, which for me can more typically be referred to as an intervention. It's because of this that I have been drawn to using interventions in OD as a theme to help review the field and critically examine how some of these interventions can deliver results that directly impact the effectiveness and efficiency of large organisations. However, for all the good that a field such as OD produces, there is always a flip side. I intend to explore both the good and the bad.

As a perpetual student of the field, I want to become more aware of the benefits and drawbacks that such a new science or collection of old sciences can contribute in helping organisations and people. By exploring these questions, I hope to create a path that leads from definition to understanding about the field and its application.

In exploring interventions in OD in this chapter, I feel it's important to acknowledge that the field is not just about interventions. There are limitations to using interventions in OD as theme; however, I feel that interventions in OD play a front line role as it's often the first experience a client has of what OD is about. I must acknowledge that a key limitation is that many of the base concepts that allow the field to define itself are not intervention orientated. I will explore this further in the development of my own map of interventions in this chapter.

To assist me in scoping out how I will cover the field using interventions as a theme, I will use the model as defined by Cummings and Worley (2001) (see Figure 15. 1).

Cummings and Worley (2001) see interventions (Figure 15.1) as being able to impact several organisational levels over a range of organisational issues. Despite what appears to be the mechanistic simplicity of the model, Cummings and Worley (2001) have identified five key factors that may support or hinder success around application of interventions.

- Contingencies related to the change situation
- Readiness for change
- Capability to change
- Cultural context
- Capabilities of the practitioner

Their model covers a substantial portion of the field of OD as seen through the eyes of an OD interventionist. I will use the subheadings of (1) Human process interventions (2) Techno- structural interventions (3) Human resource management interventions and (4) Strategic interventions as signposts to mark out the extent to which I will critique the field of OD.

A further limitation of using interventions as a theme is the perception that this may be too wide to appear to be effective as a method to critically review the field. I will therefore not be dwelling on interventions entirely but using them to explore further the concepts as they have emerged. That being the case, I will still lay the foundation by defining interventions and

Figure 15.1 Types of Interventions and Organisational Levels

TYPE OF OD PROCESS	Primary Organisational Level Affected		
	INDIVIDUAL	GROUP	ORGANISATION
Human Process Interventions			
Process consultation	x	x	x
Third-party intervention	x	x	
Team building		x	
Conflict resolution intervention		x	
Large-group interventions			
Techno-structural interventions			
Structural design	x	x	x
Downsizing	x	x	x
Reengineering		x	x
Parallel structures		x	x
High-involvement organisations		x	x
Total quality management			x
Work design			
Human resource management			
interventions	x	x	x
Performance management	x	x	
Career planning and development	x		
Managing workforce diversity			
Strategic interventions			
Integrated strategic change		x	x
Transorganisational development		x	x
Mergers and acquisitions			x
integration			x
Culture change			x
Self-designing organisations			x
Organisational learning and			
knowledge management			

their relationship with the concepts behind them and some of the issues this has presented for the field. I will also aim to explore where interventions sit in the field, definitions and practices of OD.

The ranges of interventions available demonstrate how easy it is to mistake interventions for OD. As I said earlier, this can easily create an image that the field is nothing more than a collection of interventions. So what's missing? I will tackle this question later in this chapter.

WHAT IS ORGANISATIONAL DEVELOPMENT?

"Everything changes, nothing remains without change" (Buddha)

One could speculate that the origins of people and organisation development date back to the time of Buddha. Even in Buddha's time, change was a concept that created perceived imbalance in the way people lived. No matter how safe, secure, predictable, and stable people's lives can be, we will still have to cope with change at points in our life along the way. Change is a normal and essential part of life, yet, ironically, when we're in the middle of it, it feels anything but normal. I feel the field of OD has a role to play in helping individuals, communities, and especially organisations learn how to navigate change more effectively. Throughout my time in the field, I have worked in the realm of the interventions in OD and in some cases delivering the change and in others easing the impact that change creates and more recently actually feeling the change first-hand.

One of the most influential perspectives on managing change is what we fondly call organisation development or OD. Organisation development is a relatively new field of study when compared with other areas of social science, yet it borrows many familiar foundations. Although one could trace the roots of the field back to the early writers on management and organisations, such as Fayol (1949) and Weber (1928), I prefer to think of the field as having its modern roots in the writings and practice of the past 50 years.

In the 1990s and into the twenty-first century, the field can lay claim to exploring other areas such as appreciative enquiry, culture, leadership, etc., and still continues to grow and push its boundaries through evolution and innovation. In recent years the field has been accused of losing its way (Bradford & Burke 2004). Ron Carucci (2003) intimates that the field of OD is at a crossroads where today and tomorrow's leaders of organisations need to see the value of where P&OD can impact organisational efficiency. As he goes on to say, "the big consulting firms are quite successful at rearranging things but we, as OD practitioners, seem to be called in to clean up the mess after they have all left. Is this all the progress we have made"?

As a practitioner in the field, I'm keeping an open mind. I've had first-hand experience where long-term OD plans have brought about significant improvement to an organisation. Conversely, I've been involved in the aftermath when organisations such as IBM, BCG, and McKinsey have met their contractual obligations and moved on to their next assignment. Nevertheless, despite the critical rhetoric I will no doubt create in this chapter, I do see a positive future for the field. The vast majority of organisations refer to people as their key resource and by default the intellectual capital they contribute to an organisation's success is no longer "a nice to have" but a baseline of many organisational values and philosophies.

Already many OD practitioners are growing from a new breed of professionals who, despite not having a strong behavioural science background, can bring a new angle to the profession. The rise in development programmes such as those offered by the Roffey Park Institute, Sheffield Hallam University, and Manchester University offer new opportunities for the field to be seeded from a new bloodline of HR professionals, managers, etc. As Carucci (2003) states, this might be what's needed to "re-boot the field".

MY DEFINITION OF P&OD

Over the last 19 years, I have worked in varying interventionist roles in OD. These roles have been in several different organisations and cultures in a range of different business sectors and during that time several characteristics of OD have emerged in my mind as summing up what it means to me.

TO ME OD IS ABOUT

- People and how they relate to each other and the organisation.
- Implementing and coping with change and in particular assisting the human condition to accepting change.
- Helping the business/organisation survive and prosper through impacting the culture.
- Human resource development and human potential growth.
- Demonstrating how one person can make a difference.
- Unlearning ineffectual behaviours.
- The effective use of interventions as a means to grounding the theory and concepts of the field.
- The long term not the short term.

Comparing my observations with other writers in the field of OD, I have made several observations.

- Writers such as Cummings and Worley (2001), and French and Bell (1995) all state that OD is a long-term process involving change and planned activities associated with cultural impact.
- The same aforementioned writers all make reference to interventions in OD as a means to shaping the organisation. Interventions are seen as a phase, step, or delivery mechanism that brings OD into the heart of the organisation.
- Ulrich and Smallwood (2003) demonstrate the value that human resources can have on the bottom line and what happens if we only focus on the explicit, easy to measure assets, thus ignoring the impact human resource development can have on an organisation.
- Covey (2004) explores the power that one person can have on him or herself and on his or her organisation or community.

In summary, most of the field matches my interpretation of how I view OD, albeit with one exception. The role and value of interventions in OD are somewhat blurred in the field. Although there has been much writing about interventions in OD, there appears to be missing stands of data around its effectiveness and location in the field. Even the word *intervention* can be misinterpreted and appears to have gathered a meaning of its own within the language of OD.

THE VALUES OF OD

In defining OD, I feel it is essential to reference the key values on which the field has been formed. French and Bell (1995) view three key values as having significant roles in creating an identity of the field of OD:

- Humanistic values
- Optimistic values
- Democratic values

Whilst I identify with the values as defined by French and Bell (1995), I sometimes struggle with how well organisations have embraced all three. In my experience as a practitioner, many other factors often drive the need and success of an OD intervention and often rather than complement the three values they actually challenge the foundation on which they are built. The closest I saw in my career to humanistic, optimistic, and democratic values being adopted was in the public sector; however, even in the NHS there were complex hierarchies of power, control, management, staff, and the unions that made this difficult. In profit-making organisations, the same issues exist thus challenging the premise on which these fine values were based.

From these three values, what particularly stands out to me as presenting the biggest challenge to the field are the collective topics that create humanistic values. French and Bell (1995) break down the area of humanistic values through the use of the following descriptors:

- The importance of the individual.
- Respect for the whole person.
- Treat people with respect and dignity.
- Everyone has intrinsic worth.
- All people have potential for growth and development.

One of the areas I will explore throughout this paper is the challenge that modern interventions in OD present around the original humanistic, optimistic, and democratic values on which the field has been built. In particular is the focus on the bottom line. This raises the question of whether or not OD can meet the bottom line and at the same time maintain its value set.

MY MAP OF INTERVENTIONS IN PEOPLE
AND ORGANISATION DEVELOPMENT

As I mentioned in the introduction of this chapter, my entry into the field of OD was fairly typical as an implementer of interventions. Most of my career I've been involved at the sharp end of OD as an internal consultant. As a purveyor of interventions, it's easy to lose sight of the foundations on which these actions are based and purely focus on the client and the assignment. To this end, I have developed my own map of OD using interventions in OD as a theme to help communicate my view of the field.

My map of people and organisation development as represented in Figure 15.2 consists of four boxes. It unpacks the field by looking at the underlying concepts on which the interventions are built in both the areas of people and organisation development.

The aim of the model is to demonstrate the linkage between the concepts, which, in my opinion, define the fields of Personal Development (PD) and Organisational Development (OD) and the interventions. By doing so, I hope to demonstrate the relationship the concepts have with the interventions and how the interventions by design embed the concepts into the practice of P&OD.

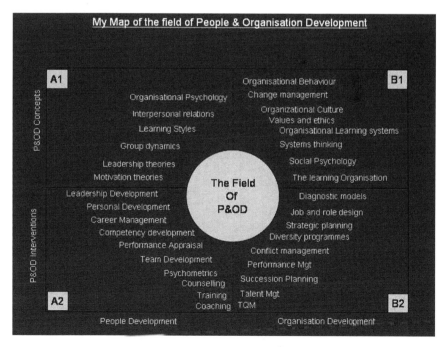

Figure 15.2 My Map of the Field of People & Organisation Development

The separation between the two fields of PD (boxes A) and OD (boxes B) is illustrated through the use of a broken line. This signifies a blurring between the impacts these fields can have on the organisation or an individual. Although I believe that certain concepts and interventions can have a strong influence to impacting only on an individual or the whole organisation, it is important to point out that people interventions can have an impact on the organisation and vice versa. In my experience, most of the organisations I have worked for have focused on the interventions not necessarily realising the complexity of the concepts that support the intervention. As a result of the intervention not being anchored in the base concept, this has in some cases reduced the effectiveness of the desired outcome.

I believe there is a strong differentiation between the concept and the intervention. In the diagram, this is illustrated by the hard line that separates the concepts (A1 & B1 boxes) and the interventions (A2 & B2 boxes). The concept may describe a model or approach that can be used to shape an organisation possibly through an intervention or collection of interventions, e.g. a change management programme.

One of the fundamental areas of misunderstanding is clarity between the definition of what OD is to the client and the role of the intervention. Many of my clients have believed that the intervention is OD. For the majority of clients, their perception of involvement in OD is when they are directly impacted by the intervention or when they deal with a consultant.

This has led me to the following viewpoints:

- There is confusion about who the stakeholders are in OD.
- OD practitioners have the capacity to create the image that the intervention is OD.
- Practitioners do not always understand the base concepts behind the intervention.
- The field may potentially be losing its accessibility to those whom it originally grew to support.
- We have difficulty in seeing the relationship between the intervention and the concept and the impact this can have on the quality of advice provided by OD practitioners.

Marshak (in Wheatley et al. 2003) reinforces my thoughts on where the field is today.

"Today, we have practitioners using interventions without understanding the values they are based on. We do not have practitioners looking for new theory."

We appear to be moving to a market-driven environment where mainstream is more appealing than the margin. In my opinion, Marshak (2003) has seen the impact that customer driven OD has had on the field. This has been demonstrated by the popularity in the use of mainstream interventions such as team building, psychometrics, organisational change models, etc., all seen as a means to quick resolution of what are often very complex people and organisational issues. An example of this is the value that interventions such as Open Space as popularised by the like of such as Harrison Owen and David Cooperidder and today practiced and written about by consultants such as Sue Belgrave (2014). This immensely exciting technique for large-group interventions is sometimes viewed by large traditional organisations as fringe, unstructured, and loose ended. Open Space, for example, works on a premise of emergent change and many organisations want predictability of outcomes as time is viewed as money and these techniques are viewed as indulgent, unstructured, and undisciplined. I of course disagree, having used this to benefit several large groups in my career.

During my time as a practitioner in the delivery of OD based interventions, I have been driven by the definition of intervention effectiveness by Cummings and Worley (2001). Their thinking brought forward three criteria which I feel contribute to an effective intervention.

1. Relevance of an intervention to the organisation and it members.
2. Knowledge of its intended outcomes.
3. Ability to enhance the organisation's capacity to manage change for now and the future—a learning organisation.

Throughout most of my career, these broad definitions of what leads to effectiveness have been instrumental in my values and beliefs around what makes an effective intervention, and, ultimately, a contribution towards organisation development; because without these guiding values, I would be no better than a salesman of a collection of magical tools. I often joke with my team about the word "entertrainment". Of course the word is made up, but what many clients seek is something that in itself is simple, fun to do, and provides learning. As we know through life, not all learning is fun, neither is it simple or easy. In fact, the worst times are often when we have the most focused learning. The question this raises is do we always link the intervention with organisation outcomes?

In recent years I've grown more disillusioned with the effectiveness of interventions as tools for change. Organisations have a need for quick-fix solutions that fit into the time horizon of the financial year. This can appear contrary to the premise on which people and organisation development is built. Evidence of this can be seen in the trend towards fast-moving business cultures driven more and more through the use of hard quantitative measures. As a result, organisations are showing a trend towards "quick-fix" solutions that tend to be expressed in OD terms as interventions. Indications that support these changes are, for example:

- The use of business planning in the public sector.
- The popularity of business tools, e.g. the balanced scorecard.
- The increasing use of real-time technology to record behaviours, e.g. recording of transactions for training purposes in call centres, the

use of electronic measurement of behaviour taken by pilots of commercial helicopters, and the use of quotas by the police to measure performance.

- The increase in democratisation in large organisations, e.g. employee consultative committees, diversity networks, pro-employee legislation.
- The increasing focus on competency at work.
- The use of communications technology, e.g. email, video conferencing, the mobile office.

These changes in organisations have placed greater pressure on the effectiveness of OD interventions to demonstrate return on investment and "earn its keep" and show their efficiency. Are we approaching change any differently than we have in the past? How many companies are still focused on short-term financial goals (because they're clear and measurable) rather than long-term employee engagement (because it doesn't fit in the financial year). It's a battle of profitability versus value-added interventions.

As a result, the field appears to be caught in a struggle to:

- Define clearly what an intervention in OD is.
- Measure the success of an intervention and its impact on OD.
- Cope with the unpredictability of interventions in organisations.

3. WHAT IS AN INTERVENTION IN OD

For the purpose of this chapter, I feel it is important to define the concept of the intervention, pulling together various definitions with the aim of exploring the relationship between interventions and OD. I also intend to share my views on what interventions are in OD and where they are located in relation to the field.

The term intervention has a wide-ranging definition and can mean many things to many people. It can range from a simple question to huge and complex change management programmes over an extended period of time.

"The range of actions designed to improve the health or functioning of the client system" Harvey & Brown (1976).

My view of interventions is based around the following assumptions:

- Interventions can sometimes be hard to define.
- Interventions can be deliberate or accidental.
- Interventions can focus on individuals, groups, subsystems, or the total organisation.
- An intervention is not organisation development.
- Interventions should be relevant to the issue.
- Interventions can emerge from within the organisation.

For me, an intervention is a tool, act, or process that has been identified using a behavioural or scientific approach to reach a conclusion that by application of the intervention can bring about a change that produces an improvement in a system, process, output, or person. An example is how we use data. Is the data that we use to diagnose what is the best intervention, e.g. existing data such as a rise in accidents at work, more complaints from customers, or high staff turnover rates, or is it created data sets such as organisational surveys of interviews with cross sections of the organisation.

The first challenge is how organisations show the application of the OD concept through an intervention that will impact business improvement. The second challenge is to prove the effectiveness of the intervention through evaluation and validate the concept on which the intervention was based. (See Figure 15.3)

My view is that organisations only focus on the first challenge and demonstrate ignorance around understanding and application of the concept. Many factors contribute to this from the competence of the organisation's internal or external consultants, the strength of its leadership to support an intervention, the perceived impact on the bottom line, and finally the sheer trust and hope that an intervention will fix the problem like waving a magic wand. It's similar to what it must be like when we all go to the doctor hoping what is wrong with us will be put right by a simple course of pills rather than a life-changing intervention.

I see interventions as the tools of OD. Without these tools, OD would be nothing more than theory and conceptual models. This belief is reinforced by French and Bell (1995) who define an OD intervention as:

> sets of structured activities in which selected organisational units (target groups or individuals) engage in a task or a sequence of tasks where the task goals are related directly or indirectly to organisational improvement. Interventions constitute the action thrust of organisational development; they are making things happen and are what's happening."

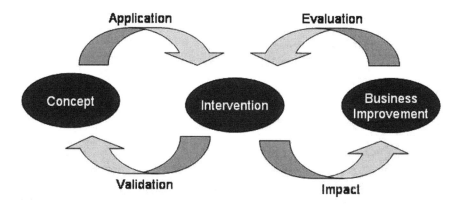

Figure 15.3 An Intervention in OD

French and Bell's thinking does seem to borrow much from earlier thinking in the field from Drucker and Management by Objectives.

My view is that interventions can focus on individuals (PD), groups (PD & OD), and/or the total organisation (OD). In the next section of this chapter, I will explore these areas further and aim to demonstrate the link between interventions and OD.

Albeit the fields are intertwined, interventions in P&OD can be perceived as separate, giving the impression that there are two distinct fields and not one as I presupposed in the earlier part of this essay. Interventions play a significant role in P&OD shaping in many clients eyes the nature of the field.

As referenced earlier in Figure 15.3, the concept and the intervention can sit separately; however, to the client, often the intervention is the concept thus leading to a misconception in basic understanding of what organisation development is.

INTERVENTIONS IN OD

Organisational development is essentially about a planned effort to help people work and live together in an effective and productive manner over a period of time in their own organisation. Hanson & Lubin (1995)

In my opinion, the modern practitioner must be able to communicate on a simple level while appreciating the roots that brought about his or her role in working with these tools and concepts and not profess to be a miracle worker who can cure all ills with his or her magic elixir of interventions. That moves to looking at the role of the consultant.

A more current description as professed by French and Bell (1995) still continues to build on Beckhard's original definition of OD. It gives a clearer picture by anchoring the role of the consultant-facilitator while bringing in some of the concepts, e.g. visioning, empowerment, learning, problem solving, etc., on which interventions might be based.

> Organisational development is a long-term effort led and supported by top management, to improve an organisation's visioning, empowerment, learning, and problem-solving processes, through an ongoing, collaborative management of organisational culture with special emphasis on the consultant-facilitator role and the theory and technology of applied behavioural science, including participant action research. (French & Bell 1995)

Much has been written about the consultant-facilitator role. This body of work is helpful in locating where interventions reside in the field of OD. Over the evolution of the field, there has been movement from the "touchy feely" approach taken by consultants with strong humanist values, to a more bottom-line, return-on-investment focus. I would argue that this has placed more of a spotlight on the interventions in OD as having to provide a return in investment. This in turn has raised the profile of interventions in OD to a level where they are now viewed as essential tools for success by practitioners and clients alike. The volume of consultants who now specialise in one aspect of the field, e.g. coaching, change management, team building, performance management, demonstrates where the field and its relationships with interventions may be heading.

HUMANISTIC VALUES VERSUS THE BOTTOM LINE

More and more I hear the disposable term "soft skills or woolly thinking" used to describe the types of interventions that are driven by the social science aspect of OD; and for many clients, we the practitioners are seen as occupying the space of the tribal shaman. Needless to say, I have often wondered if these interventions, shrouded in a cloak of humanistic intent, actually impact the bottom line.

Evidence of this is indicated in research produced by Ernst and Young (2000).

They have concluded that "the shareholder value model has changed and non-financial performance has become increasingly important" Ernst and Young (2000). In their "Measures that Matter™" investor diagnostic tool, they have demonstrated the link that "soft stuff" can have on shareholder return. Amongst other things, they specifically mention "The Strength of Company Culture", which includes areas of OD, such as teamwork, quality of employee training, incentive performance systems, and social policies. Ernst and Young (2000) identified "a common hierarchy of critical Measures that Matter that analysts and buy-side investors respond to" (see Figure 15.4). Surly this must bode well for the field of OD, especially for those organisations that are driven by shareholder value.

However, picking up a copy of a recent edition of the *People Management* journal, I felt that there is still some work ahead. Strap lines such as "race for the prize", "hire for best results", "turn around a failing department" proliferate through the writings of a professional journal that cohabits the same space in OD as Ulrich and Smallwood.

Linking OD's humanist values to strategy in some corners must be likened to finding the Holy Grail. Change programmes that help position organisations strategically and gain a better fit with the external environment possibly will help demonstrate the value OD can add. Developments in interventions such as integrated strategic change (ISC) and transorganisational development (TD) may herald a vehicle for further pushing the boundaries of the field and thus demonstrate the impact OD can make on an organisations' long-term strategic goals. Cummings and Worley (2001) said, "The choices OD practitioners make in incorporating technology into change management processes will have an important effect on feelings of inclusion, influence, and participation." This area of intervention presents

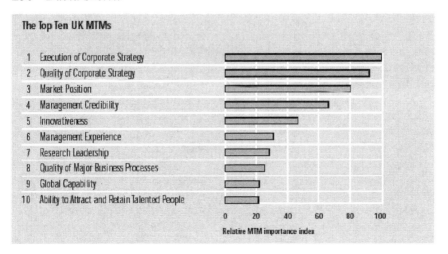

Figure 15.4   The Top Ten UK MTMs

a challenge for OD professionals. Can they prove their effectiveness and value-added contribution in these strategic areas of impact such as:

• The external environment
• Business strategy formulation and shaping
• Organisation and cultural change

If they can impact these focus areas, then surely the value that OD can bring to the bottom line can be interwoven into the fabric of organisational change, building on its humanistic values that deliver to the level of effectiveness desired by many of today's Managing Directors and CEOs.

In concluding this section, I described from my perspective the dilemma facing the field of OD between the humanistic values that appear to be in conflict with the increasing drive for organisational effectiveness. This section has raised the question in my mind of how traditional OD values can coexist with the drive for value and leads me into exploring who OD actually serves.

THE FUTURE OF OD

As P&OD enters the twenty-first century, it exists in a world that, for many reasons, is in turmoil through political, economic, and environmental uncertainty. Wheatley (2003) echoes the uncertainty that exists within the field and its purpose for doing good. How much of the field truly is about the benefit of mankind over profit or politics? Has the individual been lost in the machine of the organisation?

Has Wheatley (2003) perhaps missed the point of a field that is evolving to match the needs of its clients? In a market-driven environment where consultants themselves have a need for economic existence, is this change in the field a natural growth or a disabling feature of a nirvana that was never to be in a capitalist-driven world. Worley (2003) reinforces this thinking by concluding that there are several dilemmas facing the field which may lead change in how it is perceived in the future. They are:

- Globalisation of commerce and work.
- Increased infiltration of technology and in aspects of life.
- A more diverse, educated, and contingent workforce.
- An increase in networked organisations.
- Increased conflicts between positivism and social constructionism.
- Increased conflicts between values of performance versus process.
- Increased conflicts between values of egalitarianism versus concentrated wealth.
- Increased interest in ecological sustainability.

Is Wheatley's (2003) oversimplification of the purpose of OD accurately reflected in the organisations I have worked for or has she avoided the fourth observation that OD is about improvement? Whether that improvement is in safety, profit, personal growth, survival, or renewal, I believe that the missing fourth assumption, that the current purpose of OD is about improvement, has more significance in the twenty-first century than writers are prepared to credit it.

The missing fourth assumption is an area that was not explored until the late 1970s through the work of Porras and Berg (1978) who on exploring this area of research found:

- Little research existed on the effectiveness of OD
- Most of it was of poor quality
- There was a wide range of unsubstantiated beliefs about the efficacy of OD
- Some believe that OD makes only people in the organisation happier
- Others note it may change individual behaviour but not improve the organisation's performance
- Only groups benefited

This work perhaps demonstrates that a field claiming to understand the concepts of planned and emergent change has been perhaps caught off guard and is now playing "catch up". Mitchell (in Wheatley et al. 2003) talks of the field as being "in a mid-life crisis"; he goes on to say that there is a genuine need for effective and competent OD practice. He says if we can learn how to deliver to the market through demonstrating value, we may be able to progress its evolution. I do think this is slowly beginning to change with the increase of OD training programmes, such as those at Roffey Park and Birkbeck College in the UK. Also more and more senior OD roles are not part of an HR function but instead report directly to the senior leaders. These are indicators of slow realisation as to the impact the field can have on business improvement in both the private and public sectors.

I do believe that there are examples of good practice that demonstrate that the field of OD is beginning to figure out how to combine its values with that of value-added return. For example, in my current organisation, the behaviour around safety is viewed as being a key issue that not only attends to basic needs as set out by Maslow (1943) in his hierarchy of needs, but has a major cost impact on the organisation. I would like to illustrate this through case study 1.

Case study 1 is an example of the use of a range of OD interventions used to impact a culture change in an industry where the ultimate cost is the loss of life. This kind of culture change surely embodies the humanist values of P&OD, whilst addressing the economic drivers that create value in the business. In this case study it's hard to prove whether the business

---

CASE STUDY 1

Behavioural-Based Safety at Chevron Upstream Europe Ltd

The behavioural-based safety programme that was introduced to raise the profile of health, safety, and environment throughout the organisation has already demonstrated an impact in reducing safety incidents in its first six months of inception. Over one million man hours of work have been conducted without a lost-time incident or injury. The aim of the programme is to increase the data around avoidable safety incidents in furtherance of "Target Zero". The base belief that had to be instilled into the organisation is that accidents are avoidable. Focus around leaders modelling the beliefs and behaviours associated with this culture change have been essential to embed this culture at the highest levels of the organisation. Interventions used to achieve this have been behavioural interviews, coaching, feedback, psychometric testing, training, employee engagement in design of the programme, reinforcement-based leadership, and regular communication. Further research has shown that this positive impact is not just a demonstration of the Hawthorne effect but is a result of the aforementioned OD interventions. This has impacted both the needs of people in terms of safety in addition to reducing the cost associated with safety incidents as they occur. Much of what had to be achieved was through behavioural change. Most of the focus was on leadership behaviour in setting the role model for employees to follow. A culture of positive reinforcement was created through the use of results based leadership. Ulrich, Zenger & Smallwood (1999)

needs drove the humanist values or whether the values drove the business to change. Whatever the case, the quantitative measures have demonstrated sustainable success in safety behaviours through the organisation and those contract organisations who partner with Chevron.

Now that I have briefly explored the purpose of OD, the next step in this discussion is to identify who owns or serves the field.

WHO OWNS P&OD

The purpose of this section is to explore the impact the field brings to those at the receiving end. To help critically analyse the effects of this impact, one must first identify who owns or influences OD to the benefit or detriment of the client. Additionally I would also like to explore if a win-win outcome is always possible, especially in light of the previous discussion around the challenges between humanist values versus the bottom line.

In exploring the concept of ownership of the field, I am presented with a limitation in this thinking. Is it possible to own something that itself is not concrete in its existence? Perhaps the semantics of the word "owned" may prove a challenge to define. For the purpose of this paper, I intend to use the model in Figure 15.5, as shaped by my own thinking in the field, to assist in the framing of how I view ownership of the field and use it to explore how the clients as defined in Figure 15.5 impact the field of OD.

THEORISTS AND WRITERS IN THE FIELD

During my literature review, it emerged that many of the founding writers of the field are themselves practitioners. I would have thought this would lend itself as an advantage in those practitioners being grounded in the everyday

Figure 15.5 Who Owns P&OD

Aspects of OD		Client
The intellectual and conceptual development of P&OD	Owned/influenced by	Theorists and writers in the field
The practice and interventions of P&OD	Owned/influenced by	Consultants and practitioners
The contracting of services from the field	Owned/influenced by	Organisations and the leaders
The consequences of P&OD interventions	Owned/influenced by	Organisations, their employees and society, the total system

challenges that face large and small organisations alike. On the positive side, the huge volume of publications produced each year push and expands the field by seeding new ideas, sharing experiences, and challenging the current thinking of the day. Surely this is a good thing. However, how much of those consuming this body of knowledge do so with a critical mind? How many of our CEOs and MDs jump on the latest bandwagon having read a paperback on organisational change purchased at their local airport only to return to their organisation and suggest the implementation of what appears in theory to be a cunning plan. In my experience, an example of this phenomenon was the release of Peter Senge's (1990) *The Fifth Discipline.* Many raved about it but in reality struggled to interpret his thinking into practical application until he brought out *The Fifth Discipline Field Book* (1994) that was less conceptual and more applied. Was his act one of genuinely adding to the field or just a clever marketing ploy? I prefer to believe that Senge applied his own thinking in learning theory and, based on feedback from his first publication, created a more accessible piece of work for practitioners who wanted to act rather than reflect.

CONSULTANTS AND PRACTITIONERS

I myself am a practitioner and am the first to admit that as a body we are capable of positively impacting people and organisations, but we are also guilty of myopic, incompetent behaviour. More and more our clients perceive us as a service where value for money and customer satisfaction are the key drivers for success. Perhaps this has come about as a result of the status we have created. Perhaps this is an argument that is located by the complexity of how we work in organisations and the need for a common map to help unpack this thinking. Competence of OD professionals is perhaps another approach that can be used to bridge this gap. The challenge here is that in the industry of OD, many (intervention led) specialists are rising to the surface, e.g. coaching, team building, organisational change, etc. This appears to be market driven by the client who wants an immediate solution. Perhaps the future of OD will focus around intelligent buying of OD expertise and the wider development of professionals entering the field to increase the breadth of understanding.

The internal consultant is driven by the organisational politics and relationships that exist with the strong probability that he/she may become ethnocentric after several years of occupying the same role. Likewise the external consultant may be driven by economic drivers and success measures in addition to the challenge of creating or maintaining a good reputation in the organisations in which they work. I myself have seen this first-hand where the external consultant goes native or, in my opinion, starts to see the world from my perspective. Is this such a bad thing? Surely the simple solution to this is better partnering and alignment of both internal and external to the ultimate benefit of the organisation. I wish this were easy but often external consultants occupy a magic credibility of what is promised when compared with their internal peers.

ORGANISATIONS AND LEADERS

I believe that leadership has a significant role in shaping the purpose of OD as purchasers of OD service and as clients. Leadership at the highest level can define the purpose through the actions taken to shape the organisation towards its vision. This is of course assuming the organisation has a clear vision of where it wants to go. According to Kotter (1999), strong leadership and strong management are key ingredients to the successful management of change.

The leadership within most organisations often holds the budget and purchasing decision authority to employ specialist OD support. As mentioned earlier, leaders/managers are often driven by time and immediate bottom line results. A consequence of this is the need to use interventions that create instant fix solutions. As a further consequence the intervention then gets mistaken as OD.

ORGANISATIONS, EMPLOYEES, SOCIETY, AND THE TOTAL SYSTEM

How much is the field doing to create a positive impact that produces a win-win solution for the whole organisation? Hultman (2003) has observed the negative impacts of P&OD interventions, such as downsizing, right sizing, restructuring, self-management, and automation.

He goes on to say the consequences have been:

- Organisational mistrust
- Worker alienation
- Corporate wrong doings and corruption
- Poor sense of belonging
- Technology reducing social interaction

He believes it's the role of OD professionals to begin to tackle these issues in organisations. By doing so, he sees the whole organisation as this client.

I subscribe to this view and feel that both practitioners and writers in the field of OD have a sense of duty to represent the field and its values in relation to the clients' needs and perceptions. At the end of the day, the field has emerged to service the needs of those who draw on it for the mutual benefit of people, the organisation, and society.

AND FINALLY . . .

In this sections, I will present the key findings I have arrived at while writing this chapter.

1. OD is a field in its own right but borrows from so many other fields of social science which gives it added depth and complexity.
2. Interventions in OD can stand on their own and add value to small components of an organisation but may or may not be a part of a more holistic strategy. Sustaining the value in the intervention is the challenge.
3. Perhaps a drive to creating more informed clients in the space of OD might help the practitioner better frame what the field can do for the customer. This could be achieved by including more about the field in leadership programmes, MBAs, and airport bookshelves. After all, this is an inclusive field.
4. I have discovered that concepts, theories, and practice lie at the heart of OD deployment. Practitioners need to take more responsibility for understanding the roots of theory that directs their interventions. This hopefully will lead to better informed interventions that deliver value.
5. Humanistic values do exist through the practitioners in the field today, but there is a conflict at times between these and the need to create value, especially where profits and targets are a strong element of an organisation's culture.
6. Interventions are in most cases the lens by which clients view OD. We need to keep this at the forefront of our minds as practitioners of the field as we work in large organisations.
7. As a result, I have concluded that the clients' needs and perceptions are critical to the success of OD in organisations and communities. After all, it's because of the client that we exist.

At the beginning of this chapter, I set out to answer the question "Is OD just a big bag of interventions"? To me the answer is no; there is considerably more complexity to the field. However, it is a matter of perspective. Depending on your role, knowledge, and involvement in OD, you may answer this question from a different point of view. One creates this point of view through knowledge and understanding. I have begun to understand the need to push deeper into this knowledge through critique, analysis, challenge, and exploration.

As a student of and a practitioner of OD, I have gained an insight into the academic depth on which the foundations of the field are built. By having improved my understanding of the values contained with the field, I feel this will influence my practice by helping me ground the theories I have explored and provide a deeper understanding to competently apply the appropriate intervention.

To finish, I want to close with a quote that for me sums up how I feel about the field from my perspective as a practitioner.

"An ounce of action is worth a ton of theory".

Fredrick Engels

REFERENCES

Belgrave, S (2014) Large Group Interventions: A Potent Alchemy (159–178). In E Griffin, M Alsop, M Saville and G Smith. Gower: Farnham.

Bradford, DL and Burke, WW (2004) Introduction: Is OD in crisis? *Journal of Applied Behavioural Science*, 40(4), 369–373.

Covey, S (2004) *The 8th Habit*, London, Simon & Schuster.

Cummings T & Worley C (2001) *Essentials of Organisational Development & Change*, Ohio, South Western Thomson Learning.

Fayol, H (1949) *General and Industrial Management* (trans). Pitman: London.

French W & Bell C (1995) *Organisation Development*, New Jersey, Prentice Hall.

Hanson P G & Lubin B (1995) *Answers to Question Most Frequently Asked About OD*, USA, Sage Publications.

Harvey, DF and Brown, DR (1976) *An Experiential Approach to Organization Development*. Reading, MA; Prentice Hall.

Kotter J, (1999) *John P Kotter on What Leaders Really Do*, USA, Harvard Business Review.

Maslow, AH (1943) A theory of human motivation. *Psychology Review*, 50, 370–396.

Porras J & Berg P (1978) *The Impact of Organisation Development*, Academy of Management Review 3(2), 249–266.

Senge, PM (1990) *The Fifth Discipline: The Art and Practice of the Learning Organization*. Century Business: London.

Weber, M (1928) *General Economic History*. George Allen & Unwin: London.

Wheatley M, Tannenbaum R, Griffin PY, & Quade K (2003) *Organisation Development at Work*, San Francisco, Pfeiffer.

Articles

Church A, Burke W W, & Van Eynde D, 1994, Values, motives and interventions of organisation development practitioners, *Group and Organisation Management* 19, 5–15.

Ernst & Young, 2000, *Measures that Matter™—An outside-in perspective on shareholder value recognition*, http://www.ey.com/GLOBAL/content.nsf/UK/CF_-_Library_-_MTM

Porras J & Berg P, 1978, *The Impact of Organisation Development*, Academy of Management Review 3(2), 249–266.

Postscript

Bernard Burnes and Julian Randall

SHARED PERSPECTIVES

> Life can only be understood backwards; but it must be lived forwards.
>
> (Søren Kierkegaard[1])

> No battle plan ever survived the first encounter with the enemy.
>
> (Quote attributed to Field Marshal Helmuth von Moltke)

Change, like life, is something that is much easier to understand in retrospect rather than at the time it is being undertaken. It is more difficult to tell someone what they should do in the future than what they should have done in the past. This is why, despite all the time which is rightly spent on planning, in essence, change is about predicting the future: 'If we do X, will we get Y?' Consequently, though change agents may have a 'battle plan', as events unfold, this will need to be revisited and creatively amended as unexpected and often novel problems arise and have to be dealt with. It is this mixture of unpredictability and creativity which makes the process of change so variable. Indeed, it might seem from reading the chapters in this book that each person who leads or facilitates a change initiative does so in their own inimitable way and that there really are no common rules or guidelines for managing change. Certainly, each change agent develops their practice based on their own background and experience and applies it in the distinct set of circumstances in which they find themselves. The result is that the same type of change can be managed differently depending on the people involved and the circumstances. This does not, though, necessarily mean that the outcome will be different, but it does stress that experienced change agents adapt their practice to the needs of the situation. What the contributors to this book have shown is that whilst they may not share a set of common rules for managing change, they do share some common perspectives on how change should be practised, which are as follows:

1. Take nothing for granted—always challenge assumptions, whether these assumptions are about the nature of change, the circumstances

in which change takes place, your own assumptions about the situation and what needs doing, and what other people tell you about what needs doing.

2. Changing behaviour is central to successful change. As Schein (1988: 12) observed 'all organisational problems are fundamentally problems involving human interactions and processes'. Therefore, it is necessary to understand the current behaviour, identify the desired future behaviour, and ensure that the change process is geared to achieving this.

3. Change is a participative, learning experience, where people need to be enabled to share their stories and attempt to come to a common view of what needs to be done. Therefore, encourage and facilitate communication and openness. This process can be slow and frustrating, but it will avoid problems and save time at the implementation stage.

4. Be patient—do not rush the process of change. However, always have the end result upmost in your mind and see the change process through, but be aware of the temptation and pressure to declare victory too soon.

5. Change is usually a team effort. Make sure that the team comprises people with the necessary knowledge, skills, and aptitudes. Take time to build them into a team.

6. Understand the context in which the change is taking place and recognise that what worked well in one context may be disastrous in another.

7. Problems and obstacles are normal. Make sure that unresolved issues and problems are identified and stay on the agenda. Do not let people ignore or bury these.

8. Change practitioners will be treated as role models and other participants will take their lead from them. Act and behave as you want others to act and behave. In particular, recognise that change often raises ethical issues. Change practitioners have to be aware of what their values are, what the organisations values are, and if the change process challenges these and how they can and will respond. Recognise that your credibility is a key component of your effectiveness as a change agent.

9. No change agent will be successful all the time and no change agent has the experience, talent, or aptitude to be effective in all change situations.

10. Build your personal resilience. Leading change is stressful and physically and emotionally tiring. Stay physically fit, make time for yourself, seek emotional support, and, remember, you are allowed to have fun.

Bearing the earlier points in mind will not guarantee success; change involves far too many variables and no one has or could have sufficient experience that they could cope with all change situations. However, the contributors to this book have literally hundreds of years of hard-won practical experience between them. Therefore, treat their advice with caution, but ignore it at your peril.

We introduced this book with Barack Obama's 2008 campaign slogan— '*Change we need*'. Let us close it with a quote from Michelle Obama.[2] In 2012, in support of her husband's campaign for a second term of office, she stated that:

Change is hard and change is slow.

NOTES

1. Kierkegaard, S (1843: 306) *Journalen* JJ:167. Søren Kierkegaard Research Center: Copenhagen.
2. Quoted in Swaine (2012).

REFERENCE

Swaine, J (2012) Michelle Obama: 'Change is hard and change is slow'. *The Telegraph*, 5 September. Available at http://www.telegraph.co.uk/news/worldnews/us-election/9521734/Michelle-Obama-Change-is-hard-and-change-is-slow.html.

About the Editors

Bernard Burnes is Professor of Organisational Change at the University of Stirling. His research covers organisational change in its broadest sense. His work is published in leading international journals. Bernard is the author of *Managing Change (6th edition)*, Series Editor of the *Routledge Studies in Organizational Change*, and Joint Editor of the *Routledge Companion to Organizational Change*.

Julian Randall is Senior Lecturer in the management of change at the University of Aberdeen and obtained his PhD at the University of St Andrews. His research interests include the perceptions of individuals affected by imposed change and its influence on their evaluation of their jobs, work, careers, and the organisation. He has published on these and related topics in *Organization Studies*; *Organization, The Journal of Organizational Change Management*, and the *Journal of Qualitative Research in Organizations and Management*. He is programme leader of the Masters in Management Consultancy degree.

About the Contributors

Richard J. Badham is currently a Professor of Management at the Macquarie Graduate School of Management. He is the co-author of the *Harvard Business Review* (2012) article on leadership and transformation 'Fire, Snowball, Mask and Movie: How Leaders Ignite and Sustain Change', as well as the popular text on leadership and change, *Power, Politics and Organizational Change* (Sage, London 2008). He has held positions as Visiting Professor at Yale University, the David Goldmann Visiting Professorship in Business Innovation at the University of Newcastle, UK, and a Senior Von Humboldt Fellowship at the Technical University, Berlin. He has worked as a consultant to the European Commission, the West German Government, Ford, James Hardies, and Hoover, as well as numerous other government agencies and corporations in Australia and worldwide. He has been Associate Dean (Research) for the MGSM, Director of the Centre for Managing Change, was the Foundation BHP Professor in Management at Wollongong University, and has held international editorial board positions on six international research journals. He is the author of over 100 books and articles on change, innovation, and organisational politics and is internationally recognised as a leading authority and popular speaker on leadership and organisational change. He is currently working on organisational change as drama, and the role of paradox and irony in leadership performance.

Stephen Banyard is the former Director General of Personal Tax HM Revenue and Customs. Before joining HMRC, he was a post-doctoral research scientist working on the structure of large protein molecules. He joined the then Inland Revenue in 1974. He has held a number of posts in HMRC, including Tax Inspector, Regional Director, and Director of Operations, where he was responsible for 47,000 staff.

Nic Beech is Vice Principal and Head of the College of Arts and Social Science at the University of Dundee. He trained in philosophy and social anthropology before switching to HR and change management at Strathclyde and St Andrews. He has published widely on various aspects of management and is a Fellow of the Royal Society of Arts, Chartered Institute of Personnel and Development, and Academy of Social Sciences. He is presently Chair of the British Academy of Management.

David M. Boje is a public intellectual. He is giving a keynote in 2015 in Lyon, and he has given four keynote presentations at conferences in 2014 in countries around the world. He holds the Wells Fargo Professorship, Distinguished University Professor and Bill Daniels Ethics Fellow in Management Department at New Mexico State University. Professor Boje also has an honorary doctorate from Aalborg University, with a special affiliation to the Material Storytelling Lab founded by Anete Strand. He is informally known as the 'godfather' to the lab. Emerging in New Mexico is the 'Embodied Restorying Processes' (ERP) lab, which is affiliated with the worldwide 'Material Storytelling Lab' community. The New Mexico ERP Lab is also working with student veterans and their family members. ERP and Material Storytelling work are being combined with Equine Assisted Growth and Learning Events (EAGLE) using horses in work with veterans and their family members, followed by the sandtray work (**http://peaceaware.com/eagle**).

Tricia Boyle has worked as a consultant for over 25 years. She is Head of a small Organisational Development team for NHS Fife in Scotland. Prior to joining the NHS, she ran her own consultancy. Tricia's OD team provides an internal consultancy service for the chair, CEO, and the director of organisational development at NHS Fife.

David A. Buchanan is Emeritus Professor of Organisational Behaviour at Cranfield University School of Management and Visiting Professor at Nottingham Business School, Nottingham Trent University. He works freelance as a consultant, presenter, and author, specialising in change management and organisation politics. He has a doctorate in organisational behaviour from Edinburgh University and was Director of Loughborough University Business School from 1992 to 1995. He has held visiting posts in Australian and Canadian management schools and works regularly in Australia. He is author/co-author of over two dozen books, including the best-selling *Organizational Behaviour* (with Andrzej Huczynski; eighth edition 2013). He has also co-authored several books on change management, including: *Take The Lead* and *The Expertise of the Change Agent* (with David Boddy), *The Sustainability and Spread of Organizational Change* (with Louise Fitzgerald and Diane Ketley), and *Power, Politics and Organizational Change: Winning the Turf Game* (with Richard Badham). He has also written numerous book chapters and articles on organisational behaviour and change and research methods.

Patrick Dawson is a Professor of Management at the University of Aberdeen. He holds a PhD in industrial sociology from the University of

Southampton and during his early career worked at the University of Surrey and the University of Edinburgh. He moved to Australia in the 1980s where he took up a position at the University of Adelaide. In studying change in the UK, Australian, and New Zealand based organisations, Patrick has worked on a number of Australian Research Council (ARC) and Economic and Social Research Council (ESRC) funded projects in collaboration with scholars at other universities. He has examined change and innovation in a number of organisations, including LG Electronics, Pirelli Cables, BHP Billiton, Royal Dutch Shell, British Rail, Aberdeen Asset Management, British Aerospace, Laubman and Pank, General Motors, Hewlett Packard, Central Linen Services, State Bank of South Australia, Illawarra Retirement Trust, TNT, and the CSIRO. Since taking up the Salvesen Chair at Aberdeen, he has held Visiting Professorships at Roskilde University and the Danish Technical University in Denmark, an Adjunct Professorship at Monash University, and a Professorial Fellowship at the University of Wollongong. He has published over 60 refereed academic journal articles, numerous book chapters and books, and he is regularly invited to present keynote addresses at major international conferences.

David Ennis is a former Managing Director of Oki (UK) Ltd, based in Cumbernauld Scotland. He originally moved to Oki as their Director of HR and Corporate Affairs. Prior to that, he worked for Philips Electronics and Plessey Telecommunications. Currently, he is an associate with his son's company, NSDesign, an SME digital consultancy founded in 1999. He is also an Honorary Professor at Stirling University.

Tonya L. Henderson is an international speaker and consultant on the topics of complexity and organisation development. As CEO of Gly Solutions, LLC, she applies her education and experience as a management scholar-practitioner, certified yoga instructor, veteran naval officer, and aerospace subject matter expert to help organisations and individuals find their own creative solutions to today's business challenges. For more information, visit www.glysolutions.com.

Phil Jackson has worked as a consultant for over ten years specialising in developing communication, self-awareness, and mindfulness. Prior to that, he held a number of management posts at Unilever, including Head of Manufacturing Outsourcing Operations. He holds a PhD in Chemistry and an MSc in Organisational Psychology.

Robert MacIntosh is Professor of Strategic Management and Head of the School of Management and Languages at Heriot-Watt University. He holds a PhD in engineering and has worked at the Universities of Glasgow and Strathclyde. His research interests centre on strategy and organisational change. He is a Fellow of the Institution of Engineering

Index

Note: Italicized page numbers indicate a figure on the corresponding page. Page numbers in bold indicate a table on the corresponding page.